Let's
Rock this
year!

XOXO

♡ Sage

Praise for

WOMEN ROCKING BUSINESS

"Sage Lavine is pioneering the women's business movement, making a compelling case for bringing feminine values of sustainability, generosity, spiritual fulfillment, and social and environmental awareness into the business realm as a way of creating entrepreneurial ventures that are both lucrative AND aligned with the balance humanity is longing for and in need of."

— Marci Shimoff, best-selling author of
Chicken Soup for the Woman's Soul and *Happy for No Reason*

"Women Rocking Business is a perfect blend of rock-solid business sense, spiritual philosophy, and personal experience woven into a practical formula for a successful livelihood and life! In a well-researched and easy-to-use guide that you'll want to keep at your fingertips, Sage Lavine draws upon her experience of feminine principles in the business world to give new meaning to one of life's most fundamental questions—how do we honor our truest nature while making a living for ourselves and our families? From engineers to homemakers, from politicians to healers, I recommend this book to everyone who is ready to unleash their life's potential without compromising their personal integrity to do so!"

— Gregg Braden, best-selling author of
The Divine Matrix, The God Code, and *Deep Truth*

"Sage is the ultimate leader of women entrepreneurs. Her heart is completely dedicated to her clients, students, and readers. She brings a pure and committed love to the templates, systems, and structures she creates for women who are ready to build a thriving business. More importantly, she believes in women's fundamental greatness. As you read this book, you'll feel her belief in you so strongly that you won't be able to help but believe in yourself, too."

— Lynne Twist, best-selling author of *The Soul of Money*

"Women have been the financial underdogs for millennia. Thankfully, Sage Lavine is here to change that painful legacy. Her outstanding new book, Women Rocking Business, powerfully helps women heal their relationship with money by building a business that brings them financial success while being a powerful contribution to the world. You can give more from a cup that is full than from a cup that is empty. Women Rocking Business helps women to understand that the path to earning money can be one of deep spiritual fulfillment. What Sage Lavine has put together with this book will be a prayer answered for women all over the world."

— John Robbins, best-selling author of *Diet for a New America*
and *Voices of the Food Revolution*

"*Sage Lavine is helping to redefine the very nature of business. She's facilitated tens of thousands of clients in transforming their lives and building vibrant businesses that align with their values. Now, she's here to help you. With clarity, vulnerability, and practical strategies that are tested and proven, Sage will walk you down the path to building the life you deserve. Yes, you CAN have a thriving life, do work you love, and make a contribution on the planet.* Women Rocking Business *will show you how. If you want to do yourself the biggest favor ever, read this book.*"

— Ocean Robbins, CEO of The Food Revolution Network,
co-author of *Voices of the Food Revolution*

"*In her book,* Women Rocking Business, *Sage shines a light on the challenges that hold most women back in business, and she provides practical, tangible solutions to support the emerging woman entrepreneur get out of her own way and build a business in alignment with her authenticity and generosity. She shows women how they can give back to others as they grow their business, helping them expand their vision to be bigger than themselves and their clients. This book is the answer to many questions women entrepreneurs have had for years.*"

— Doug Abrams, co-author of the #1 *New York Times* bestseller *The Book of Joy*

"*Sage does an incredible job illuminating the truth that women are uniquely positioned at this time in history to play a unique and essential role in the future of this planet. She provides a step-by-step system for women to make their unique creative contributions by launching successful businesses in ways that feel congruent and aligned with conscious values. By reading this book you're sure to discover an even greater possibility for your financial success, brilliance, and impact than can be imagined.*"

— Claire Zammit, Ph.D., founder, FemininePower.com,
and creator of the Feminine Power courses for women

"*Sage Lavine is a fresh and feisty transformational voice and I'm so glad she created this extension of her brilliance in this magnificent book so you can say a big YES to your wildest business dreams and make them REAL.*"

— SARK, author/artist Planet SARK

"*In her book,* Women Rocking Business, *Sage reveals business-building secrets rooted in feminine values that will not only help the emerging woman entrepreneur connect to her creative unconscious, but put her on the path to her full potential and true destiny as a successful, thriving business owner.*"

— Lisa Sasevich, "The Queen of Sales Conversion"

WOMEN
ROCKING
BUSINESS

WOMEN ROCKING BUSINESS

THE ULTIMATE STEP-BY-STEP GUIDEBOOK
TO CREATE A THRIVING LIFE
DOING WORK YOU LOVE

SAGE LAVINE

HAY HOUSE, INC.
Carlsbad, California • New York City
London • Sydney • Johannesburg
Vancouver • New Delhi

Hardcover ISBN: 978-1-4019-5226-6

10 9 8 7 6 5 4 3 2 1
1st edition, September 2017

Printed in the United States of America

*I dedicate this book to all women everywhere who
have had the gumption, the passion, and the heart
to start a business that contributes to the world.
I dedicate this book to my clients, who never cease
to inspire me, and who have joined with me to help
women to start businesses in Rwanda, Zimbabwe,
Indonesia, Ecuador, Liberia, and all around the world.
And finally, I give a special shout-out to the women in
my life who have had my back . . . and my front, and
my sides . . . as I've grown into the woman I am today.
You know who you are. I've got your back too.
(And your front . . . and sides. Always.)*

CONTENTS

FOREWORD

It was early morning as we paddled our canoe down the Amazon River. The rising sun cast a golden glow on everything. Pink dolphins leapt out of the water. Our guide from the Achuar tribe pointed out macaws on a faraway branch and the mating song of the cicadas. We were surrounded by a constant buzz as we paddled deeper into the rain forest.

I was here in the Amazon rain forest with a couple dozen leaders all committed to helping preserve the jungle ecosystem by aligning our businesses with values of sustainability, social justice, and spiritual fulfillment. I sat next to Sage Lavine, discussing in hushed tones how to best create deep, connected women's communities and how to balance the busy schedules of a CEO with time for restoration.

It was the perfect setting away from our usual world to reflect on how important that collective and restorative energy is. Gliding through the rain forest in a canoe put us in touch with our own innate rhythms and our connection with nature, and how it all operates in collaboration.

In our fast-paced Western business world we so often think that we have to do it all on our own. We have to get ahead. There is a masculine energy that propels us this way. Yet here in the quiet space of the Amazon, we could reconnect with what matters most and what will work, in our lives and our businesses.

It's a crucial time for this conversation, about how to create successful, sustainable businesses that contribute to, rather than detract from, our world. The book you hold in your hands is a guidebook for doing just that. *Women Rocking Business* provides a revolutionary approach to creating a business that honors your innate feminine values. In these pages you will discover how your natural tendencies as a woman give you a cooperative advantage in business. This book is full of practical "how-tos" that will help you become a thriving entrepreneur from a place of *empowering* others rather than *powering over* them, a place of *collaboration* rather than *competition* and *contribution* rather than *greed*.

I've often seen people who have success at the expense of their happiness, which isn't really success at all. That is not what Sage teaches in this book. She shows you a way to rock your business while also rocking your life. Sage is one of those rare leaders who walks her talk. She cares about the thousands of women who seek out her mentorship. She cares about the planet. She cares about you: She knows that when you get the support she provides in this book, you, too, can rock your business and make the difference you're here to make, all while experiencing happiness and spiritual fulfillment.

I first met Sage almost four years ago. Months before our trip to the rain forest, Sage came to my house for a masterminding day. Although we had different businesses and experiences, we were all in the business of transformation.

During that day of masterminding, we brought forward what we each had to share. My business partner, Debra Poneman, and I contributed a longer-term perspective of having been in business for decades. I shared wisdom from having created and run multiple million-dollar businesses over the past 35 years and from being a best-selling author and selling millions of books. Sage and her colleague Vrinda Normand brought in refreshing, innovative, younger perspectives and more advanced understandings of marketing, technology, and business. Sage and Vrinda had also both created million-dollar companies as young women in their 30s, which in and of itself is an incredible accomplishment. They had also made it their mission to give back to the world. Our day together felt like a meeting of the elders with the next generation.

What I saw in Sage that day was a deep passion for the nearly 100,000 women she reaches on a weekly basis, and a commitment that fuels everything she does. Sage is a lifelong learner dedicated to transformation and growth. We can't really expect our customers and clients to grow and change if we're not committed to doing the work alongside them, can we? Sage listened attentively to my suggestions and then applied them all to her life and business right away. She has continued to create extraordinary success because of her willingness to learn, implement, and transform.

Since that fateful day of masterminding, I've been honored to be an elder guide to Sage on her authoring journey. I also turn to her for advice and ideas around business. I'm always delighted by her knowledge base and suggested strategies. She brings unique perspectives on technology and systems that I haven't been exposed to or understood without her guidance. Sage is both a consummate learner and teacher, willing to learn new ideas and share her unique perspectives and expertise that have helped me grow my businesses.

Just like we had a guide on the Amazon River who helped us navigate the unfamiliar terrain and showed us things we would not have seen on our own, so too is it imperative to have a guide in business. The wisest, most successful people are those who learn from the people who have what they want. Mentorship is critical to our success. We shouldn't even try to reinvent the wheel. Having a guide is the shortcut to creating what you want, in your business and in your life.

It's no accident that you picked up this book. The guidebook that you hold in your hands will inspire, educate, and entertain you as it also breaks down the daunting task of building a business into realistic, bite-size chunks. The time is now for women to design businesses that are in true alignment with feminine values, rather than discarding those values. I believe this book will play an essential role in supporting you and many other conscious women entrepreneurs around the globe to redefine the playing field and the game of business itself.

Please read this book. You don't need to try to figure out how to create success on your own. You can trust that Sage is speaking from experience that is tried and true and that you will be guided in the absolute best way possible—for your success, for your fulfillment, and for your future clients and customers. Here's to the rocking business that's waiting for you!

Marci Shimoff
Transformational leader and professional speaker
#1 *New York Times* best-selling author of *Happy for No Reason,*
Love for No Reason, and *Chicken Soup for the Woman's Soul*
San Anselmo, California

PART I

SETTING THE STAGE FOR SUCCESS

Chapter 1

FROM DESIRE TO DESTINY

"Desires are like stepping stones on the path to your destiny."

— JANET ATTWOOD

I was lying on my back one summer evening in Santa Cruz, staring up at clouds passing overhead. It sounds like an idyllic moment of relaxation, right? Well, not exactly. My neck was out, and I was in terrible pain. I was exhausted, stressed, and broke, and I couldn't move my head.

Full of visions, aspirations, and a bit of naïveté, I had just sold everything I owned, moved into an RV with my husband, and driven across the country to Santa Cruz. I was set to start my dream business and leave my legacy! Instead I found myself broke and burned out. Struggling to launch my business and finally give the gifts I knew were inside me, I felt like a total failure. A friend had told me, "Sage— follow your desire!" But at that moment, "desire" was about as far from my consciousness as Iceland or Timbuktu.

Why had my neck twisted into knots? I was in the midst of my first major business project, an interview series I was putting together for women entrepreneurs—and to say it wasn't going as well as I had hoped is an understatement. I had invested thousands of dollars in the project with very little profit to show for my weeks of effort. My husband was furious, and I was deeply ashamed that I wasn't contributing to our financial resources or helping to pay off the nearly $35,000 of debt we had accumulated in moving to Santa Cruz.

Meanwhile, I was awakening to the crushing truth that our marriage was over. We had grown apart, and despite several years of attempting reconciliation, we had become two very different people. While I didn't want to admit it to myself, I was ready to move on, and I needed the finances to do it.

At the same time, I was terrified to make the kind of money that would buy my freedom. I had resisted success for months, keeping the big dreams at bay as an excuse not to leave my husband and best friend of 10 years. Even as I longed for the financial success that would give me the freedom to start a separate life, a part of me wanted any excuse to avoid the terror of going it alone. After all, my husband had believed in me when nobody else did, and even though we wanted different things in life, we still loved each other fiercely.

There was no denying what I felt deep inside, though. I was meant to help women step into their greatness through building a business they loved. And how could I look my clients in the eyes and tell them to live their dreams when I wasn't living mine in my marriage? It was time for me to step into the power I knew was within me and create my own income. Only then could I move beyond the safe container of my marriage into what I really wanted.

Ohhh, sister! This was one of the hardest decisions I've ever had to make, and I couldn't have done it without the women in my life, my amazing clients, and my extended female tribe—a tribe I'm going to lovingly invite you to join throughout the course of this book.

That summer evening, staring up at the Santa Cruz sky, I felt so sorry for myself. Then I remembered my spiritual work and turned my attention inward to a connection with something bigger than me. I found the part of me that was holding on for dear life, clenched in pain, and I turned toward it. Embracing my own fear and shame, I offered myself some kindness, and a flood of tears followed. The sweet pressure release that comes only from a good, long, messy cry opened up my consciousness, and I slowly began to unwind and feel my body again.

In that deep and profound surrender, I turned toward myself. In that moment of reconnecting with myself, I suddenly felt connected with all that is. I felt connected to all women, everywhere, who had struggled with money. I felt connected to my grandmother and my great-grandmother . . . I could even, in that moment, perceive the millions of women around the world who are stuck in uncomfortable and even abusive situations because of a lack of money. At that moment, the sun beamed through the clouds, and I glimpsed a future that would allow me to make a greater contribution and reach great fulfillment.

So like any self-growth junkie dedicated to pursuing (insert sarcastic tone here) "an exalted life of purposeful conquest and magical manifestation," I decided to make a deal with the Universe. In all seriousness, that night, I turned my life over to something bigger than myself and asked for help. I made a deal with God, whispering to an angel-shaped cloud that was passing overhead: *"If you can get me out of this pain, God, if you can help me make my own money and find freedom, I'll dedicate my life to helping women around the world who are struggling and stuck because of financial dependence."*

And so it was that within moments of my plea, I had an idea that would bring me more than $100,000 of income in less than three months. In that flash, I saw clearly how I could use the women's interview series I had just launched to attract my soon-to-be clients, creating immediate cash flow and changing the future of my business forever. And it worked. I moved out of the RV and into a gorgeous ocean-view home in Santa Cruz, and the financial freedom that had once been just a dream began to become a reality. I believe the commitment I made that night gazing at the clouds has made it possible for me to (1) help tens of thousands of women launch global businesses and (2) build my own million-dollar company.

I had always dreamed of making money online—money that showed up in my inbox. I had heard about this phenomenon from colleagues and business gurus. But I always thought it was only for the computer geeks of Silicon Valley who had cracked some sort of magic, secret Internet code with highly complex passwords and mad technology skills.

Nevertheless, I went ahead and launched my business based on the idea I received from that divine guidance, and lo and behold, it took off right away. I made tens of thousands of dollars online in just a few weeks. It was like a miracle to me, kind of like winning the lottery.

In my previous life as a schoolteacher in Iowa, it had taken me more than three years to make what I made from that one program that sprung from my divine inspiration. And not only was I making more money than I ever imagined in such a short time, but I was serving women I loved working with from all over the globe. In fact, I had engaged an online tribe of more than 5,000 women almost overnight. That number would grow to nearly 75,000 readers as my company became a million-dollar organization in just a couple of years.

Does it sound impossible? It isn't! Stay with me, and keep reading. I'll show you how you too can create incredible success in your business.

YOU CAN DO IT TOO—REALLY, YOU CAN

So you might ask, "Can a woman like me, with just the spark of an idea, actually start a business and make money?" Yes! Can those of us who have bodies that still get twisted up from stress, who have failed marriages, who have relied on others for financial security, or who are fundamentally imperfect in a myriad of ways *actually* start and run successful businesses? The answer is yes! You don't need to have reached some distant peak of intellectual nirvana or spiritual enlightenment to build a successful business and make a massive contribution on the planet.

If I can do it, you can do it. I promise!

What you're about to experience through reading this book is a road map that has helped thousands of my clients build successful and sustainable businesses. These clients include authors, health practitioners, consultants, coaches, manufacturers, retailers, real estate agents, day spa owners, healers, clothing designers, aspiring public speakers, restaurant owners, and many other types of professional women. They've all chosen to thrive through building businesses on their own terms. This road map can work for you too—*really!*

Over the last decade, I have invested nearly $500,000 in my own business training, and I have more than 18 years of personal-growth education under my belt. With this knowledge, I've built three successful businesses of my own, which has put me in a unique position to show you, step-by-step, how to begin making money using your gifts. On the pages that follow, I'll share the very best of what I teach my clients over the course of several intensive business training programs and our Entrepreneurial Leadership Academy.

Women Rocking Business will provide you with an in-depth how-to guide that's filled with integration exercises and real-life case studies you can apply right away to help you build your own business. As you read these pages, you will:

- Heal any places in your life where you've been hurt by money so that you can make more of it.

- Learn how to build a support network of Entrepreneurial Sisters so that you don't have to feel alone in your business endeavor.

- Clarify your offering for the world.

- Choose a business direction.

- Discover the secret to not burning out.

- Learn how to use the power of the Internet and online marketing to find and enroll your ideal customers.

- And much more!

With this map and the support systems I will lay out for you, you'll always have a plan you can return to as your business grows and develops.

Chapter by chapter, I will invite you to challenge the core beliefs that may be holding you back from building the business you dream about. Perhaps you were taught to work hard with your nose to the grindstone. Maybe you were told that work can't be fun or that you have to be "realistic" about what's possible. Maybe you were encouraged to be nice, to be quiet, to minimize your accomplishments, and to dim your own light.

For 20 years now, I have been working in the fields of women's empowerment and women's leadership, and I've spent the last seven of those years completely immersed in helping thousands of women start and grow businesses that are successful beyond their wildest dreams—in spite of (and building upon) their limiting beliefs and the real-life "shero's" journeys they've been through.

You will come to see that each precious moment of your own shero's journey has provided the building blocks for your business and the authentic marketing platform that will attract your ideal clients, customers, and students.

How to get the most VALUE from this book

You'll get the most bang for your buck by reading this book from cover to cover, chapter by chapter. Each chapter includes self-reflection exercises and templates for clarifying your branding message and marketing plans. I promise we'll get to everything that's important for your next step. But I'll encourage you to slow down enough that you can tease out the message and business direction that not only lies within your heart, but that— most importantly—speaks to the hearts of your waiting clients and customers.

The degree to which this book will change your life is the degree to which you're willing to follow the steps and *complete* the exercises. And so I ask you, will you commit? *The people who are waiting for you are depending on your ability to actually do the work.*

WOMEN HAVE PARTICULAR GIFTS FOR BUSINESS

But wait a minute—don't you have to curb your femininity in order to be successful in business? That's what we've all been told, right? In years past, as we entered the business environment, women had to shed aspects of feminine creativity and intuition in order to survive. We've dressed in both the literal and metaphorical male power suit and lived by masculine rules. Countless women still struggle with the fear that to succeed in the marketplace, they have to sacrifice their true nature, even sell their souls.

Yet when you look out across the world of startups, entrepreneurial endeavors, online and home-based businesses, and self-employed independent contractors, you see women rocking and improving the world of business. Over the last 15 years, women have stepped into entrepreneurship in significantly greater numbers than men at a rate that's 1.5 times the national average.[1] And women have good reason to start businesses: We're creators and visionaries, but we're also pragmatists. We're starting businesses because we want it all—the career *and* the family—and there's no reason why we shouldn't have it.

We're starting businesses because we understand the challenge of facing a three-hour commute while raising children and still maintaining some time for ourselves. We're starting businesses because we're sick and tired of being in a position of monetary dependency, and we're ready to claim our financial freedom and self-determination. We want to be the masters of our own schedules. We want to share our deeply innovative gifts with the world. We want to work for ourselves on our own terms without compromising the natural female instincts inside us.

Throughout history, women have been accused of people-pleasing, conflict-avoiding, and perpetually putting others' needs before their own. But guess what? It's exactly because of these very qualities that we're now excelling in business.

Women are gifted at prioritizing the needs of others. We have an intuitive understanding of how to create meaningful connections and exceptional working relationships with clients and colleagues that give us what I lovingly refer to in chapter 9 as "a cooperative advantage."

It's true that women have unique talents we're meant to bring to the world of business. Yet according to the report "Women-Owned Businesses in the 21st Century," put out by the U.S. Department of Commerce, our businesses are more likely to fail. The report reveals that a staggering 95 percent of us don't break through the six-figure income barrier, go on to have the larger impact we want to have, or make the contributions we desire to make.[2]

Well, I'm here to tell you that you can overcome these odds! I've found in my work with thousands of female entrepreneurs over the years that when we remain in alignment with women's values, we can build businesses that flourish.

So this book isn't about teaching you how to be successful at business according to men's rules. Nope! It's about teaching you to *be successful at business as a woman—as your true self*—and helping you become an influencer yourself, changing the way business today is actually done. I will lay out a specific plan for building your business in a way that honors work-life balance, so your work can support you financially *and* fit into your life. You won't have to settle for a life that fits around an overly busy work schedule.

You'll learn principles to bypass many of the roadblocks that women encounter when they attempt to learn business strategy, marketing, and sales through old-school, traditional pedagogy. It's a new day, and the opportunities are great. We now have the world at our fingertips, which brings us both great possibility and a very real responsibility.

The approach in this book honors your innate feminine values while helping you empower yourself and at the same time empower others, rather than having *power over* them. I'll show you how to run a successful business as a place of *collaboration* and *contribution* rather than *competition* and *greed*.

Women thrive on collaboration. That's why I've built a community of women who help one another, and you can become a part of it for your own benefit and the benefit of the other women in the community.

Women carry an innate awareness of the needs and challenges of our times and often feel a deep sense of social responsibility. We have an opportunity to build businesses that champion and usher in a much-needed social change.

Over the years, together with others, my company has raised hundreds of thousands of dollars for women and children in Indonesia, the Amazon rain forest, and Liberia. I'll show you how to align with organizations so that your fund-raising efforts for them can actually help you build your business. As you give back, you will also receive and grow!

The Dalai Lama has said:
The world will be saved by the Western woman.

I don't believe the Dalai Lama meant you or me specifically. He meant all of us as a group. We, as a gender and as a society, now have the collective awareness, strength, and compassion to be the problem solvers and healers the world needs. Of course, we aren't obligated to save the world. In fact, I believe if we truly want to help heal the world, we have to do it from a place of joy, through blissful contribution. The world doesn't need more people who are out to "rescue" the "helpless." Instead, in the words of beloved author and philosopher Howard Thurman, "what the world needs is people who have come alive" and can contribute to the empowerment of others.

I've seen firsthand that when women learn about marketing and entrepreneurship through this lens, they're better positioned to implement entrepreneurial strategies and create success.

You'll begin to see the exchange of money in business as not just for material gain but also for spiritual fulfillment. I'm committed to providing you with a wake-up call, to lighting a fire under your butt, so to speak. I challenge you to proclaim what you're meant to say and give to the world so that you can make the difference only *you* were born to make.

WHAT ABOUT MEN? CAN THEY USE THESE TOOLS AS WELL?

Men can absolutely use the tools laid out in this book to help themselves be successful. Because we're all a unique combination of masculine and feminine qualities, we can utilize both masculine and feminine tools to create our own version of success.

In fact, some of my most trusted business mentors are men. I turn to men in part because some of them have been at it longer than a lot of us women have! In fact, throughout history men have frequently paved the way. I believe we as women thrive even more when we have men who support us and believe in us.

DESIRE IS YOUR YELLOW BRICK ROAD

So you know you want to succeed in business, and you now know that being a woman can be an advantage in many ways. But is there some "secret sauce"? People ask me about this all the time: "How did you come to train thousands of women to start businesses? How did you get where you are today?" The answer is: I followed my desire.

My friend and mentor Janet Attwood, the best-selling co-author of *The Passion Test,* has helped thousands of would-be visionaries, including me, launch successful livelihoods. Her method involves doing a thorough inventory of your passions and using those impulses and insights to make major life and career decisions. Janet once told me something that forever changed my life. "Sage," she said, "your desires aren't necessarily your destiny. Your desires are stepping stones on the path to your destiny."

Wow, did I need to hear that! You see, nearly a decade ago, I was lost. When I quit my teaching job, I didn't know what to do with myself at first. I knew deep down I needed time to explore my interests before going full bore on my next career path. Finally I allowed myself to do something I'd been longing to do for years—I let myself paint. I had studied art in college, and putting color on canvas nourishes a deep part of my soul. Even though I knew that choosing the career path of an artist would be too isolating for my personality, something told me that if I just allowed myself time to paint, more would be revealed.

My husband and I sold everything we had and moved into my grandpa's motor home to "follow our dreams." That utopian vision didn't last, as you've already seen, but I did make progress with my artwork. So I dove straight into creating my first batch of paintings, and before long I was making greeting cards and prints, selling them in bookstores and health food stores. I even got to the point where I was making several thousand dollars a month from my art!

I loved painting, but something in me remained deeply unfulfilled. The truth is that I'm too people oriented to be trapped behind a canvas day in and day out. I felt there was something else for me to do.

I told my art teacher, an incredible artist named Mara Friedman, about my journey. Her jaw dropped open in awe. "It's rare to see an artist monetize their art within just a few months of launching their career. Would you teach a class for young artists about how you made money from your art so quickly?" she asked.

Happily, I said yes.

Teaching that class was more rewarding for me than anything I had done in a long time. To support these young women in their creative process, to help them believe in themselves, see their own value, and lay out plans for making money, was like a dream come true. I was home.

In following my passion for art, I discovered that I'm not just an artist—I really am also a teacher. Just sitting behind the drawing board all day doesn't light me up enough—I'm meant to inspire and educate groups. And while I loved teaching high school, in the K-12 school system I wasn't able to teach the subject matter that's meaningful to me. I despised teaching to the standardized test. With the class for artists, helping them launch their art businesses, I began to discover my passion, and it would continue to evolve until I knew just where I belonged—teaching creative female entrepreneurs how to make money and build businesses that give back. In order to discover what it was inside me that desperately needed expression, I had to follow my desires like my own yellow brick road, one step at a time.

So your desires alone might not be your destiny, but I believe that in following them, you'll be directed toward your true path and your next chapter. Ultimately, if you choose it, you'll be led to launching a business that will leave a legacy.

You'll need the fuel of your passion and desire to propel you to true success, where outer-world achievements will be equaled by inner achievements of meaning, fulfillment, and significance. It's the act of trusting what you want most that puts you on the journey of launching the right business for you—a business that will pull you out of bed in the morning, propel you through the darkest of times, bring you infinite joy, and satisfy your heart.

You may currently be going through your own personal or career transition, or you may be dreaming of doing something significant with your life that's different from what you're doing now. Or perhaps you want to skyrocket your already established business to a new level of contribution and success. Wherever you're starting from, within you lies a seed of desire that will point you toward the opportunity that awaits you. As I've often heard said, every break*down* precedes a break*through* to where you need to be for greater levels of fulfillment.

What Is DESIRE?

The word *desire* comes from a Latin root (*sidus*)
meaning "star" or "heavenly body." Perhaps that
heavenly body is guiding us from above?

My friend Derek Rydall, an incredible teacher and author,
has a spiritual definition of the word. "De-sire" can be broken down
to "of the sire," which translates to "of the Kingdom of God." To
me, this makes perfect sense. How else is God, Goddess, Source,
the Universe, or whatever you might call the Supreme Intelligence
and Creator of our world, able to communicate with us except
through our desire? Yet so many of us trample on our desire by
ignoring it, denying it, or feeling unworthy of it or separate from it.
And what's worse, we aren't taught to search inside for it.

My first question for you is: What makes you come alive? What is your deepest desire for your business and your life?

Case Study: Entrepreneurial Goddess Emily Utter

You don't have to see the entire vision right now. Even if you're not yet sure what your business wants to be, if you trust this process, it will help you make that discovery. You may only be aware of a piece of what you want, but that's enough to begin. One of my clients, Emily Utter, looked me in the eyes after one of our client retreats and said, "Sage, I'm not even sure what this business is supposed to be. All I know is that I want to work with people I love, and I want a business that brings me freedom!"

I could relate to her on every level. So many of us crave a business that allows us autonomy, choice, and a flexible schedule. At the time, Emily was a consultant who was bored with her work, always needing to push the agenda of her clients while secretly desiring the freedom to travel the world and help people in a more meaningful way.

Well, that's exactly what she created. Emily called me earlier this year on her way to Thailand and shared, through tears, that she had just completed her first online course to generate over six figures in income in just a few months. She was on her way to Asia to celebrate.

Emily is like me, and she may be like you too. She wants to give fully and help people change their lives for the better, but without compromising her freedom. We laid out a schedule and plan for her similar to the one I'll introduce in chapter 7, a plan that's allowed her to work 12 days or less per month with the flexibility to travel internationally, attend workshops, go to festivals and events, and launch a business—now approaching seven figures—leading workshops and online courses that support adventure-seeking entrepreneurs.

The two of us recently made the journey to the Burning Man Festival in Nevada with our fishnet stockings and fur coats. Emily and I share a desire to create a business that gives us the freedom to explore all of life, and that's exactly what we're doing. To find out more about Emily's work, visit www.emilyutter.com.

Emily and I didn't get some special certification that allows us to do what we love with a schedule that gives us freedom and abundance. What we did can be taught and learned so that you can have it too. That's the purpose of this book!

THE JOURNEY WE'LL BE TAKING TOGETHER

I promise to do everything in my power to help you discover your deepest desire, build your business, and thrive financially. I promise to show you a formula for reaching your clients and customers in a way that is authentic to you, that honors your feminine nature, that keeps you connected instead of isolated, and that also utilizes your inner masculine nature when appropriate. I will lay out a balanced plan that allows you to become all you can be, while still taking good care of yourself.

So, Entrepreneurial Goddess—is it okay if I call you that?—let's start by walking you through an exercise of visioning what you want your life and business to look like. Whether you have the desire to birth a purposeful new business or take your current business to the next level, I'm going to encourage you right now to trust that desire.

TAPPING INTO YOUR INNERMOST DESIRES

With "of the Kingdom of God" as our translation for *desire*, let's assume for a moment that the Universe, God, Goddess, or whatever name you have for Source is using your desires to communicate what you need to do. You're designed to be a channel for your gifts, from which your purposeful business arises, and this begins with getting in touch with your innermost desires.

What do you already know you'd love to do? Let's say you know that you want to be onstage, or to be sitting in a garden for hours counseling people about deep matters of the heart, or selling your favorite homemade scones at a café of your very own. Maybe you know you want to work three days a week or to generate enough money to donate to the women's shelter down the street.

For now let's suspend the need to strategize or plan and just focus on capturing the *essence* of your desire. Begin right now, right where you are. I believe the fact that you're reading this book is evidence that you have everything you need to fulfill your deepest desires and most magnificent expression of your purpose, already tucked away in the center of your soul.

Keep in mind that books are transformational tools, meant to be written in, marked up, highlighted, and underlined. So don't be precious about these pages! Go for it!

During the following exercise,
slow down your mind to the pace of your pen,
leaving space for the wisdom of your spirit to come in!

INTEGRATION

Tapping Into YOUR DESIRE

This process is about uncovering your deepest desires
and visions for your next business chapter. These
questions are powerful. Trust the process!

1. What in your life is holding you back from living your desire?

2. What needs to change/shift to allow you the space for your desire?

3. What is it about your career path that isn't working?

4 . What do you want? Write it down. Give yourself an entire page or pages to reflect on this. We weren't taught to reflect on what we want as a regular practice, so be gentle with yourself if it feels clunky at first. Do this repeatedly. Check in about your desires weekly.

5. Describe, in writing, three dream business visions you've had.

6. How do you most want to serve and contribute to people?

7. What do you want your business to *feel* like?

8. What would your ideal work schedule look like?

9. If you were doing exactly what you want in your life, you would be:

10. As you experience success, how do you want to incorporate giving back to the world?

ARE YOU READY TO MAKE A COMMITMENT?

Now that you have a better idea of your desires, I'm going to be bold and blunt: I challenge you to commit to the process in this book all the way through to the end. Your customers will thank you for it, as will the future you, who will be ecstatic to wake up every day doing what you love! Doesn't that sound amazing?

The first step to making this commitment is to sign a commitment contract. Keep in mind that contracts are binding—they mean something. Signing a contract and following through will strengthen your relationship with yourself and your ability to achieve business success. Signing a contract and *not* following through will ultimately weaken your relationship with both yourself and your future customers/clients.

Sister, there's no better feeling in the world than waking up to a business of meaning and clients you adore! Are you ready?

Women Rocking Business Commitment Contract

Welcome! I'm thrilled to have you on this business-building journey! Congratulations on saying YES to yourself, your dream, your future customers, your impact, and your income! Please read these commitments out loud (in front of a mirror is powerful), and POST the contract somewhere you can see it.

I, (state your name)_____, hereby commit to myself, my future customers and clients, and my business. I am willing to do whatever it takes to create a financially sustainable livelihood doing what I love. I'm willing to take massive action even when it feels uncomfortable. I'm committed to working through the steps laid out in this book even when I find myself stuck in resistance, disbelief, or self-doubt.

I commit to being gentle with myself, to stepping forward even when it feels unfamiliar or scary, and to staying out of overwhelm by doing one thing at a time.

I commit to taking responsibility for my life, my business, and my results.

Finally, I commit to loving myself and my dreams, no matter what.

Signature: _____

Date: _____

Let's do this thing, Goddess . . . together!

Love, Sage

Still feel confused about your desires and how they relate to your business direction? I invite you to hop online and grab my Virtual Guidebook, where you'll learn my three-step process for "Purpose Clarity."

All you have to do is go to the website listed below and you'll get access to a purpose clarity audio I recorded that will walk you through a three-step clarifying process for what is next in your career and business.

Each chapter includes online breakthrough bonus trainings!

At the end of each chapter, you'll have an opportunity to interact more deeply with the chapter contents by claiming free audio trainings, money breakthrough exercises, sisterhood masterminding templates, a recipe for creating your marketable mission statement . . . and more! Here's your first gift, sister:

Women Rocking Business VIRTUAL GUIDEBOOK

BREAKTHROUGH BONUS TRAINING #1:

A Purpose Clarity Audio

With this book, get exclusive access to the
"3 Steps to Clarify Your Life Purpose & Make Money Living It"
audio interview with Sage and Darius Barazandeh

(You're going to love this!)
Grab it here: www.womenrockingbusiness.com/guidebook

Chapter 2

REWRITING YOUR MONEY STORY

"Making great money is part of our spiritual path."

— KENDALL SUMMERHAWK

Sitting in a café with my friends in Bangkok, Thailand, at age 23, I thought I knew everything. I had it all figured out.

Money? I didn't really respect it much at that point in my life. I had chosen freedom. I was traveling the world. I was a spiritual seeker learning to live with less. When I needed it, I made just enough to save for an international excursion, and then off I would go.

Once we had ordered our Thai curry, my friends and I began to mock the droves of robot-like humans back home forced to show up for work each day in cubicles while we lounged around in our outdoor gear, reveling in our freedom. The next agonizing decision of the day? Whether to visit a temple outside of town or catch a bus to the island of Phuket for some scuba diving.

That's what it was like for me for quite a few years. I made money into an enemy. As a young woman, I believed I could either be free and broke or be rich and enslaved to the source of my income. So I chose freedom and traveled the world, trusting that I'd always have just enough dollars (or euros, yen, or baht) when I needed them.

The simple, freedom-based life I created for myself reinforced the belief that I would have to sacrifice my happiness if I wanted to be wealthy. I thought in order to live on my own terms with a schedule I loved, I had to let money run through me like a sieve.

This relationship with money was instilled at a young age. Like most of us, I was raised in a family that didn't always value money and didn't teach me how to have a healthy, thriving relationship with it. In my case, my parents were anti-materialistic and ecologically minded. Rich people were a common object of jokes and judgment around our kitchen table. My family prided itself on finding the best deal at Goodwill and traveling around the world on a shoestring. There's nothing wrong with these values. I still brag to my friends when I find a cheap plane ticket; I love a good bargain! In fact, I'm grateful that my family valued freedom, and we got to see a lot of incredible places.

But the "freedom" my family stood for was somewhat of an illusion. As long as they were repelled by money and what it stood for in their minds, they weren't free at all. And I inherited that mind-set.

As you can imagine, I had to do some "inner work" to become an entrepreneur and build a million-dollar company.

What about you? Where are your blocks to having the wealth you want to create?

WHAT'S YOUR RELATIONSHIP WITH MONEY?

Before we start to clarify your business direction and marketing strategies, it's essential you consider your relationship with money.

Most of us would love to have more money, but we don't consider how much our feelings about it block us from having more. Far too many of us have inner conflicts about wealth that prevent us from manifesting it in our lives. We harbor deep shame and disempowering beliefs about our ability to generate money, and we equate our inner value with the numbers in our bank account. We beat ourselves up when we think the numbers are too low and feel guilty when we think the numbers are high. And "low" and "high" are hardly absolutes. Ask two people for their low and high numbers, and they're almost guaranteed to give you different answers.

Most of us have been hurt or disappointed by money throughout our lives. But if you want more money, you have to first *"bless that which you want,"* as the Hawaiians say. Noticing what emotions money elicits from you is the first step to improving your relationship with it and healing any hurt you've had because of it.

So I have some questions for you: What happens inside you when you think about money? What physiological sensations do you notice when you ask people for money? Do you get nervous? Excited? Do your muscles contract? Do you feel empowered? Or does your stomach tighten into knots?

Remember: In its simplest form, money is neutral. It's just scraps of paper and long number sequences in the unseen world of Internet banking and invisible financial systems. We're the ones who choose to associate money with worry, shame, and blame—then blame it for not showing up for us.

You may even be actively pushing money away, if you associate it with values like materialism and consumption. Maybe you don't want to be a part of the cycle of greed you see taking place in our world, so you sit on the sidelines, forgetting that you could do a lot more good if you were to embrace money as a spiritual tool you can use to contribute to others.

Regardless of your individual relationship with money, you've no doubt developed less-than-healthy patterns with money over the course of your life. You might unconsciously push money away because you've been raised to believe it's bad to want it. Maybe you live in a chronic state of not having enough, where the desperation for money becomes almost habitual. Before long this can become an unhealthy, self-perpetuating cycle, causing you to spend or give away any extra that comes in. You might find that you rely on adrenaline to drive you toward pulling together next month's rent or car payment. Or maybe you hoard what you make, fearful of spending it on the little luxuries that can make life a bit sweeter.

Let's explore what you can do to treat money better and help it treat you better in return, shall we?

> Reverend Deborah Johnson, my beloved spiritual counselor and the minister at my local nondenominational church, Inner Light Ministries, says:
>
> *"If money were a person, consider how you're treating money. It's no wonder money doesn't want to play with you! You're blaming it for all your problems!"*
>
> How are you treating money?

CULTIVATING A MIND-SET OF ABUNDANCE

We're all capable of having a beautiful relationship with money that's full of gratitude, love, and adventure. But to do so, we have to consciously cultivate an *abundance mind-set.*

You can do this. I promise! Just stay with me.

If you've never had your own business before, we need to help you create an entirely new relationship with money. Being self-generative is a new skill. If you've always received a paycheck and haven't created your own income as a businesswoman, you'll be learning to rely on your own resources and connection with the Universe, the Divine, or whatever name you have for Source to generate enough money to buy your lunch and pay your bills. And if you like to eat organic food, like me, you'll need a little extra. So let's get you living in abundance!

What's more, as a business owner, all of your unconscious places about money will be brought to the surface so that you can heal them. Sounds like so much fun, doesn't it?

I promise you, it's worth it.

And you're not alone in your money "gunk." We all have places where we go unconscious about money. We stop paying attention, we overspend, or we hoard. As you become aware of your patterns and consciously work on your mind-set, your relationship with money will get healthier.

ASSESSING YOUR MONEY GUNK

Over the next few pages, I'm going to challenge you to take an honest assessment of your beliefs and fears in regard to money. Then you'll have the opportunity to reclaim your financial power and step into your next chapter as a wealthy business owner. Sound good? Doing your work around money is kind of like cleaning out the garage—you have to make more of a mess before the piles start getting organized in their Rubbermaid tubs. But the end result is order and spaciousness!

The healthier your mind-set is around money, the more confidence you'll have to implement the strategies to create your dream business. There's a saying that goes:

"If you always do what you've always done,
you'll always get what you've always gotten."

If your old money mind-set hasn't allowed you to reach your goals, it's probably because your subconscious desires are at odds with your conscious intentions. It's like trying to drive a car with an empty tank.

As your issues about money come to the surface, you'll have the chance to heal long-held beliefs that have limited you, maybe for years. You'll have the opportunity, should you choose to accept it, to bring what's truest and most valuable inside you out into the physical world—to finally make your life purpose a moneymaking vocation.

Perhaps you have a dream of opening a restaurant that will provide a space for people to break bread together, or maybe your dream is to serve others through your writing or workshops you lead. Regardless of the nature of your business idea, it lives in a deep place within you. And you're in the process of reaching inside your heart, extracting that dream, and asking the world to give you money in exchange for your gift. My dear, this takes a tremendous amount of courage! So the more we can optimize your "inner game" of business, the easier it will be for you to receive money in exchange for that precious gift of yours.

And if we're going to talk inner game, there's no better place to start than with shame.

OVERCOMING MONEY SHAME

My parents were often controlling and secretive when it came to money. When my friends began to wear designer jeans, I was desperate to have that little triangle on my butt that indicated I was, indeed, cool. I begged for those designer jeans. I mean, my entire social identity and future were riding on it!

But my mom refused. For years she preferred to take me shopping and choose what I bought, and she let me know there was no way we had room in our budget for designer jeans. Years later, we implemented a clothing allowance, and I was finally able to make my own decisions. But I still felt a secret need for Mom's approval of what I bought.

When I was a kid, Dad had to approve every purchase made in the family, which put my mom in an awkward position because she was in charge of taking care of my brother and me. When Mom took us shopping for school clothes, she often asked us to remove the tags as soon as we got home so the new clothes would look like they'd been in our drawers all along. This way, Dad wouldn't know how much money we'd spent.

Years later, I found myself in a marriage where my husband was in charge of our money. When I left my job teaching school to launch my business and money got tight, I found myself right back where I was as a young girl. I would secretly buy myself something new, smuggle it into my home, dispose of the tags, and hope my husband wouldn't notice. Deep inside I was harboring beliefs that I might not be capable of making and managing my own money, along with an underlying shame about spending money on myself. The story in my head was loud and clear: "There's never really enough, so you have to sneak around to get what you need."

One day I finally realized what I was doing and that I'd never make the kind of money I wanted if I harbored lies about it (however insignificant they might seem). So I decided to tell my husband everything. Through tears, I showed him the inventory I had listed on a yellow legal pad. It added up to a little over $1,000 of spending over the previous year without his knowledge. Looking back, I'm not sure if he felt sorry for me or figured I had punished myself enough, but by the end of the conversation, we had both let it go.

It's only natural that until we acquire financial maturity, we give our power away to the source of our money. After all, most of us are conditioned that way as children. This also explains why it's natural to feel fear and vulnerability when you ask for money in exchange for your services. It can be terrifying to take full responsibility for your own financial well-being, especially if a healthy way of doing so wasn't modeled for you as a child.

Most of us weren't taught much about making and managing money. We were supposed to somehow just assimilate that knowledge from our parents, who likely never developed a healthy money mind-set from their parents either.

We re-create our childhood money story in adulthood . . . until we do inner work.

So it isn't surprising that I re-created my childhood money reality as an adult. I depended on my mom well into my 20s to help support me financially. She even bought my plane tickets during my early adult years so that I could fly home to see my family. One day, for whatever reason, I allowed myself to feel the agonizing pain of not being able to afford my own plane ticket. I saw how, because my mom had purchased it, I would adjust my travel dates to fit her schedule and spend less time with my friends during my visit home. I felt I owed my mom that much.

When I allowed myself to evaluate what I was doing, I realized that money had represented my mother's love for me. I was unconsciously keeping myself from accumulating money because a deep need for love was met when I received those plane tickets, along with other small loans and items she would purchase for me when my finances got "tight."

Once I stepped away from my teaching career and regular paycheck to launch my business, the pattern became crystal clear. Within months, I realized I had to put an end to it once and for all. I gathered my courage and told my mom that there would be no more plane tickets. "I'm finding a way to buy my own," I declared. I admitted to her that I wanted to feel her love for me outside of our dynamic of financial rescue. Tears and tenderness followed that conversation, and in the end, I broke free from an incredibly disempowering financial relationship with my mom.

Our relationship today is far better than it's ever been because money no longer plays a role in it. Now I feel my mom's love through her phone calls, her hugs, and her curiosity about every area of my life. I proudly flew her out to see me last year and took her to my favorite spa. I truly believe it was because of my deep commitment to financial autonomy that my business began to take off.

YOUR MONEY GUNK INVENTORY

Write down your answers to the following questions. It's helpful to keep your answers because you may have additional insights later when you reread what you've written.

1. What beliefs did you acquire growing up that may be limiting your money consciousness? (Examples: Rich people are bad. Making money is hard work. Wealth is a representation of consumption, and I don't want to contribute to the problem.)

2. What did your parents and other early influencers tell you about money, and how has this history affected your ability to generate and keep money today?

3. Describe three of the most painful money moments in your life. What happened? How were you let down by money?

4. What money patterns play out in your life over and over? Do you have any idea where the patterns originated? If so, write down your thoughts. If not, simply ask for the answer to come to you. Then wait for it as a lightbulb moment or maybe in a dream.

5. What relationship will change when you make more money? Most of us have at least one primary relationship, if not more, that will drastically change as we begin making significant amounts of money. When we address money dynamics in our relationships head-on, we step into empowerment around money rather than give our power away to it (or to whoever has provided the money in our lives). Once you do an inventory of relationships that may shift when you make more money, you can address the dynamic head-on and heal what needs to be healed so you can attract as much money into your life as you want!

MONEY AND HAPPINESS

When I first met my dear friend Marci Shimoff, she invited me and a couple of her girlfriends to her gorgeous home in San Anselmo, California. The moment I walked into her home, I felt surrounded by wealth and spirituality—even a sense of Goddess Power. The tall ceilings, Buddha statue, and sweeping views of the San Francisco Bay Area were complemented by gorgeous landscaping, an inviting pool, and a hot tub out back. We shared an incredible lunch together and swapped ideas about our businesses all day long.

After sitting in the hot tub and having a heart-to-heart with several of Marci's friends, I was filled with the elation of girlfriend love and inspiration. But I left with curiosity: How did this heart-full woman, who was so full of happiness, get to where she is today?

Several months later, we were both invited to Ecuador with our mutual friend, Lynne Twist, and I had the opportunity to hear about Marci's life as we sat on a bus bouncing through the Andes. I was surprised to learn that this woman—who now glows so brightly—was born an unhappy camper. She was mildly depressed throughout her early years. When she was 22, she decided she wanted to create a life of happiness, so she set five goals for herself to achieve that:

1. To build a successful career helping people

2. To have a happy marriage with a man she loved

3. To enjoy many wonderful friendships

4. To live in a comfortable and beautiful home

5. To have the equivalent of Halle Berry's body (she told me that with a chuckle)

Marci went to work to accomplish those things that she believed would make her happy. By 1998 she just about had it all. Three of her books were in the top five on the *New York Times* bestseller list at the same time (she went on to write five more bestsellers), and she had a great life partner, wonderful friends, and a comfortable home. Although she says she didn't have Halle Berry's body, she was grateful she had a healthy body. She had everything a woman needed to be "happy" by textbook rules. Heck, by her own personal rules!

Then one day she had her wake-up call. She had just finished speaking to 8,000 women, and after her talk, she'd autographed 5,432 books. She felt like an author rock star. But after signing that last book, Marci went up to her hotel penthouse suite and broke into a flood of tears. She realized she had everything on her list, but she still wasn't happy. Something was missing. She'd been living by the myth that success would make her happy, and the spell was broken.

Marci started digging deep, going to the well within herself to find the true source of happiness. Over the next years, she studied the vast research on happiness and applied what she learned from it. As a result, she began deeply experiencing the happiness that came from within, from being connected to her soul and doing what her soul is here for.

As she found this new, more lasting experience of happiness, she was also catapulted to a higher level of success. She was featured in the book and movie *The Secret,* and her new book, *Happy for No Reason,* became another *New York Times* bestseller.

I was enthralled with her story as we lurched down a steep road past Mount Cotopaxi, just south of Baños, Ecuador. She turned toward me and said, "People who are truly happy and successful have done both the inner work to know their soul and the outer work to express themselves in the world." Then she looked deeply into my eyes and said, "Successful people are willing to do what everyone else is not. Sage, it seems to me that you're headed for success and happiness and everything you want in life. You've been willing to take actions that others aren't willing to. And you're committed to helping others do the same."

Have you ever had a moment like that, when you feel seen and validated by someone who's been there? Someone who knows it isn't easy to stick your neck out or stand onstage with butterflies in your stomach? Someone who understands how vulnerable you can feel when sharing with the world something precious that you feel you just have to share?

I'm grateful for Marci to this day for seeing me and for doing her work to help pave the path.

Marci also shared some interesting findings about money and its relationship to happiness. The happiness research clearly shows that money doesn't make us happy. However, the research also shows that happiness does help us *attract* money. In fact, happier people on average make approximately $1 million more over the course of their lifetimes. Everyone wants to be around happy people, so clients and customers are more attracted to businesses with happy people!

Happiness has other fringe benefits too. It brings greater productivity, more effective leadership, and better health. Happy people are one-third less likely to get sick, and they live on average nine years longer.

So, my dear Goddess sister, clearly we don't want to go after money just for the sake of money. And many of us are discovering that as we seek meaning, fulfillment, and a deep connection with our soul, happiness will follow. Then happiness can open the door to more money, freedom, and true wealth, both inside and out. And you know what? You are worthy of this—I promise!

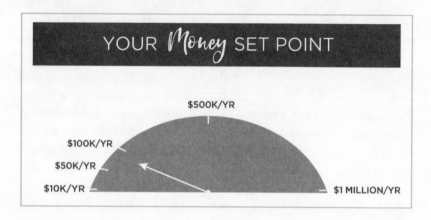

WHAT IS YOUR MONEY SET POINT?

We all have a money set point. In other words, we get used to a certain amount of money we're comfortable allowing into our lives. Then, because we're habituated to that amount, we find a way to spend or give away any surplus that comes our way. This often happens when people win the lottery. Within five years or less, they're back to where they began financially. Similarly, when our income drops below our money set point, we kick into gear and make up the difference by getting another job or cutting our expenses to return ourselves to our comfort zones.

Before I understood the concept of having a money set point—and before I invested in mentorship with someone I trusted to show me how to reach my financial goals—I attempted to grow my business haphazardly. I tried some things over here and over there but didn't manage to create the momentum I so deeply craved. I was struggling to pay my bills, felt like a victim to money, and secretly wanted a man to rescue me from the entire mess.

So I recommend becoming aware of your own money set point. Then you can practice, visualize, and take strategic action toward expanding it so that you can receive and keep larger amounts of money.

Calculate Your Monthly Money Set Point

1. List the gross amount of money you've received each month during the past year. Include spouse income, salary from a job, unexpected income—all of it!

2. Add the totals from your five highest months over the past year, and divide the grand sum by five. That's your money set point!

   My money set point is: $_____ /per month

NOTE: I like to calculate a money set point based on monthly income rather than annual income because when we think about our income per month, it's easier to increase it over a short amount of time. To determine your annual money set point, just multiply by 12.

My Money Set Point Example: When I first started my business, I had been comfortable making about $2,750 per month as a school-teacher. My grandfather had died the year I launched my coaching practice and left me $10,000. So my money set point at that time was:

$2,750 x 5 for the 5 top-earning months + $10,000 inheritance
Divided by 5 = $4,750 per month

I was blessed to have received the inheritance from my grand-father that helped me experience the luxury of a little more money.

When I moved to California and started my business, I knew that $2,750 a month wasn't going to cut it. I realized I needed a minimum of $5,000 per month to be comfortable. Once I knew my money set point, I was able to commit to and create income recipes that helped me generate $5,000 per month or more within a year of launching my practice.

My income recipe at the time was simple. (I like simple numbers.) I wanted to enroll 10 clients who would invest in a six-month training program with me at $500 per month each. It took me about nine months to find and recruit those 10 clients, but once I knew how much I needed to make and had a recipe—a plan to achieve my goal—and a mentor to hold me accountable, the money flowed.

The clearer and more confident I became about how much money I wanted to make, the more I made. I didn't start making $5,000 per month all of a sudden, and I didn't "accidentally" build a million-dollar company. Those financial goals were deliberate and strategic.

MONEY LOVES CLARITY!
Get specific about your money goals,
and brainstorm ways of meeting them.

STRETCHING YOUR MONEY SET POINT

Now that you know your money set point, the next step is to stretch it. What would you like your new money set point to be? In other words, how much money would you like to be making? Be realistic, but stretch yourself. I needed to get to six figures ($100,000 per year) before I could get to seven figures ($1,000,000 per year). What's a new money set point you can imagine yourself reaching but still feels exciting and abundant to you?

$$ Your New Money Goal $$

Old Money Set Point: $_____ per month

New Money Goal: $_____ per month

Now brainstorm three to five ways that you could createthe income to reach your new money goal.

Examples:

- If your new money goal is $7,000 per month and you work with private clients, your income recipe could be to enroll 14 clients paying you $500 each per month.

- If you're an artist and your new money goal is $10,000 per month, your income recipe could be to sell 20 prints per month at $500 each or sell 2 originals per month at $5,000 each.

Brainstorm . . .

- Income Recipe #1:
- Income Recipe #2:
- Income Recipe #3:

CHARGING WHAT YOU'RE WORTH

I'm here to put a stake in the ground for you, dear one, to have more money. I believe one of the most spiritual things you can do is to charge what you're worth! I want more money in the hands of women like you, who are going to go out and change the world with your wealth!

Furthermore, when you commit to your purpose and surrender your life over to Universal intelligence, it's my belief (and my experience) that you'll be financially taken care of.

Case Study: Entrepreneurial Goddess Rachel Augusta

My beloved client Rachel is an incredible animal healer and communicator. She has worked with many furry friends that have cancer, helping put that cancer into remission. She's helped animals to walk again after two months of paralysis, cured PTSD and trauma in animals, and prevented death due to sudden heart failure in dogs, cats, rabbits, horses, and various pocket animals in at least 500 cases. Impressive, right?

When Rachel first joined our Entrepreneurial Training Academy, despite her amazing gift, she was making only about $1,500 a month but was hesitant to raise her rates. Living in Minnesota, she was surrounded by people who were often leery of energy work on animals, thinking it was dubious, fake, or even witchcraft. Furthermore, how could she turn away pet owners in need when their furry friend was on the brink of death? She found herself charging less when it meant saving an animal's life.

Through coaching with my team and working with our prosperity principles, Rachel finally realized that she had to handle her own finances if she was going to step fully into this miracle healing work for pets and their owners. She was going to have to be healthy, vibrant, and easily able to pay her rent and get herself a massage. That's the only way she could show up for her clients. Like my friend Derek Rydall says, "You can't be the light of the world if you can't pay your light bill!"

Rachel embraced this and summoned the courage to raise her rates. Then she did so again. I recently invited her into the "hot seat" on one of our group calls, and she proudly announced she had made $7,500 last month by giving herself a raise. She was glowing. This was the highest income level she had ever hit in one month of her business.

The best part? When Rachel is being paid well by her clients, she has room to support friends and their treasured pets on a scholarship rate when she needs to. She now confidently considers herself the energetic emergency room for all animals. Her approach is grounded in physics and can be easily explained through science.

To find out more about Rachel's work, visit: www.RachelAugusta.com.

GIVE YOURSELF A RAISE!

Again, money is just energy, and when we give our life force energy in a way that contributes to others, we invite energy to come back to us as an exchange. For myself and many of my clients, the more willing we've been to allow the Divine to do its work through us, the more we've been able to allow ourselves to be provided for.

How can you do this too? You just have to be willing to ask for your value in exchange for your contribution. In other words, charge what you're worth.

I believe the Universe *wants* you to have what you need, and then some. I believe the Universe wants you to have excess. Just stop and contemplate that for a moment. What if it's true?

How much more could you give to your clients and customers
if you were living in total abundance?
This is what it's like to give from a cup that runneth over!

Stair-Stepping Your Prices

I'm a big believer in "stair-stepping" your prices, especially if you're selling a service. The last thing you want to do is cringe or expect objections when you tell a client your rate. So start at a rate that feels comfortable to you—a rate that you can quote as easily as you say, "Please pass the salt" at the dinner table. Then, with every few customers who hire you or buy your product, give yourself a raise.

TAKING FINANCIAL RISKS

Of course, it takes a little bit of gumption to raise your rates and put yourself out there as an entrepreneur, charging money for that delicious gift inside you. The good news? Research shows that 87 percent of women see themselves as financial risk takers, compared with just 73 percent of men.[3]

I've seen it in my clients over the years. We're better risk takers, more likely to see the big picture and take a long-term view, and less prone to overconfidence. Women are already taking the lead, and the legions of women entering the business world are ready to value themselves and what they have to offer! You've got this gumption inside of you too, sister.

WHAT'S YOUR "WHY"?

Is it uncomfortable to imagine making more money? Is it exciting? To interrupt the patterns that perpetuate financial lack, some of us actually have to be taught to *desire* money. Knowing why you want more is the first step. Consider: Why would *you* like to have more money?

What if you had enough money to . . .

- Go on a luxurious vacation anywhere in the world?
- Invest in as much bodywork, massage, or healing as you desire?
- Hire a personal chef?
- Buy whatever clothes you want?
- Give to whatever charity your heart desires?
- Send your kids to the best schools and colleges?

Perhaps none of those things are what motivate you, but if you have a desire to make and keep more money, it's important to consider why you want more. Most of the women I work with are more motivated by the idea of freedom than by the acquisition of more expensive cars or fancier jewelry. We want to be able to work when we want, with the people we want, and on our own terms. We aren't always lit up by the possibility of a higher number in the bank account, but we may get excited about the chance to travel, give back, or send our kids to college.

Regardless of what motivates you, when you know *why* you want the money, it's much easier to take the steps to increase your income. Knowing your *why* actually pulls you toward your money goals.

> *WHY would you like to have more money?*
>
> *WHAT will you spend your extra money on?*
>
> Brainstorm here:
>
> _____
>
> _____
>
> _____
>
> _____

MONEY IS LIKE GLUE

We're more likely to attract money when we have something for money to "stick" to, such as a goal of taking an exotic vacation, saving for a down payment on a house, or sponsoring a child in Africa.

The same is true for your clients. Allow me to introduce you to a simple marketing principle: your potential clients will invest their money in your services when they're connected to *their* why.

The wise entrepreneur takes the time to find out what motivates their potential clients and customers: The Realtor knows that a family wants a big enough yard to put up a jungle gym for their kids. The healer knows her client wants to be healthy enough to run a 10K. The weight loss mentor knows her client wants to lose that extra 12 pounds before her wedding.

When you take the time to connect your potential customers to their bigger *why*, they'll be much more likely to invest in your services or product. We'll chat more about this in chapter 8.

MONEY IS A TOOL

Having money at your disposal is a positive thing, in large part because you'll do good deeds with the extra finances you accumulate. Yet some of us unconsciously push money away because we don't want to become part of the materialistic, consuming, power-hungry world we live in. We carry an unconscious fear that when we become wealthy, we'll lose track of what's really important. We think we'll become power-hungry money moguls. In my experience, this just isn't so.

Once you're wealthy, you're going to be the same
gorgeous, heart-full woman that you are now!

As long as we carry a fear of losing ourselves in the acquisition of money, we allow others with less awareness to hold most of the world's wealth. We leave the moneymaking to people who may not choose to do the right things with it. You can impact the world in a much greater way when you have a financial surplus at your disposal. Money is a tool—like a hammer—one we can use to either build things up or tear them down.

I'm confident that you, my dear Entrepreneurial Goddess, will do amazing things with your money, so let's put a plan in place to help you attract and keep more of it! In order for you to embrace your wealthy, heart-full, spiritual future self, I absolutely must tell you a story about my dear friend Lynne Twist.

Case Study: Entrepreneurial Philanthropist Lynne Twist

Lynne is the best-selling author of *The Soul of Money* and by far the most influential money mentor I've had in my life. I believe she's the ultimate Goddess Philanthropist of our time. She's dedicated her life to changing the planet, ending world hunger, and saving the rain forest. In doing so, she's built several multimillion-dollar organizations that give back to the causes she loves.

Lynne is the most incredible fund-raiser I know, raising millions of dollars for causes she believes in with confidence and ease.

I've never seen anything like it. She invites audiences to give more, and the rapport she has with them inspires people to dig deeper. More often than not, she doubles or triples the original amount she had in mind.

She isn't afraid to ask for money and redistribute it to the people and places in the world that need it. We could all aspire to emulate her relationship with money. Lynne loves money, and money loves Lynne back!

When we look at the developing world, we often see societies based on consumption and materialism. Walking through a shopping mall and witnessing the "more, more, more" mind-set can be a soul-crushing experience. But if you're anti-materialistic to the point of judging others, you risk unconsciously pushing money away.

Lynne is a great example of a woman who has chosen to stand for sustainability rather than against consumerism. Twenty years ago she founded an organization called Pachamama Alliance, a nonprofit that's dedicated to protecting the Amazon rain forest, the precious lungs of our planet, in Ecuador. The mission of Pachamama Alliance is to bring forth an environmentally sustainable, spiritually fulfilling, socially just human presence on this planet.

The Pachamama Alliance partners with the indigenous Achuar people of the rain forest, working together with them rather than adopting a "rescue" mentality. This dynamic alone has created a new paradigm and financial dynamic for social justice leaders and nonprofits across the globe.

Bringing wisdom back to the United States from deep within the heart of the Amazon jungle, Lynne's organization realizes that while the accumulation of money isn't the end goal, we must create ample resources to address the issues our planet is facing.

Lynne is acutely aware of the struggles that plague the world— poverty, global warming, war, homelessness, and hunger—yet she continually operates from a place of abundance for both herself and the causes for which she stands. She taught me early on in our friendship that if I was going to be of service to the planet, I needed to make peace with money. I had to break my own story of "not-enoughness" and insufficiency. I had to embrace the fact that at the end of the day, I had enough, there was enough, and I wasn't the victim I made myself out to be in my mind.

You're Wealthy NOW

Here's the truth: if there is food in your fridge, if you have shoes and clothes, if you have a bed and a roof, you're richer than 75 percent of the people in the world. If you have a bank account, money in your wallet, and some coins in the money box, you're more fortunate than 92 percent of the people on the planet.

You and I may have gone through some very difficult times with money, but we're *not* victims of money. We're resourceful, capable creators of our own financial reality!

MONEY AS A SPIRITUAL PATH

If you've had struggles with money, you now have an opportunity to learn from the struggle and even grow spiritually. That may sound surprising; we're hardly taught to think of money as spiritual. But what if it actually *is* spiritual to desire money, to make money, and to give back in a way that lets your income grow?

In addition to fund-raising for my friend Tika's Hope for Women organization in Bali, my company raises money for an organization in Ecuador called the Jungle Mamas, a group of women who are fighting to protect the Amazon, their precious rain forest home. It's been an honor to know these women, to give to them, and to support women leaders who have devoted their lives to the most pristine jungle on earth.

I've found that as I include these women in my wealth vision, I've become wealthier. As I give back, more money comes my way.

It's almost as if the Universe trusts me to do the right thing with the money, so my container grows.

Through Lynne's mentorship and several trips to Ecuador by her side, I've learned to surrender my life force energy to being a positive force for good. I've strengthened my faith in the belief that as I contribute to the world, the Universe will care for and provide for me. I've come to deeply understand and embrace the old saying, "It's in the giving that we receive."

I've found from working with women entrepreneurs for the past decade that once our needs and the needs of our families are met, we tend to reach a limit as to how much money we're interested in generating. So when we, as women, adopt a humanitarian cause or service-based mission above and beyond our immediate client base, we rise above our typical income levels. Now we have a reason to generate more. The truth is that women love to give back, and we're often the donors of the planet. In fact, in a recent study, the *Huffington Post* discovered that 64 percent of donations are made by women globally.[4]

I ask my clients who take my yearlong business training programs to choose a humanitarian cause that they will support with their business profits. Often it's in choosing a cause and including that cause in their message that they reach a new level of success, visibility, and recognition in their positions as business owners.

As women, we're wired for service. While the average entrepreneur may aspire to just break even, women entrepreneurs are lit up and turned on by the possibility of building a business that makes a powerful contribution to the world. We're on the planet to give. When we give back to the world through our businesses, especially to a cause greater than ourselves, we actually increase our capacity to receive and grow our income. We're able to release any old patterns of feeling victimized by money and grow into a more empowered relationship with our finances. And that, my dear, is how money becomes a spiritual path!

INTEGRATION

Your Financial Inventory

1. How much money would you like to be making in your business within one year? Three years?

2. Extra credit: Find someone who is creating that kind of money in her business, and take her out for lunch. Or even better, hire her to mentor you!

3. What's your favorite charity or service-based mission in the world? What do you wish you could do to better the planet? Write it down. That's the first step to making it a reality.

Women Rocking Business VIRTUAL GUIDEBOOK

BREAKTHROUGH BONUS TRAINING #2:

Three Money $ Breakthrough $ Exercises

Grab these three Transformational Money Experiences!
My clients tell me these are game-changers for them!
Grab it here: www.womenrockingbusiness.com/guidebook

Chapter 3

READY...
FIRE...
AIM!

*"It is better to be boldly decisive and risk being wrong
than to agonize at length and be right too late."*

— MARILYN MOATS KENNEDY

I met the author SARK on a cruise ship from Seattle to Alaska, and we had an instant connection. I've always looked up to her as an artist, a thought leader, and a pioneer of creativity. I buy her books as soon as they come out and devour them page by page, wondering, "How does she come up with this stuff?!" When I met her, I immediately fell even more in love with this gorgeous, buoyant being.

During our first conversation, I asked her, "What's your secret to success?"

She leaned in very close and looked at me with her bright eyes. "I make it up!" she said.

Girrrrl, SARK was speaking my language! The truth is we're all just making it up all the time. So maybe we don't need to stress so much about having it all "figured out." Here's my question to you: What do you want to "make up" next in your life? What beautiful next step do you want to create for yourself?

Over and over again, I tell my clients to stop trying to figure it all out at once. Your business will evolve one client, one customer, one sale, or one project at a time. You'll derive more clarity from a week of trying out an idea to see if it's a fit than you will from years of thinking about it.

Now that you've done some work around healing your relationship with money, you're ready to dive into your business dreams. So here it is, Goddess—my invitation for you to be IN ACTION. This is the next inner game strategy you need to ensure your success.

If there's a business idea that's been tapping you on the shoulder for a while, the time is now. I wish you were here sitting in this coffee shop with me right now so that I could look you in the eyes and say:

"Sister, clarity comes from taking action
and not the other way around!"
In other words, stop overthinking it!

You and I are friends by now, yes? Allow me to boldly light an energetic fire underneath you to urge your commitment to action. Don't try to meditate your way to clarity.

As I've said before, don't expect to have your 10-year business plan drafted before you even start, and don't expect to know exactly who your customers are. Don't put that pressure on yourself and your tender, growing dream right away (especially if you haven't had a ton of experience running a business or working with customers). That would be like expecting a 16-year-old to know exactly what she wants to do with the rest of her life before she starts college. I know there are those rare teenagers who set out to become a doctor or own a restaurant and end up doing exactly that for the rest of their lives, but they're few and far between.

I like to refer to our businesses as "evolutionary," and that makes you an "evolutionary entrepreneur." What if you've been called into the next chapter of your livelihood to help your customers evolve, help yourself evolve, and help the planet evolve? This means that you can relax into the transformation that you and your business will go through. And you have an incredible opportunity to build a business that will evolve with you, so give yourself permission to start somewhere—anywhere!

What if, my dear, you gave yourself the gift of launching your next mini business project without having it all figured out? Invite some friends to your living room to tell them about your new chapter. Practice with some colleagues. Host a mini open house at the library or in a local community center. Announce your new service or product, and start practicing with potential clients. You don't need a fancy website or business plan. You don't need 10 pages full of client success stories or customer testimonials before you get started. All you need is your passion and willingness to put yourself out there. Then be willing to receive support and feedback.

I know there will be naysayers, but don't let them hold you back! If someone in your life has an opinion that's less than supportive, just say, "Thank you for sharing," and turn toward the people who *are* willing to support you. These are the people you can lean on—the ones you *know* are on your team.

WHAT'S IN THE WAY OF YOUR CLARITY?

Once again: "Clarity comes from taking action and not the other way around." Make that your new mantra. Perhaps you're waiting to feel like you're "ready." (Good luck with that. Hope you're enjoying your life when you're still waiting 10 years from now.) Maybe you're hoping one day the clouds will part and a sense of perfect clarity will fly down from the heavens like a white dove, creating a nest within your heart to accompany you to your next glowing summit of success. Sister, this isn't how it goes, so let's have a heart-to-heart, you and I, on the topic of clarity.

"Why Haven't I Figured It Out?"

One of the most common blocks to clarity is that self-critical voice, or the "gremlins," as some of us like to call them. I've noticed that many of my clients criticize themselves for not having "made it" or "arrived" at some utopic vision of success, fame, or financial freedom.

Can you relate? Perhaps you're beating up on yourself for not going faster or achieving more. Or you're being hard on yourself for the time you've spent in your life searching. Your gremlins might sound something like this: *"Why haven't you figured it out? You're [insert your age] years old! Why are you still struggling with what you should do for a living? It's too late; you're hopeless! You can't start over now. What about that expensive Ph.D. program? What about your engineering degree? You should be far along at an engineering firm by now,"* and on and on.

My gremlins can be ruthless with self-criticism when it comes to my career. When I first started my business, at age 36, I had a deep fear that I was too old to start over and launch a new business. I left a secure teaching job and a master's degree behind—education that I hadn't even finished paying for!

My gremlins used to bark at me, sounding something like this: *"You thought it was so much fun being a wilderness guide for women in the Canadian Rockies all those years before teaching. But listen here, dearie, that was a royal waste of three years of your life. You got paid diddly-squat, and then your 'brilliant' self spent five more years teaching high school when you knew the whole time you really wanted to start your own business. And what do you think you got out of those years traveling around in your grandpa's motor home to Utah, the Grand Canyon, and Oregon? You've made your bed, and now you have to lie in it. You're trained to be a teacher. Just be grateful for your job, and go teach those high schoolers!"*

Downright mean and nasty, right? Especially to the adventurer and seeker inside me. Am I ever glad I didn't let those voices win. The voice of fear—your own personal gremlins—simply get louder when you try anything new. When we stretch outside our comfort zone, the gremlins kick up, hoping to pull us back to safety. Fear is going to be present as you begin taking the bold actions to build a business. The only rule here, dear one, is that fear doesn't get to drive.

> ## "It's too late! I'm too old to start a business!"
>
> If your fear voice is telling you that you're too old or
> it's too late, please remember that the searching you've done
> in your life hasn't been for nothing. Divine law tells us that nothing
> is wasted in life. If you've been seeking variety, trying on different
> careers, dabbling in this, and dabbling in that, celebrate all that
> you've explored! Your soul has gotten what it needed to become
> the woman you are today, ready to step into the next level of
> commitment and build a business you love.
>
>

Looking back, I can see how my experiences, although I can be good at making them wrong, have perfectly prepared me to play the role I'm playing. Here's a quick inventory:

- **Experience A:** My stint as a wilderness guide

    How it prepared me: I took dozens of young women backpacking in the Canadian Rockies for weeks at a time. It taught me what I'm truly made of, as well as how to lead women.

- **Experience B:** My career as a science teacher

    How it prepared me: I mastered facilitating learning experiences for others and creating content. I learned to break down complex ideas so that people can understand them and how to guide a group through a self-discovery journey.

- **Experience C:** Traveling in a motor home for a year

    How it prepared me: My aluminum home on wheels gave me time to see the world and meet all kinds of new people. I often felt as if I were without a purpose, floating from place to place. I secretly wished I was more connected to the world around me, more productive, and more purposeful, instead of planning yet another lonely hiking trip. What developed in me during that time was the burning desire to build a business that would change lives. When I find myself overwhelmed, I frequently remember that having a purpose is a gift, even when it feels hard. I'd rather do my traveling on my flex week and have a life I look forward to returning to on the other side.

Yes, I spent time pouring my heart into my jobs and frolicking around the world, and, yes, those experiences singularly prepared me for what I'm doing now. They helped me truly appreciate the difference I get to make with my business. Yes, yes, yes!!!

Never underestimate the power of giving yourself a . . .
YES!!!
"Yes" to all of your life experiences.
What have you not said YES to within your own journey?
What are you still making yourself wrong for?

All right then, girlfriend, let's assess: How have your life experiences contributed to what you want to do next? Take a moment to do your own inventory:

- Experience A:

    How it prepared me:

- Experience B:

    How it prepared me:

- Experience C:

    How it prepared me:

What did you discover, my dear? Can you see that your inner explorer has been committed to getting you exactly the experiences you needed to complete your life mission on the planet? I hope so!

But Don't I Still Have to Figure It All Out First?

Have I mentioned that clarity comes from taking action and not the other way around? I've said it before, but I'll say it again because I've seen so many women get stuck on this one: Trying to figure it all out before you take the first step will not only slow you down but keep you stuck. Often the steps ahead can't reveal themselves until you take that first step.

Trying to figure out your destiny is futile. Instead, trust that your desires are leading you to the right next step that will take you to the right place. Even if a choice seems to be a mistake, I guarantee that it will teach you something important. (Did I say that nothing is wasted?)

I'll never forget the day my friend Holly looked me in the eye and said, "Sage, you're never going to feel totally ready. Just don't let it stop you." So even if you don't feel like you're ready, even if it isn't perfect yet, it's time, Goddess. It's time to get out there and take the next step. Trust me, you can do this!

THE SHADOW OF PERFECTIONISM

Why do we think we have to be polished, prepared, and groomed, with *i*'s dotted and *t*'s crossed 101 percent of the time? If you have such perfectionistic tendencies, I'm sure it's because you want your work to be as great as it can be. There's nothing wrong with that, per se, so let's take a moment to honor the perfectionist in us, shall we?

After all, some of the greatest experiences of our lives have occurred because other people have held themselves to a high standard of excellence. Behind every truly brilliant movie, every amazing work of art, and every meal that's so good it brings tears to your eyes lies a perfectionist. Some dear human was so attached to it being right that they didn't settle for less.

But I also want to shine a light on the shadow of perfectionism for a moment. Maybe you're someone who does 89 things in a day, but you beat yourself up for the 11 things you don't do. Maybe you're more easygoing about your to-do list, but perfectionism shows up in other areas, like worrying about whether you have a spot on your shirt or whether you said the exact right thing when you stood up to introduce yourself at the Rotary Club lunch.

What if you allowed yourself to be imperfectly human? Remember: you are a gorgeous work in progress!!!

READY . . . FIRE . . . AIM!

Be willing to fall on your face.
Allow some room for mistakes.
Then you can embrace the risk taking
that's required to build a business.

YOU CAN DO THIS!

The danger of perfectionism is that it can keep you from getting your magic out into the world. That's because perfectionism and procrastination are friends. Did you know that? They're like the evil stepsisters in Walt Disney's *Cinderella*, working together to keep your inner rock star from shining as bright as she can!

I have clients come to me all the time with oodles of content they've spent hours creating . . . in a closet. Wonderful stuff that they've poured their hearts into. The problem? They're not selling it, sharing it, or using it to serve anyone. It's tempting to hide out behind your computer, working on your website, meandering around social media, creating theoretical products, or even writing a book! Have you ever known anyone who's spent months or years writing a book, yet nobody has read it aside from their mother, dog, and best friend?

It can be a seductive mistake to create content in a closet. Sometimes the insides of those closets are very beautiful! But they're also dark and safe. The truth is that those products, books, and other creations are going to be much more marketable when you create them out in the open and involve your customers in your process from the start.

If the closet creator sounds like you, I urge you to stop hiding out and be willing to get out there. Just get people's input before your products and services see the light of day. That will give you valuable information you can use to improve the quality of what you're creating.

But wait . . . what if people steal my idea before it's gotten off the ground?

I've also had clients tell me countless times, "I can't tell anyone about this concept I've created because it's so good, I'm afraid they'll steal it and go do it better!" I invite you to challenge the gremlins who voice that fear. It's just another strategy to keep you from moving forward. The truth is that you are *so* much bigger than one concept. What's the worst that could happen? You'd have to come up with another idea. And before you say, "I don't know if I can," let me say, "You can! You have more ideas inside you than you know!"

It's a little tricky to be the best-kept secret when you're trying to make a living. Get out there!

"I'm Not Original Enough"

How many of us fear that our message isn't unique, and therefore we have no right to put it out into the world? Any good publisher (especially my publisher!) will tell you that it's the author's stories and particular way of teaching lessons that sell the book, not the uniqueness of the concepts.

Besides that, the Universe often introduces an idea into the world in a variety of ways through several people. So know this: You're original enough just by virtue of being you. Who you are is original and unique, and your story is unique. Nobody else on the planet can be you.

Look at Pepsi and Coke—they're almost exactly the same, but people are loyal to one or the other. They're both successful companies because their marketing is different and appeals to different customers.

There's a concept similar to mine (which I did *not* invent) called "Build the plane as you fly it." Sure, there's some overlap, but no one teaches in exactly the same way as me. I bring my background and personality to everything I do, and so will you. And the people who resonate with who you are will find you and hear you.

Good Is the Enemy of Great

So often we aren't taught to go for "great," so we accept the career or relationship that's "good" or "fine." My client Willow Brown was in that camp. She deeply wanted to reach more people and have a bigger impact on the planet, but she already had a successful acupuncture practice, working four days a week.

When I first met Willow, she had just let go of her 16 years of teaching yoga and qigong so she could free up more time alongside her acupuncture work to share her true passion—the teachings of Taoist sexology. Though she loves her acupuncture practice and loved teaching yoga, she longed for that feeling of bringing true transformation to a group. She always knew she was meant to bring all her knowledge together and teach the global community in a way that would support a shift in consciousness around health, sexuality, and sensuality.

I worked with Willow to strengthen her vision of how she really wanted her work life to look. She knew that these longings to teach on a broader scale weren't going to go away. So she slowly pulled back from her acupuncture practice to just three days a week, sometimes two, in order to focus on bringing her bigger work to the world. It's always a risk to step away from the familiar and build something new. Willow is an extraordinary example of the courage it takes to build that bridge to a new career chapter.

Because of Willow's extensive background in acupuncture and Eastern medicine and her work as a doula, throughout the years she had accumulated a vast understanding of women's health and sexuality and all the hormones and emotions that go with it. She knew deep down that she was meant to help women access the medicine that resides in their own bodies, so she finally took the leap and began teaching her own version of Taoist sexology. After all, she'd been personally practicing it and loving it since she was 21. So it was about time, right?

Willow needed more of an audience, however, so even before she felt completely ready, she began using the tools we teach in our training programs. She crafted a talk that she delivered in the San Francisco Bay Area to potential clients, as well as online. Willow admitted to me how nervous she was to give her first few talks. She was afraid someone would know more than she did and challenge what she said. But she did it anyway!

This is a perfect example of "READY, FIRE, AIM." Willow's willingness to take a risk and step out before she had it all figured out paid off. She recalls her first speaking engagement at a local healing center titled "3 Keys to Hot Spiritual Sex." More than 20 people attended, several of whom went on to hire her. Since then she's led talks and retreats in the Bay Area; Park City, Utah; Athens, Georgia; and Luang Prabang, Laos. As I write this, Willow is making plans for her next trip, to Java, Indonesia!

Willow is now inspiring women globally to understand their bodies, endocrine systems, and meridian systems. This allows them to access their most authentic inner wisdom and greatest creative power that comes from their sexual glands, organs, and desires. She teaches women how to harness their sexual vitality and how to use that energy to create the life they yearn for with grace and equanimity, from a place of deep acceptance.

Willow has shared the stage with visionaries like Mantak Chia, Alison Armstrong, and Shakti Malan, and her business is on an entirely new trajectory. She has now trained dozens of women through her Taoist Sexology Mastery program and added more than $50,000 of income to her business. And she's still just getting started! She's constantly inspired by her new work and is able to relax into a life that allows her to travel and teach.

Her clients now call her and say, "I'm pregnant!" or "I had a superior orgasm last night!" That's the real payoff for Willow. You can find out more about her work at www.yinwellness.com.

IT'S TIME TO *FIRE*

Now, it's time for you to try on the mind-set of "Ready, Fire, Aim." Sister, trust me. I'll say it again: you don't have to know exactly which road you're taking to take the first step. Follow your desire, and beta test an idea like Willow did. The people you're here to serve deserve to be included in your process. It's the beauty of building the plane while you're flying it rather than building a plane that you don't even know could make it off the ground.

Start by opening up about your ideas and dreams to a friend you trust—or even a potential client. Then the ideas will become real, and you'll no longer be in the dreaming stage. You'll be in the firing stage. Just don't wait to take aim first!

Successful people are successful not because of their talents but because of the choice they made to show up, over and over and over again. Successful people didn't figure it all out and hide in a closet until one day they miraculously had thousands of raving fans. Remember the old saying: we work for years and years to become an overnight success.

Yes, it takes courage and guts to show up and try out your idea while you still have your training wheels on. But that's what is necessary for success.

Right here, as you're preparing to launch your business or take it to the next level, I invite you to give yourself permission to not be perfect. Give yourself permission to show up and take imperfect action, to figure it out while you're on the path, and to build the plane as you're flying it. And the next time that internal perfectionist rears her perfectly groomed head and says, "But I want it to be perrrrrfect," let her know that your leadership, skills, and capacity to wo-manifest will get polished in the experiences of life that are waiting for you. Your soul will be shined to perfection simply by showing up (imperfectly).

And when you do your best, whether it's a home run or a fall on your face, you get to show up having done your best. That's not only all that matters, it's what it's all about.

INTEGRATION

Taking your next few BOLD Action Steps

Action Challenge #1: Put together an experimental program/ service or an open house for your business idea so that you can take it for a test drive with practice customers. Our daughters and sons play "candy store" in our living rooms. Why can't we?

Then ask for feedback from these customers in real time. Get success stories and testimonials from those who have sampled your work. This way, you'll design the most effective products or services possible for your future client base. As you get a little experience, you can even choose to charge a nominal fee and get paid to do research for your own entrepreneurial education!

Action Challenge #2: Find a business owner who is successful with a business similar to the one you dream about. Invite this person to lunch and ask questions, or ask if you can shadow her (or him) for a day.

Action Challenge #3: Go to a networking event and practice telling people what you do, even if you're making it up!

Action Challenge #4, for service providers: Offer people free breakthrough sessions where you show up and serve them. Walk them through a process you've created, or just wing it! (Yes, that's right, I said, "Wing it!") If they like your session, ask them to write you a testimonial.

Voilà! You're already on your way!

Women Rocking Business VIRTUAL GUIDEBOOK

BREAKTHROUGH BONUS TRAINING #3:

Sage Lavine interview with Neale Donald Walsch:
"The Spiritual Solution to Confusion"

This video interview I did with Neale is among my favorite interviews of all time. There's no better man to help you find clarity by connecting to the Divine than Neale Donald Walsch.

Grab it here: www.womenrockingbusiness.com/guidebook

Chapter 4

BUILD A SUPPORT NETWORK OF ENTREPRENEURIAL SISTERS

*"If you want to go quickly, go alone.
If you want to go far, go together."*

— AFRICAN PROVERB

When I first went off to college, I was desperately homesick. It turned out that the daughter of my dad's girlfriend was also going off to school in Ames, Iowa, so we decided it would be better to room with someone familiar rather than a total stranger. That's how Carlie became my freshman year roommate. Unfortunately, I soon found out that a total stranger would have been better.

Carlie was incredibly charming and totally gorgeous, but she had backstabbing and mean-girl tendencies. She had this way of going behind my back and gossiping about me to a mutual friend or snapping back at me with cutting words just when I was struggling with a moment of self-doubt. Then, when my father and her mother broke up, her behavior toward me got worse. She began to strategically leave me out of our posse's evening or weekend plans at times when I was feeling the most alone.

Still, when I hung out with Carlie, I felt cool because I thought *she* was cool. And although I got better grades and accolades, she knew how to dress better than me, she knew how to flirt with boys, she was big-eyed and slender with a short pixie haircut, and she just had a way of magnetizing fun. All of that seemed so much more compelling than good grades and art awards.

So I rode on her coattails the first few months of college. We partied together, drank together, and woke up with awful hangovers in our college dorm room bunks. We met boys together and formed the freshman tribe that we all need to make it through that first year away from home.

But ohhh, Goddess! Carlie and I were like oil and water! Looking back now, I can see my people-pleasing insecurities very clearly, and I can see that her need to put down other women was just her way of finding a sense of false confidence.

When I was truly ready to have friends in my life who treated me with love and respect, I moved across campus, away from Carlie and my freshman tribe, and I began my search for a new community. Eventually I found an incredible group of new friends with whom I shared many college memories, but I still didn't feel quite at peace with the way things had ended with Carlie. Then, one day, I ran into another member of the freshman tribe, who informed me that once I left, Carlie had turned on her too and begun pulling the same stunts. My friend apologized for not seeing through Carlie before and not standing up for me.

What a life-changing moment that was for me, to experience such validation. I hadn't just imagined Carlie's lack of kindness. I'd been seeing it clearly all along.

Looking back on that experience, I see that Carlie was my beloved teacher, and the gift for me was that the mistreatment stopped there. While I had been treated badly by other girls all through grade school, high school, and my first year of college, something changed the day I moved out of my dorm room and told Carlie never to contact me again. A warrior of feminine love awoke inside me, and I've become dedicated to creating a tribe of women allies ever since. Now I'm proud to say I have the very best girlfriends in the entire world. (If you have great girlfriends too, then we can all be friends, okay?)

What about you? Have you experienced this same kind of mean-girl syndrome? If you haven't, you're one of the few. Just about every woman I meet has a story about a mean girl in her past.

Or perhaps you were on the other side of it. Maybe you carry a history of causing some hurt to women in your life, intentionally or unintentionally. You probably became aware at some point that your behavior came from an insecure part of you. Growing up is hard, and there have likely been times when you didn't bring your most loving and whole self to the party. Some of us have even been on both sides of the mean-girl scenario, shifting back and forth between victim and instigator.

Today I recognize that both Carlie and I participated in the dynamic between us, and I'm thrilled to now be in a place where I can take full responsibility for the victim role I played in our little drama. There's nothing wrong with getting caught in a victim mentality temporarily, as long as we catch it and learn from it! After all, women have been victimized throughout history again and again. It makes sense that we would re-create these scenarios in our lives in order to understand fully how to take back our power. But we can more fully reclaim our sense of inner strength and confidence when we support one another.

Throughout the course of my life, I've had women both stand by me and abandon me. Women have been my biggest cheerleaders and most ruthless enemies. Some women can be brutal, bitchy, and backstabbing. But others can lift us up out of the most painful despair with a nurturing love that heals, transforms, and changes our lives.

In your life, perhaps you've been both supported *and* disappointed by women. Maybe along the way, there was someone who knocked you down a few notches when you became too expressive, too loud, too big for your britches, or even too mature or independent for the comfort of a girlfriend.

And goodness, dear sister, I hope you've also had the experience that there's no better support on the planet than an invested, dedicated, and loving girlfriend who believes in you with her whole heart!

What if you could multiply that girlfriend until you had a whole tribe of loving women who support you? Women whose vocabulary does not contain "mean-girl syndrome"? Doesn't that sound amazing?

WHY YOU NEED A TRIBE OF SUPPORTIVE WOMEN

I'm here to tell you that such an amazing tribe can be yours. I've gone from being the underdog among my woman peers—at times feeling squashed and minimized—to being a leader of women. I've been studying the most successful women on the planet for two decades. I've done more than 150 interviews with self-made women with six- and seven-figure incomes during my "Women on Purpose" online series. They all say the same thing: "Don't try to do it alone. You can't! A tree doesn't grow without roots. Get anchored. Let other women support you on your journey."

In fact, in working with my clients for the past decade, I've seen that success comes easier for women leaders when we prioritize supporting other women and allow them to support us in return.

We've already talked about the mind-set of generating money as a spiritual path and a balanced schedule and relationship to work so that you don't burn out. The next step in attuning your mind-set for success is to create the emotional support system you'll need to sustain you as a leader—especially from the women in your life.

HEALING OUR WOUNDS ABOUT OTHER WOMEN

If feelings come up for you as you read this chapter, do your best to breathe and stay connected to those emotions. Express them as it's appropriate for you. I assure you I won't leave you stranded here! This book is meant to be a healing journey for you, sister.

You may have resistance to the kind of support I'm suggesting. After all, if you've been burned by women, maybe you haven't yet had a truly close girlfriend. This chapter will at least get you started on clearing out that resistance. Maybe you even resist support because you feel guilty for having been a mean girl to someone else. Know that whatever you did in the past was due to your own insecurities and hurts. Now you deserve the kind of tribe I'm talking about.

Whatever comes up for you as you continue reading, rest in the knowledge that it's part of the alchemy that will prepare you for true leadership and greatness.

Because I know what it's like to be on the receiving end of women's competition and wrath, and because I've found my way to keeping my heart open toward women throughout the pain, I've learned how to create and hold a safe space of community for my women clients. I instinctively know how to shine the light of truth on gossip and design an environment where every woman feels safe to show up. It's a place where every woman feels protected enough to ask for support and put her vulnerable self out there, even as she offers support to others.

But my level of mastery at creating women communities came *only* because of the pain I've been through. Again, one of my biggest wounds emerged as my biggest gift. *In other words, what you've been through in your life will emerge as the golden lining of your business message.*

WHY WOMEN?

I'm often asked why I've chosen to work primarily with women. Here's my answer: Once upon a time, an Indian guru was asked, "Why are there more male leaders than female leaders in the world? Why is it that the leaders of the Eastern traditions have been primarily men? It has been mostly men who have brought the wisdom of the East to the West, including Wayne Dyer, Deepak Chopra, B. K. S. Iyengar, the father of yoga, and more."

In his Indian accent, the guru responded, "The reason there are more men leaders than women is this: Women are like crabs in a pot. If you put crabs in a pot to boil, you don't need to put a lid on the pot because as soon as one of the crabs crawls up to escape the pot, another crab will just reach up, grab its leg, and yank it back down into the pot. Women don't like other women to get too much more successful than they are. It's threatening to them. Men are more forthright in their competitiveness. They say, 'Brother, I'm going to take you down.' Women are more subtle but more incessant in their competition with one another. And for this reason, it's difficult for women to be big and shiny in the world. They don't want to lose the love of their tribe, so they keep themselves small."

When I heard this story, I shed some good, cleansing tears. I wept for all the times I had felt this way, for all the times I had been on both ends of this women's inferiority/superiority story. I wept for the times women had pulled me back into the pot and the times I had pulled other women back in without even meaning to.

I've told this story to women all over the world—my sisters in Thailand, Bali, and India and the indigenous Achuar community in Ecuador. Every woman could relate to it on some level. We've all been knocked down a bit, and we've all done some knocking at times when we weren't feeling like our strongest selves. The truth is that we women have played a role in keeping our own gender down, and we are the ones who will turn it around.

So where do these women's wounds come from? Where did we learn to compete, to turn our backs, start rumors, gossip at the expense of women we love, and close our hearts down?

Perhaps some of us saw the way our mothers or grandmothers were with other women and adopted some of their disempowering behaviors. For example, I have an incredible mom who loved me and was kind to the women around her. But Mom didn't help me cultivate my sense of inner power as much as I would have preferred. She was quite controlling, and she always wanted to quiet me down. "Be a lady," she'd say. "Don't be so loud; don't show off like that!" She often thought it was "too much" if I became excited about a theater production at school or a win on my debate team.

Meanwhile, I witnessed the small ways Mom would minimize herself. She is an incredible schoolteacher, her students love her, and she's a gorgeous woman. However, as a child, I didn't see Mom owning her greatness. Instead I saw her people-pleasing and over-giving. I imprinted on her behaviors, and the people-pleasing part of me developed. It's taken me years to learn to stop over-giving, to ask for what I want in life, and to set boundaries. Now Mom and I have heart-to-heart talks about these behaviors and encourage each other to ask for what we want in life.

After weathering several disempowering dynamics with girlfriends in my younger years, including the one with Carlie, I came to understand how to choose friends, how to train others to treat me the way I wanted to be treated, and how to recognize relationships that allowed for an equal energy exchange between two souls. I got very good at acknowledging those around me, seeing their greatness, and reflecting their beauty. And I asked for the same in return.

When I shifted this painful dynamic inside myself, I attracted women friends who blew me away with their commitment and integrity. An example of this is my first entrepreneurial friend, Holly. Holly is a daring soul with bright eyes and long brown hair, and we became instant friends when she walked into my yoga class one day years ago. Over a five-hour breakfast, we decided we'd been witches in a past life together, burned at the stake for giving our gifts, and that in this life neither of us would allow such a thing to happen to the other.

Not long after, Holly and I put together our first women's workshop, in which we facilitated deep connection exercises with our female students, teaching them the power of vulnerability and the healing that can take place when women stand by and for one another.

The best part? Holly and I have hired each other. I hired her to facilitate my first vision quest experience. Recently Holly hired me to help her grow her business. Now she leads priestess and sisterhood retreats alongside me, and I've had the honor of supporting her to grow her business, double her income, and transform more women through her programs. She leads retreats in Glastonbury, England, and takes several months off every year. Holly is living the life she's dreamed of for years.

SUPPORT FOR THE FEAR OF FAILURE . . . AND THE FEAR OF SUCCESS

Holly and I have vowed to stand by each other as we've both built our businesses. Incredible friends like her have promised to love me whether I fall on my face in front of a roomful of people . . . or become an "overnight" success and land an interview with Oprah.

This is so important because becoming too successful can leave us abandoned by the people closest to us who may not feel comfortable with our good fortune. The truth is that some people in our lives will judge us at both ends of the spectrum—when we're weak and when we're strong.

Failure and success can be equally scary when you really decide to go for it in your business. Failure, of course, comes with its dose of shame and indignity, but the fear of judgment that comes with success can be just as crippling. Add to that any feelings of not deserving your success, and you might just crash and burn without supportive sisters.

I've needed my friends like Holly to promise me they aren't going anywhere, no matter where the ride takes me. This loyalty has anchored me enough to take the big risks. We women have to remember that we're meant to stand behind one another on this path to our dreams. It's how we won the right to vote in the United States, and it's how we've gotten where we are today. It's also how we'll make new strides tomorrow.

Even though the past few decades have seen an emerging force of women leaders and earners, we still take a back seat to men in most of the world. In the United States, we earn 83 cents on the dollar compared with men. There's no way around the fact that we've inherited a set of limiting beliefs that devalue our gifts and diminish our worth, both in our own minds and in the minds of men. It's up to us to work together and find our power.

Of course, we also need to learn to support ourselves. We do. But in our modern world, in my experience, far too many of us think that we're independent and unstoppable all the time. I've found that we have a much more sustainable strength when we surrender to the truth that we need one another and allow ourselves to be supported.

Let me also be clear that in making a case for building a sisterhood, I'm not making men wrong. We need our men! As women, we're standing on the shoulders of men who love and adore us, who have fought for us, and who have even given their lives for us. And there may be men in your life who can be phenomenal allies in your business.

However, when it comes to our healing, so many women leaders have found that the true medicine is other women. When women bond with and empower one another, stand by one another on our path to leadership, and pick one another up when we stumble, we heal one another from the places where we lacked support in the past. We become an unstoppable force.

Of course, not all the women in your life are going to be able to support you as a leader. If these women aren't stepping onto (or already on) a path of leadership or entrepreneurship themselves, they won't understand how much courage it takes to do what you're doing. I recommend you choose your sisters wisely, and take care in selecting those you reach out to in times of need regarding your leadership or business. Starting a business is a vulnerable process, and you'll want to protect the sapling you've planted until it grows deep roots. One of the key ways to protect its fragile new branches is to turn for support only toward those who will understand how to provide what you need.

"Don't feel obligated to spend time with people
who pull you off the path of your life purpose."
— Doreen Virtue

FEMININE POWER

My friend Claire Zammit completed her doctoral dissertation in women's leadership and women's power. She has dedicated her life to helping women access the power they need to self-actualize.

As founder and CEO of Feminine Power training courses for women, she has reached hundreds of thousands of women leaders over the past decade. Through her work, Claire has observed that even though women are launching small businesses in unprecedented numbers, 95 percent of women never break through the six-figure barrier to experience the greater success and impact we know we're here to make.

However, she has also discovered that when women extend themselves to stand with and for one another's success, they can gain the confidence and power to rise above the disheartening statistics and attain the success they're ready for. By enlisting the support of other women, we heal the female-competition wounds we've been brought up with. As we gather in support of one another, we create a collective awareness that allows us to rise above the old ways of being. And as we heal disempowering paradigms, we step into our potential, our message, and our leadership.

Bear in mind, too, that while you may not share in my passion to grow women's companies, it's likely that more than half of your customers will be women, taking into account that women purchase 83 percent of all goods and services in the United States. Women are simply the buyers and economic engine of the Western world. So any fear you have of being judged by your customer or fan base as you embark upon your journey to success will likely be remedied by forming alliances with other strong and talented women.

In my entrepreneurial women's workshops, we like to say that we're all here to hook our little crab legs over the edge of the pot and chuck one another *out* one by one. We're not going to pull each other back down into the pot anymore. We're in this together, and when we're united, we can ALL change the world and become the women we've been waiting for . . . together!

Even Research Shows We Need Each Other

In a world cluttered with iPhones, iPads, smartphones, and laptop computers, the *Huffington Post* recently published an article stating that "relationships have been sacrificed on the altar of technological efficiency." Over the past 25 years, with the rise of the virtual office, we now belong to fewer clubs and groups, get together with friends less often, know fewer of our neighbors, and spend less time with our families. Without a sense of belonging or connectedness, we risk feeling more anxious, depressed, and alienated. The article argued that the strongest predictor of a fulfilled life was to build healthy relationships with others at home, at work, and in the community.

It turns out there's a relationship between friendships and stress. Furthermore, women react to stress differently than men. This difference is due to the proportions of hormones that are released into the bloodstream. According to the article:

When men and women are stressed, the hormones cortisol and epinephrine are released together, which raise a person's blood pressure and circulating blood sugar level. Then oxytocin comes into play, which counters the production of cortisol and epinephrine and produces a feeling of calm, reduces fear, and counters some of the negative effects of stress. Men release much smaller amounts of oxytocin than women, leaving them to feel more acutely the effects of the flight-or-fight response. Men tend to respond to stress by escaping from the situation, fighting back, or bottling up their emotions.

Women, on the other hand, are genetically hard-wired for friendship in large part due to the oxytocin released into their bloodstream, combined with the female reproductive hormones. When life becomes challenging, women seek out friendships with other women as a means of regulating stress levels. A common female stress response is to "tend and befriend." That is, when women become stressed, their inclination is to nurture those around them and reach out to others.[5]

Studies have also shown that women who have a strong, supportive circle of friends outlive women who live in social isolation—by many years. In fact, the more friends women have, the less likely they are to develop physical impairments as they age. Not having friends or confidantes was found to be as detrimental to our health as being overweight or smoking cigarettes.

In her book *Best Friends: The Pleasures and Perils of Girls' and Women's Friendships,* Ruthellen Josselson reminds us that when women get busy with our work and families, the first thing to go is our friendships. It's common to lose sight of the strength the women in our lives provide us, but then we miss out on the healing benefits we derive from those friendships. As the research suggests, women especially—and more than ever before—need to prioritize friendships with other women and build these important bonds to protect our physical and emotional well-being, as well as our ability to achieve success.

Case Study: Entrepreneurial Goddess Rebecca Snowball

My beloved client and colleague Rebecca Snowball has often told me that the sisterhood she experienced in our business training programs was an essential ingredient in supporting her to take her yoga business to the next level at a critical moment in her life. Rebecca has always loved teaching yoga and has attracted many dedicated students over the years.

When I met Rebecca, she was teaching yoga full-time, driving from studio to studio and private client to private client, pouring her energy into her teaching and working long hours. She was making money as a yoga teacher, but not enough to thrive. She was frustrated and felt she lacked the support she needed to make a big change. Deep down, she was exhausted and ready to give up on her vision, even though she desperately wanted to contribute in a bigger way.

Rebecca admitted to me along the way that teaching yoga can be very lonely. I think a lot of women business owners can relate. Yet when she joined our program, she came alive. At one of our events, I broke the participants into groups so that they could share their mission statements. When she stood up to share her truth with the others in her group, with her hand on her heart and tears in her eyes, her group began to clap for her. I'll always remember the moment. She lit up so brightly, it was as if she'd ignited from the inside out.

Then, throughout the weeks in our program, her business began to take off. Rebecca implemented every Internet marketing tool I put in front of her as if she were gobbling up a delicious chocolate dessert.

In the 11 years she had her yoga business, she had never experienced a community to support her with the business-growing aspect of her life. Within weeks, Rebecca had more women than she could count to ask business questions of and run ideas by. They all genuinely wanted her to succeed, and she wanted them to succeed. She admitted that it felt like a sunny day after a rainstorm to have this professional network of women beaming with wisdom, know-how, resources, ideas, feedback, love, encouragement, laughter, and fun!

Within weeks, Rebecca had interviewed dozens of other successful yoga professionals and launched an online training program, the Vibrant Yoga Entrepreneur. Then she launched her own online community for yoga teachers and brought what she was discovering about community into her own teaching.

Rebecca is now reaching 2,500 yoga teachers around the country online, and she's dedicated to supporting them to create their own thriving businesses. She thrived within the structure and safe container of our training program, and gone were the days of the lone wolf in business.

Before I met Rebecca, her summers as a yoga teacher were dreadfully slow, and she often found herself back in her apron job, waiting tables. Now, I must say, there's nothing wrong with that. Work is work. However, with the business strategy she gained in our programs, the accountability, and the free-flowing support of the women growing businesses by her side, her first summer with us yielded 11 new clients and brought nearly $5,000 of additional income. That didn't even include her studio classes or private yoga clients. That summer there was no need for an apron.

She went on that fall to launch a group program called "Yoga Teachers Thrive" and enrolled 18 teachers, resulting in more than $7,000 of additional income. Her business has grown and thrived each year, and it's been a great honor to be a part of the impact and contribution Rebecca is bringing to yoga teachers. You can find out more about Rebecca's work at www.vibrantyogaentrepreneur.com.

A GLIMPSE INTO OUR ENTREPRENEURIAL WOMEN'S RETREATS

It was a Sunday night, and one of my entrepreneurial women's retreats had just come to an end. My team had been together for three days with about 500 women entrepreneurs, and we met to debrief the event over sushi and champagne. We were celebrating, feeling a deep sense of reverence and excitement at what we had just created.

During the retreat, we dove deep into what holds us back from success and the lies we tell ourselves about money and our self-worth. We felt deeply, cried, laughed, danced, healed, and made commitments. We stood on the beach in a circle and felt the power of women supporting us, having our backs . . . and our sides. We strategized about launch plans, client enrollment, and customer retention. We deepened our dedication to the purpose-based businesses that wanted to flow through us. We surrendered to the call that was bubbling up within our souls.

For the final hour of the event, I facilitated, as always, an all-room ritual. Half of the women were blindfolded while soft music played. The other half wove among the blindfolded participants, whispering words of encouragement in their ears and rubbing their backs. Tears streamed down their faces as women received the exact encouragement they needed to be able to move forward, including words of validation that many had never heard before. We were a giant family in which everyone belonged and received support.

After I brought the ritual to completion, our participants declared their biggest takeaways. With wet eyes and open hearts, they stood up one by one and affirmed that the experience had changed their lives and their ability to believe in themselves. They left with tangible tools to build their businesses, armed and ready to go get customers, and with a tribe of support sisters alongside them. The women in the room had created networking groups among themselves, ready to refer clients to one another; some had even enrolled new customers during an exercise we challenged them to try at lunch. Many women at the event had generated revenue just by attending, learning the strategies, and getting on the phone during a break to sign up a new client or customer.

These events include sisterhood, but also strategic action. I've found that when the two are partnered together, women finally feel they have the support to go out into the world and play bigger.

We wrapped up the event by acknowledging the team—our emcee, other trainers, the back-of-the-room team, the mike runners, the DJ, the video crew, and the welcome committee. I then had the honor of standing in the middle of our closing circle—a circle of 500 women, witnessing their transformation into entrepreneurial leadership. I thought about the journey it had taken me to arrive at this place. I felt the ultimate high of blissful contribution. There's no better feeling. I desire this for all of us, this feeling of just giving our absolute best and making a difference as a result.

When it's time for our training events to end, our women attendees don't want to leave. They linger because they feel like they've found their home. After experiencing a three-day entrepreneurial rite of passage like this, women know in their hearts that they can go and build their dream businesses. They know their clients are waiting. I always feel an upwelling of gratitude in my heart so big that it feels like I'll burst. I'm reminded every time that this is why I said yes to building this business. This sisterhood that's established when women come together and support one another is like nothing else

I've ever seen. Women can and are changing the world together—and you are a part of it.

YOUR TRIBE

The task that lies before you is this: Go and find your Entrepreneurial Sisters. Find your tribe! Find women who are on a path of leadership who can stretch and grow alongside you. I promise you they're out there!

Don't take criticism from those who are standing on the sidelines. Don't accept judgment from those who aren't dipping their toes in the water of risk and transformation. Ignore the naysayers and apathetic bystanders. Instead, find the players and befriend them. Find the women with grit, fervor, passion, and warrior spirit.

Choose a friend or two, and make a pact—a vow like one you would make during a marriage ceremony. Agree to stand by one another no matter what. Can you feel that in your nervous system? What would it feel like to know you have sisters standing by you on the path to your dreams? You can have that. But first you have to ask. Take the risk to design several key relationships to support you. You're worth it!

I have a sisterhood practice that might serve you. I take weekly "masterminding walks" with my entrepreneurial friend Jennifer Brewer, who is an incredible nutritionist and chef (you can check her out online; she's Chef Jenny Brewer). Jenny and I walk nearly every week for an hour to the lighthouse in Santa Cruz and back. We divide the time in half, each taking 30 minutes to vent, share, process, and dream. Then we reflect on what we heard from each other and make commitments to each other regarding our next steps. We offer feedback and share both acknowledgment and advice for how to become stronger, clearer, and even more confident. And while we bring praise and kindness to each other in spades, we also push each other. We don't let the other play small.

I treasure my masterminding walks, and I recommend that you find someone to do the same with. Be real and transparent with your masterminding partner. Vent, but catch yourself when you fall into incessant complaining. Demand more from each other. Dream together, brainstorm together, and for Goddess's sake, remind each other who you are and what you're capable of!

Remember: you have gifts for the world that are wanting to be birthed through you! We're with you. Join us at one of our Women Rocking Business events to plug into this tribe (see chapter 12's Breakthrough Bonus Training for more information on how to become part of the live sisterhood). We will be right there, encouraging you and standing right behind you. Close your eyes and feel this support now. We love you, and we know that YOU can do it!

INTEGRATION

Creating Your Ideal Sisterhood Support System

STEP 1: Healing the Sisterhood Wound

What friend or friends have attempted to knock you down your ladder of leadership? List them here, and take a few minutes to write about the pain they've caused you. Use this exercise to get the feelings out without placing blame. Try to own your experience and what you made each woman's behavior mean about you. Remember, the stories you told yourself about their behavior weren't necessarily true. *Taking responsibility for your own experience is the first step to healing.*

Her name:	What hurt the most:
(Example: Carlie)	(Example: Carlie made plans behind my back and lied about me to others. I made up stories that she didn't care about me and that I was unlovable.)

STEP 2: Sisterhood Support Inventory

What friend or friends have supported you and believed in you no matter what? These are friends you know would pick you up if you fell on your face—friends who love you and have your back. List them here, along with the gift you believe they've given you.

My dear friend:	The gift she gave me:
(Example: My friend Emily)	(Example: Emily taught me to see the best in myself and others. She saw the good in me and reminded me over and over.)
_____	_____

STEP 3: Gather Your Tribe of Sisters

If you don't have friends you can list, write down your commitment to yourself that you will find them! If you don't know where to start, look for like-minded women online who are doing things you admire, or look for a Meetup group in your area that might include female entrepreneurs. If there aren't any, plan one, and advertise it!

Once you have your list, contact these women to talk about making your support commitment to one another. Then plan regular times to get together and be there for one another.

Women Rocking Business VIRTUAL GUIDEBOOK

BREAKTHROUGH BONUS TRAINING #4:

Sisterhood Support Masterminding Template

Use this outline for a highly productive masterminding/ brainstorming/celebrating/accountability session with a fellow sister on the entrepreneurial path. You're going to LOVE this! My clients use it again and again.

Grab it here: www.womenrockingbusiness.com/guidebook

PART II

DISCOVERING THE PURPOSE OF YOUR BUSINESS

Chapter 5

YOUR LIFE AS A PH.D. PROGRAM FOR YOUR BUSINESS

*"What I think is that a good life is one hero journey after
another. Over and over again, you are called to the realm of
adventure, you are called to new horizons. Each time, there is the
same problem: do I dare? And then if you do dare, the dangers
are there, and the help also, and the fulfillment or the fiasco.
There's always the possibility of fiasco. But there's
also the possibility of bliss."*

— JOSEPH CAMPBELL

It was about 5 A.M. when I awakened to the rooster's cock-a-doo-
dle-doodling outside my window. I was staying on the second floor
of a three-story retreat center in the middle of terraced rice fields in
Bali, Indonesia. From my room I could see the silhouette of a volcano cloaked in clouds. I had always dreamed of leading a retreat in

this place. Eighteen women were flying in from around the world to attend the retreat with my co-leader, Heather Houston, and me.

Getting to that magical place on our planet had been quite a journey. When I left my husband (yes, I left him), the only clear desire I had was leading a women's retreat in Bali. It wasn't just because *Eat Pray Love* had instilled in me a good dose of Bali obsession, although that was part of it. (Thank you, Elizabeth Gilbert!) But deep inside, I felt called to create an experience of helping women clarify their purpose and next business steps on this island that's steeped in spirituality.

With Indonesian women burning incense and making offerings in every neighborhood temple, Bali is known by many as a deeply sacred and feminine island. What better place to lead a retreat for women, helping them gain clarity about their purpose? My vision for this retreat included interacting with and supporting Balinese women in some capacity. I didn't want to just bring a bunch of women to the country to be tourists. In my mind's eye, I saw Western women having an integrated experience with local women, supporting one another, and creating sisterhood together. Yet I was clueless about how that part of the vision was going to happen.

As the time for the retreat grew closer, my Internet searches for Bali women's groups with which to collaborate were proving futile. Meanwhile, I was supposed to be preparing to lead the retreat, but big waves of grief from the ending of my marriage hit me daily, leaving me exhausted and emotional.

I didn't anticipate how painful divorce would be—like someone had ripped an energetic cord out of my belly. I had no idea I was going to feel like I couldn't do anything but cry all day. Still, the post-divorce semester in the Ph.D. program of my life proved to be one of the biggest catalysts for my future business success. As brutal as it was, it catapulted me into a new version of myself and my leadership in the world, not to mention a new relationship with money. This was Sage Lavine 2.0.

I was convinced, though, during those dark days after leaving my husband, that my grief would seriously hinder my ability to lead the retreat. In a rough moment, I even called Heather and told her I wasn't sure I would be able to do it.

"Hell, no! You're not backing out on me now," she said. Then she came over and helped me pack my suitcase.

The night before I was supposed to leave for Bali, I remembered my vision of integrating Balinese women into our retreat. You know how every once in a while, an idea takes root under your skin and you just can't seem to let it go? I kept returning to this goal of finding these Balinese women for a sacred experience. I said a prayer and wrote the vision on a piece of paper, setting it on my altar. This is a common spiritual practice I've leaned on when I don't know how to make something happen. It's a physical representation of giving over my request to the Divine.

Maybe what happened next was one of those moments when the Universe delivered a miracle. Maybe not. But two hours later, a knock came at the door. It was a friend of a friend—a man named Kyer. Our mutual friend had informed him that I was on my way to Bali. He asked if I would personally deliver an envelope full of cash to a woman he knew on the island, named Tika. It was about $3,500, a bonus he had gotten from work. Kyer wanted to gift the money to Tika, who was running a women's organization in Bali. (Goose bumps!)

He handed me a Bali cell phone and showed me that Tika's number was right there. "Just call her anytime, and she'll find you to pick up the money," he said. "If I send this money as a wire transfer, they'll take at least 10 percent in fees, and she may never see it given how unreliable banks are in Bali."

I asked him to convince me there was nothing illegal about it. He did, and when he teared up as he explained how much he believed in the work she was doing there, I was on board. It turned out that Tika was the founder of an organization called Hope for Indonesian Women, and she worked with her team day and night to support women in starting businesses and leaving abusive situations. (More goose bumps!)

So, once in Bali but with a few days before my retreat would begin, I called Tika and met her at a café in Ubud. As she sat there in front of me with bright eyes, I felt I had known her forever. She was short and fiery with long black hair. She passionately explained in broken English that women in Indonesia are often stuck in abusive circumstances because of finances. It's legal to hit your wife in parts of Indonesia, and this causes some women to turn to prostitution as a way to get out and make money. Then another cycle of abuse kicks in. Tika and her team travel from town to town to educate and empower women in these circumstances. They train the women to become food vendors so that they have a source of financial freedom. Tika provides the carts, the ingredients, and the packaging. Women in Bali already know how to cook, so this is a way for them to become independent and get free from these awful situations, Tika explained to me. Then they can get stronger and create a new life for themselves.

At this point, the goose bumps were exploding all the way up and down my back. My heart broke open for these women in the same way my heart had received the awareness about women and money that day I'd lain under the clouds, making my deal with God.

All of a sudden, time slowed down and I felt tingly. It was as if I could feel my heart connected to Tika's through lifetimes of sisterhood. I was aware that I was experiencing a spiritual awakening of sorts, and there was something bigger calling me—something I was meant to pay attention to. The grief and sorrow I had carried around for weeks from my divorce began to slip away. In the days that followed, I invited Tika to bring a handful of the women she worked with to tell their stories to our retreat participants.

Soon after they arrived, we found ourselves dancing, laughing, and singing alongside these Balinese women. They shared stories of leaving their abusive marriages behind and starting their food businesses. As a group, we raised another $11,500 to add to Kyer's $3,500, which helped our new friends start up their first official women's and children's shelter.

Watching my clients and friends bond with these incredibly courageous women from Bali awoke something very deep and strong inside me. In that moment, I could feel my soul say 100 percent "yes" to this work I was being called to do.

Right then and there, I committed to doing everything I could to help these women start businesses in Indonesia, just as I would also continue to support women entrepreneurs around the globe to build businesses that give back. This giving back mentality has become a critical aspect of my company culture as we've grown, and the Bali chapter of my life's Ph.D. program was an integral moment in helping me create a business that expressed all of who I am.

> As I looked into the eyes of those women who had faced abuse and rape—circumstances far worse than my own or those of most of my clients—I decided there wasn't enough time for me to waste even one more day lost in grief for my marriage or overwhelm at the never-ending to-do list of building a business.

TURN YOUR STRUGGLES INTO A SUPERPOWER

Meeting Tika in Bali and having the honor of supporting her alongside the women in our retreat became a symbol of what I now know is possible when we as women ignite our intentions, value ourselves, and work together.

This was just one of many experiences I'd had in my life that drove me toward my mission of empowering women in their leadership and finances. As a young woman growing up, the message was clear: to be successful, I needed to find a husband, be a good wife, and have children. Then, joining a women's leadership program in college changed my world view about what women are capable of achieving when we connect with our true strength.

So I accepted a summer job as a wilderness guide before getting my master's degree, taking 23 teenage women hiking through the Canadian Rockies, carrying everything we needed on our backs. That experience helped me reclaim my power and facilitate other young women to do the same.

None of these transformative experiences would have held such significance had they not come on the heels of some serious struggle and challenge.

Here's the thing, sister: You and I, we've been through some major shit in our lives. Excuse my language, but you know what I'm talking about. Therapists call it "trauma." Coaches call it "the challenge." Spiritual people call it "the sacred struggle." Athletes call it "the grit." Whatever term you use, you've been there. And you've gone through things you shouldn't have had to go through.

That's the bad news. The good news, however, my dear sister, is that you can use the challenges you've been through as fuel for your next career chapter. You can turn any of your struggles into a superpower for your business! You now have the opportunity to go back and be a guide who helps others navigate a similarly treacherous landscape.

Now, it's true that having a Sherpa who knows the mountain, including the rocks and drop-offs on the path, may not totally eliminate the pain others have to experience on their journey to the summit, but it can definitely *lessen* the pain. At the very least, it can allow those walking the path behind you to know deep in their souls that they're not alone.

Your Life as a Ph.D. Program

My esteemed colleague, dear friend, and mentor Jeffrey Van Dyk thinks of life as a Ph.D. program preparing us for our businesses. He says the challenges we've faced in life have been like a training program, grooming us for our work's greatest contribution. More important, our response to those adversities sends each of us on a unique path where we develop the skills and abilities that are absolutely necessary for our life's work.

Jeffrey sees the first half of life as our time to acquire skills and the second half as our time to deliver our gifts. In working with his clients, he's concluded that a midlife crisis is really the time when our training program is up and we're essentially being asked to use all that we've learned to re-create our next life or career chapter. We stop asking why something happened *to* us and become aware that it happened *for* us. To learn more about Jeffrey's work, visit: www.jeffreyvandyk.com.

What Superpowers Have You Developed?

Not only have our life lessons groomed us into stronger, more capable humans, they've actually instilled in us what I like to refer to as superpowers. I know a recovered drug addict who went on a spiritual journey, got sober, and cleaned up his life. Now his superpower is helping young people get sober. I have a client who was the middle child; she never spoke up until she finally claimed her voice and found passion in her career as a singer/songwriter. Her superpower is sharing her voice; she inspires crowds around the world with her musical talent. I know a woman who felt she could never live up to her mother's expectations. Even an A on a test wasn't good enough; it had to be an A+. As a result, she developed a strategy to be a success at all costs, and that's what helped her land promotion after promotion to become the most high-powered female executive in her company. While she wasn't happy in that position, she developed a superpower that will allow her to achieve whatever she wants to create in her life.

Another friend of mine is a sexual abuse survivor who confronted her trauma head-on, healed her wounds, and turned her pain into the motivation to help others. Her superpower is helping people who have had similar experiences. She recently launched a crowdfunding campaign to raise money for a women's shelter that will provide a safe space for women and girls who've suffered from sexual violence.

What do all of these folks have in common? They turned their greatest wound into their greatest gift. Their greatest challenge became their *superpower.*

So here's the deal: I'd like to make the case that whatever you've been through has prepared you for a greater contribution, for better or worse. When you embrace this, you'll discover hidden clues to the purpose of your business.

Here's how it works: Your "shero's" journey has brought about a transformation in you. You might not see it 100 percent clearly yet, and it may not be as dramatic as the above examples. But it's true, and it's yours. Life has rolled out a curriculum—which I believe your soul played some role in choosing before you were born—in order for you to grow and evolve. It brought you to this moment. And when you find the superpower you've developed as a result of your life challenges, you'll have yet another clue about what you're here to do and be as an entrepreneur. Your business message, your core promise, your brand—the thing you most want to bring to the world—more often than not lies somewhere deep within that painful transformation you've experienced. It's the thing that—when you *do* bring it to the world—will turn heads, win you faithful followers, and attract loyal, paying clients.

What Is This Thing Called Transformation?

What do I mean when I say "transformation"? I think you'll find it more useful for me to share what I *don't* mean. I don't mean that you have it all figured out or that you've arrived at some Hollywood destination of "healed and handled."

What I do mean is that you've made progress, and you can look back and see how you operate differently in your life. And that progress or your new awareness as a result of that transformation has prepared you to bring a service or product to others.

Let me share a client story that'll explain what it means to transform your life journey into a business. Keep in mind that this is just one example; your life may translate very differently into the business journey you're embarking on.

Case Study: Entrepreneurial Goddess
Susan Peirce Thompson

To say that my amazing client, colleague, and dear friend Susan Peirce Thompson has been on a painful journey with food would be an understatement. Susan was overweight as a teenager and obese in her 20s. In adolescence, she used drugs like crystal meth and crack cocaine to manage her eating and weight. When she hit bottom on drugs at the age of 20 and got clean and sober, her food addiction exploded in full force. She was diagnosed with binge eating disorder at the age of 23 and spent nearly every spare moment bingeing, recovering from bingeing, or throwing her heart into some new attempt to lose weight. She spent decades struggling with her weight, swinging from her ideal size 4 to a size 24. When she was lost in that battle with food, little did Susan know that her shero's journey would begin with discovering the secret to losing her own weight . . . and lead her to mentor hundreds of thousands of people around the world to free themselves from food issues.

It started when she found several support systems, including various 12-step programs, that helped her understand her addiction and make new choices. Her growing understanding of the brain science behind human behavior and her commitment to setting people free led her to earn a Ph.D. in brain and cognitive sciences and become a tenured psychology professor. She then brought her knowledge into the classroom through teaching a college course on the psychology of eating. Ultimately she started offering online courses on weight loss and now runs a multimillion-dollar company, Bright Line Eating, which supports a global audience to finally lose weight and love life.

Susan's clients speak about her with tears in their eyes. She is single-handedly responsible for thousands of people not only losing all of their excess weight but reclaiming their health and adding years to their lives. Now she has a research program that is accumulating evidence to show that Bright Line Eating is the most effective and sustainable weight loss program on earth. In the years to come, her message of how the brain blocks weight loss—and what to do about it—will no doubt spread to millions of people. It was her own transformation that allowed her to understand what women in similar situations would need to heal and experience their own transformations. This is just one example of the miracle of allowing your deepest struggles to be the springboard for the message of your business.

WHAT MAKES YOUR BLOOD BOIL?

When I hang out with Susan, one of the things I love about her is how passionate and even angry she becomes when she talks about why it's so difficult for people to lose weight. In her anger, she's taking a stand for what she knows is possible—a world where people can take back their power and reclaim their bodies. Similarly, I get riled up when I discuss women and money. I want a world where every woman has autonomy and a sense of power in her relationship with money.

What makes *your* blood boil? What do you complain to your friends about? Perhaps you've been exposed to a challenge or problem in your life that made you so frustrated or angry that you knew you had to do something about it? Sometimes what we complain about inside our own heads or to our friends gives us a hint about the deeper gift we'd like to bring to the world.

My client Melissa has what you could call a raging passion for supporting women through breast cancer. You're going to love her story.

Case Study: Entrepreneurial Goddess Melissa Russell

Your life struggle may not translate directly into your message like Susan's. My client Melissa Russell supports women healing from breast cancer through her very successful and growing company called Beloved Bust. Her work includes helping her clients heal their scar tissue after surgery and recover from the trauma of this devastating disease. But unlike Susan, Melissa hasn't had the same experience as her clients. She hasn't had breast cancer herself.

She's a skilled bodyworker who had been running a thriving massage practice for over a decade. Several years ago, a mutual friend introduced Melissa to a new client (we'll call her Pam) who had survived breast cancer. Pam came to Melissa with painful swelling and inflammation after her mastectomy and reconstructive surgery. One of her implants had become infected, so she'd had another surgery to remove it. She expected to get another implant within a few months. In a considerable amount of pain, Pam wasn't fitting into her clothes anymore due to the swelling, and she couldn't move very well without feeling even worse.

As Melissa slowly began to work on Pam, she discovered that Pam felt pain at the slightest touch. With permission, Melissa investigated the scar. As she undraped the surgical site, she was knocked back with a wave of nausea at the radiation burns, scar tissue, discoloration, and leathery feel of the tissue on Pam's chest. Melissa says the sorrow she felt witnessing this trauma will always be engraved in her memory.

But then she was hit with another emotion—an overwhelming wave of anger. She heard a voice inside her clearly say, "This is not okay! What medical system is letting this woman walk around in the world without getting her scars and tissue treated postsurgery? What doctor is planning to cut even more deeply into this poor woman to put in a new implant and tell her she'll be all right?"

Melissa made a pact with herself then and there: "If the medical community isn't going to take care of these women or even inform them how to take care of themselves, then I'll do it." Melissa felt to the depths of her soul that she was being called to be a guide for these women.

Then the fear and doubt set in. Melissa was acutely aware that this was a delicate subject. "How can I sell such a thing?" she wondered. "How do I get the word out?"

Melissa knew she needed help. I'm honored to say that on her search to find a mentor, she chose our training programs. Immediately she was surrounded by the support of other women on their own business journeys.

In our entrepreneurial training academy, Melissa learned that she didn't have to promote herself with pushy sales tactics. As we worked together, she made an essential mind-set shift that we teach in our courses: She was able to tap into the truth that her future clients would be looking for answers and praying for relief, and therefore it was her duty and honor to put herself and her work out there so that her clients could find those answers.

Melissa says this perspective is very different from the traditional selling tactics she's been taught. Like so many of my clients, she's beyond relieved to realize that she doesn't have to try to "close the deal" in order to find her clients. Instead she's created an offering from her heart and learned to communicate from a place of service to those clients.

Melissa finds that her clients are isolated and often feel alone in their trauma. Now she has the skills to gather breast cancer survivors into her classes and lectures, and she can reach out through her network to grow her business. While she used to avoid marketing altogether, she now proudly markets herself by creating an environment that supports women and fills the gap left by the medical establishment, empowering women through connection, compassion, and community. This commitment will certainly carry her work far and wide to those who need it, and she doesn't have to be a breast cancer survivor to be the right woman for the job.

Melissa loves to talk about her work! Marketing herself has become one of the most joyful experiences in her life. She treasures the process of discovering her clients' struggles and getting to know their lives more intimately. And through her work, she has the honor of witnessing true transformation as her clients learn to embrace their bodies, self-treat their scars, and get back to their normal, healthy lives without the fear they carried before. The most frequent comment she hears from her clients is "I wish I had found you sooner."

What's more, Melissa has more than doubled her income from a year ago, and she's working fewer hours. She has the stability of a practice that isn't just consistent, but consistently growing. Now she's planning a project that will allow her to offer scholarships and classes to breast cancer survivors in need. Melissa says, "If one woman is out there scared and alone, so are we all."

Your Shero's Journey

You too, sister, have gone through a transformation or struggle in your life that has prepared you to help others in a unique way. Your life has literally been readying you for the gift you're meant to bring next.

It's no mystery why I attract women clients who are on a journey of empowerment and spiritual growth. Often they come to me when aspects of their personal identity or their relationships have shattered—all while they feel called to birth a business. The truth is that there's no better time to birth your business than when you're in the midst of transformation. It may seem like the worst time, but with the proper support, it's really the best. Why is it the best time? Because when you're in a life transformation, the very foundation of your life can feel like it's cracking and moving around. We need those cracks to let the light in, as Leonard Cohen put it in his famous song.

So, dear sister, as you consider your biggest life challenges, which we'll think about more formally in a moment, ponder the ways that your challenges may directly relate to those of your clients. Also consider how what you've been through may simply *influence* the way you express your message.

Now, don't worry. I'm not going to leave you in this dark place for long, reflecting on all the challenges you've experienced. We'll move on soon to considering who your amazing clients and customers are and the secrets to building this dream business. But without exploring your lovable shadowy parts, we'll miss out on the wholeness of you that will bring depth and magnetism to your business message.

FIVE STEPS TO REFLECTING ON YOUR LIFE AS YOUR PH.D. PROGRAM

These are the five steps I teach my clients for reflecting on their lives as a Ph.D. program for their core business message:

#1) Do your inner work.

You'll be a more effective leader, entrepreneur, and mentor when you do your own inner healing work to move beyond your past into a future of service. The challenges you've been through have prepared you for the next chapter of your business, but you have to be healed enough to use these struggles to serve. In other words, when it comes to your business, it's about *your customer*, not about *you.*

One of my spiritual mentors says, "You have to feel it to heal it." If you're still going through it, make space to grieve, vent with trusted friends, cry, emote, express it, dance it out, or do whatever you need to move it through you.

My chiropractor once told me that physiologically, emotions last only about 90 seconds. Isn't that *incredible*? Only 90 seconds! I had a difficult time believing it when the postdivorce emotions would hit me. But it's true; after about 90 seconds, if we continue to feel sad, angry, or (insert painful emotion here), it's because we're recirculating the story.

It's important to learn to grieve well, but there's also such a thing as over-grieving. We get stuck in overprocessing and overanalyzing the shit we've been through. At the end of the day, it's very likely that if you're reading this book, your needs are met and you have a good life. Feel what you need to feel, then get back at it. Happiness is a choice you make, and you'll help a lot more people from a place of happiness. So how do you let go and move on?

HINT: Bring your struggle into present time.

When we bring our life's struggles into present time, we can often break the victim cycle of reflecting on past pains. Remind yourself that you don't have to review what happened over and over in order to avoid experiencing it again. You already have more knowledge and experience than you did when you went through your challenges.

I recommend that you invite the little one inside you (who's probably endured more pain and challenge than she ever should have) into present time where we can love her up and help her remember she isn't alone anymore. I like to picture myself holding my little inner girl, loving her, showing her my life as an adult woman, and introducing her to my friends. I have a conversation with her and explain that things are different now. She doesn't have to stay stuck in the past.

I've experienced some profound shifts using this practice. I've been able to integrate the little-girl parts of me who scream at me and love to play the victim. I invite them to a dance of womanhood that includes my tending to them, taking care of myself, and getting my needs met.

When you can bring your wounds into the current moment and dialogue with the parts of you that want to hold you back, you'll alchemize that pain into fuel for your future. And, girrrrl, building a business isn't for the faint of heart, so you're going to need all the fuel you can get!

The ultimate gift is building a business from a place of commitment to service. When we make it about us and our past, we get in our own way. When we allow ourselves to feel our feelings, let them go, and move on to helping other people, we're able to make a real contribution to the world. There's simply no better feeling than changing someone's life for the better through our businesses.

#2) Sister, don't worry about which challenge to choose.

Your shero's journey has been full of twists and turns. All of the setbacks, bumps, and mountains have made you who you are today— uniquely able to help a specific set of people. You've been through more than one challenge in your life, however, so don't get hung up on which one to choose for your marketing.

It isn't so important *which* challenge you choose to alchemize into your message, but rather that you're willing to bring *any* of your challenges into the landscape of your business message as it unfolds. Your business and its message will evolve as your life has evolved.

Today it may be the translation of a health crisis you endured and how it's shaped your desire to help people. Tomorrow you may realize that it was your angry mother's outbursts that sculpted you into a soft-spoken woman who has finally learned to speak up for herself.

Bringing your story into your marketing is what attracts your clients. It doesn't matter which story; it just matters that you have a story. Keep in mind, though, that when you share your challenges with your audience, it's about them, not about you. When you share the details, keep *your audience* in mind. When you talk about your painful divorce, ask them what life transition they've lived through that's made them who they are today. When you share your health crisis, ask them to consider a time they were sick or facing a similar challenge and to feel the vulnerability of that.

#3) Stop beating yourself up for not having figured it out.

It's common for women to be hard on themselves for having experienced so many trials and tribulations. Maybe you've sampled a variety of career choices. Perhaps you've burned through more than two or three jobs. You may have left a very practical career to follow your passion with mixed success.

Regardless of what you've been through, consider this:
Your grandmother didn't have the variety and opportunity
that you have. Now here you are, beating yourself up for
sampling all of what life has to offer!

Our grandmothers, great-grandmothers, and great-great-grandmothers were limited to very few choices in their lives. Most of our female ancestors had one husband, and if they did have a career outside the home, it was likely one career. They didn't have the opportunities we have now or the chance to taste test every day.

These days, so many choices can feel like both a blessing and a curse. But the point is, if you've indulged in a life of sampling, of trying on careers and changing them as often as you change your wardrobe, make peace with it. Give yourself credit for partaking in the adventure of life. We're among the first generations of women to have been given this chance. Let's celebrate that!

#4) Document your process so you can create a map for others.

Notice what triggers you, what shifts you toward empowerment and healing, and what steps you take to get to the other side of pain. As you experience your life challenges, I encourage you to begin to create the map you wish you had to guide you through it.

Pay close attention to which stories run on replay in your mind. Watch your emotions and moods. Notice what you do to lift yourself up. Track your growth. Make lists. If you're in the mentorship field, create three-step processes or seven-step processes. Someday you may even be teaching these processes to others, who will be grateful to have them.

Besides helping others who struggle with similar challenges, there's another huge benefit to documenting your own healing process: In studying your process like a detective, you separate yourself from it. You observe it more objectively and stop being so caught up in the emotion of it. You realize that you're not alone, that others struggle with similar circumstances, and that you're here to help others and to be helped by others. This is true alchemy, when your commitment to service transforms your own pain into a contribution.

Sounds vulnerable, you say? Yes, it is. It's the ultimate vulnerability to take your pain and use it as a teaching path for others. But that's exactly what some of us have been called to do.

#5) Share your own vulnerability _and_ your credibility.

Vulnerability is key. The world is hungry for more vulnerability, for leaders who've stopped claiming to be perfect Barbie dolls selling a magic pill that they claim filled their life with rainbows and butterflies. The world is sick and tired of the mask-wearing leaders who don't own up to their own imperfect humanness.

When you bring vulnerability without credibility, however, people won't take you seriously, they won't feel safe to let down their guard, and most important, they won't pay you. And you have to get paid, or you don't have a business—you have a hobby!

Goddess, consider the life challenges that
have made you vulnerable
and what's credible about you.

What has your journey prepared you for?
What superpower have you acquired
as a result of your shero's journey?

If you don't know yet what brings you credibility, don't worry. Trust me—we'll find credibility in that gorgeous life story of yours! Whether you have knowledge or training that makes you credible or you're the one whose phone rings every time one of your girl-friends has a problem, I can assure you that we can establish credibility for you.

For instance, whether or not you've worked with paying clients, you've helped people. You know you have. You've supported people to make changes in their lives, so you can talk about those people, whether or not they've actually paid you. Let's explore this further.

DIG FOR YOUR CREDIBILITY

Here's an exercise I'd like you to try. Think of the people you've supported in your life. No, really. Take a breath, close your eyes, and bring to mind someone you've helped in the past few years. It could be a client, friend, or family member. Maybe it was your child. We tend to forget about them because as parents, we don't value what we do every day. Take a moment to tune in to the very real contribution you've made in this person's life.

Allow yourself to perceive who this individual has become because of your impact:

Where would this person be if you hadn't come into his or her life?

Who are they because of the support you gave them?

Who are they because of your advice?

Who are they because of the love you extended to them?

Now ask yourself: Can you really put a price tag on the transformation this person has experienced because of your support? It's essential that you allow yourself to take in how much you've contributed to this person. Tell her or his story!

Goddess, this is the secret to stepping into your own credibility now and not waiting years to perceive your own gifts as valuable. In your marketing, tell stories of people you've helped, even if they didn't pay you a cent. Tell stories of your past and your contribution to others.

- Perhaps you long to launch a business designing clothing, and you have a history of creating fantastic ensembles for your girlfriends to wear out dancing.

- Perhaps you're embarking on a business path of mentorship or life coaching, and you supported your sister-in-law to finally stop giving all her energy away to her husband and kids. As a result, she began to claim her power and landed an awesome part-time job.

- Maybe you're starting a café, and you have several decades of experience preparing amazing food for people you love.

Ask your friends or even family members for testimonials you can use in your marketing materials. You don't even need to call them clients. The bottom line is that we've all supported others, so why not use them as examples in your marketing?

Credibility + Vulnerability = A Brilliant and Effective Marketing Message

Whatever you've been through and whatever gift(s) you've developed as a result, we can make it credible and marketable, I promise. As long as you're willing to open up and stretch your comfort zone, we can find a way to position you so that people see the value of investing in you.

As they say, when the student is ready, the teacher will appear. There are students out there preparing to be supported by you—right now. Again, I promise.

There's one more way to bring credibility that anyone—I repeat, anyone—can use, and I recommend you use it: Share research that backs up your line of work. If you're a coach, for example, talk about research that attests to the effectiveness of having a coach. You could write: "The best athletes in the world wouldn't be anywhere without coaching. Did you know that having a coach will make you 90 percent more effective in your life, your business, your sport, or whatever you want to accomplish? When we tell someone we're going to do something, we're 65 percent more likely to do it. When we share our goal with a coach who can help us achieve it and hold us accountable to follow through, and when we create specific accountability plans and appointments around our goal, we're actually 95 percent more likely to follow through."[6]

With these statistics, we can't afford *not* to hire coaches, can we? I've hired coaches and mentors my entire life, and I wouldn't be where I am without their guidance.

Let's say you want to launch an organic café in your community. Well, you may share in your marketing that organic fruits, vegetables, and cereals contain significantly higher concentrations of antioxidants than conventional food. And many of these antioxidants have been linked to a reduced risk of chronic diseases and certain cancers.[7] These stats bring major credibility, am I right?

Remember: when you balance your vulnerability with your credibility, you become solid in your leadership and create an energetic field around you that invites the right clients to come in, take off their shoes, let down their guard, and stay for a while. Your credibility, combined with the humanness of your imperfect journey, creates a magnetic and marketable business message that will attract your ideal clients.

A Vulnerability–Credibility Example from My Own Life

I wasn't much of a saleswoman before my business took off. In fact, I come from a long line of educators. My mom, dad, aunt, and grandparents were all schoolteachers. They collected a paycheck and didn't ever need to learn how to self-generate financially. Most members of my family didn't approve of salespeople and made fun of marketers. In fact, my mom didn't want me to sell Girl Scout cookies because she was afraid I'd offend the neighbors.

When I launched my business helping women entrepreneurs, I was nervous that my family would judge me, and they actually did judge me a little bit. They made side remarks about how I'd better be careful not to offend anyone or be too pushy.

I got an e-mail from my mom one afternoon asking me if I didn't think I was bragging a bit on my website video and overpromising results to my clients. I remember the dark, sinking feeling in my stomach, a feeling cloaked in shame. I called a colleague of mine to get some support. Then I sat with myself and tapped into the wisdom of the clients I wanted to serve. I did take Mom's feedback into consideration and adjusted what I felt needed adjusting on the website. But I stood up for myself about the rest. Over the months that followed, I found the courage inside me to keep bringing my message even though I knew my mom and family were watching.

As my business grew into a million-dollar women's company and my family began to see my success, they became more and more supportive. Recently my mom flew out to attend one of my events and met some of my favorite clients. It was her birthday that weekend, and I presented her with a birthday cake onstage in front of hundreds of my clients. She was so proud of me, and it was an incredibly happy and fulfilling moment in my life. It was beautiful to stand onstage with my mom, getting to share what I'd created and to see her so receptive and engaged.

I often tell this story at the start of radio interviews and speaking gigs because it reveals my own vulnerability and humanity. It helps people relate to me and opens up my heart to feel connected to my audience. I tell my listeners how I struggled with shame in the face of my mother's feedback, and then I weave in, for credibility, the fact that I now have the honor of serving thousands of clients a year, running a million-dollar company.

The stories I tell onstage, on my website, in e-mails, and on video are often even more revealing, like some of the stories you'll find in this book. I've shared about my divorce, the growing pains of being a leader, and the days I want to give up and throw in the towel. But I'm committed to sharing my successes too. My goal is to always share a piece of vulnerability and a piece of credibility within the first few minutes of any speaking engagement or presentation. This automatically helps my audience trust me, see me as human, and respect me.

I suggest practicing this skill of sharing your vulnerability and what makes you credible, whether you're having a one-on-one conversation with a potential customer or you're on television in front of thousands. It's an equation that will set you up for success.

How Vulnerable Should You Get?

When you're sharing about the challenges of your life in your marketing materials, on your website, in conversations, on a podcast, or onstage, you might wonder how raw you should allow yourself to be. Remember that it's about your clients, not about you. We share our challenges with the goal of providing hope, healing, inspiration, and solutions. So here's my rule of thumb: If you still have healing and processing to do about the painful stories in your life, save them for a therapy session. I say that with absolute love and respect.

My friend (and storyteller extraordinaire) Sirena Andrea says that we want to bring emotions into the stories we tell without losing ourselves in those emotions. Don't let yourself get lost in the river of your own feelings. Go about shin- or knee-deep so that your potential client will feel your pain. You may let yourself feel the memory and the goose bumps. Your eyes may even get wet. (To find out more about Sirena's work with the power of story, go to www.sirenaandrea.com/.)

But here's where you want to turn back: if you tip over the edge of the emotion into waist-deep emotional waters, you've made it all about you. The feeling state is so extreme that your clients won't feel you holding them anymore. They won't be able to see the light on the other side of the challenge.

Use your story to help your clients see what's possible for them rather than focusing on yourself and sharing your pain. There's a fine line between telling your story to serve others and telling your story to continue healing yourself, but both will still occur when you align yourself with providing service. So try to avoid telling a story that you're still bleeding from.

Now that I've said that, don't worry about it *too much*. If you think you've told the wrong story or shown *too* much emotion, don't beat yourself up. Just use it as a learning experience, and make adjustments. It's much more important to get out there and tell your story. You'll find the right balance in the sharing of your gift and the actions you take.

Let me assure you, my dear, that you *are* the right person to build this business. Your life challenges and the wisdom you've gained have prepared you to help people in an absolutely unique way. Your customers and clients are waiting for you. They won't be able to hear the wisdom from other mentors out there. And if you're selling a product, they won't be able to solve the same problem from anyone else's product. You're the right person for their haircut, massage, or special dress. They're not just waiting for someone *like* you. There are people out there who are actually waiting *just for you*. And they need you to step up, be seen, take the risk, and get out there.

I'm with you, holding your hand. So, sweet sister, I leave you with this final reflection to help you take the next step on this journey.

INTEGRATION

Reflection: Your Life as a Ph.D. for What's Next

1. VULNERABILITY HARVEST: Write about a challenge you've overcome in your life and how it defined who you are today. Write a description of how it felt to go through your experience and what qualities you used to overcome the struggle.

2. CREDIBILITY HARVEST PART 1: What is the superpower you developed as a result of that struggle?

   Example: If you were commonly left out as a child, you may have developed a superpower that helps you notice when someone is excluding herself, or you may be tuned in to bringing everyone into the conversation around the dinner table.

3. CREDIBILITY HARVEST PART 2: What do people receive from being in your presence? If you don't know, ask them! Then write it down! Not only will you use it in your business marketing, but you'll feel great once you have it written down. You won't be able to deny it anymore.

4. CREDIBILITY HARVEST PART 3: What is the ache or frustration your potential clients might be feeling when they're drawn to your support, business, products, or service? How does this mirror the frustrations you've felt in your own life?

5. CREDIBILITY HARVEST PART 4: Imagine that someone you've helped has written you a letter thanking you for the transformation you've facilitated in them. What does it say? What are they experiencing or accomplishing in their life as a result of your contribution?

6. CREDIBILITY STATISTICS RESEARCH: Do some research on your passions, modality, or business ideas, and see what studies or statistics you can find to back up your future services and products.

Hold on to your answers from this exercise.
We'll use them to create your fabulous marketing
materials as you work on building your business.

Need more support clarifying your superpower?

Women Rocking Business VIRTUAL GUIDEBOOK

BREAKTHROUGH BONUS TRAINING #5:

Superpower Survey

To get special access to my favorite process for
asking your friends and family—those who know
you best—to help you determine your superpower,
grab it here: www.womenrockingbusiness.com/guidebook

Chapter 6

WHOM WILL YOU SERVE?

*"In business, it's better to be a big fish in a
small pond than a small fish in a big pond."*

— JESSE KOREN

Who are your clients and customers? Are they women? Men?
Moms? Teens? Entrepreneurs? Are they trying to find their voice?
Are they overworked and overwhelmed professionals? Are they simply people who are tired of driving 20 miles to the nearest French
restaurant?

What do they want? What do they struggle with? How can you
bring relief? What do you provide that solves their problems and
soothes their longings? What transformation or service will you
offer them?

When you feel into the heart of your business message, it's
important to ask yourself these questions. What do you know about
the people you want to serve? Look for the areas where you already

have clarity. Maybe you know that your customers want to be healthy. Maybe you want them to know they can absolutely find a house for their family that feels like a true home. Perhaps you know you want to support parents, professionals, or women in some way. Maybe you know you want to bring a message of self-love to the people who need it.

I urge you to consider this human being on the other end of the service or product you want to provide. Then we can work together to define your ideal customer, your core audience, or your niche—the group of people you're here to serve. Remember: they're waiting for you—not just someone like you, but *you* and *only you.*

WHAT IS A NICHE, AND DO YOU NEED ONE?

Regardless of whether you're in the restaurant business, selling real estate, or opening a bike shop, having a niche will set you apart from the competition and save you money.

I define "niche" as *the problem you solve and for whom you solve it.* Choosing a niche is really just a decision to focus on a group of people within your target audience to whom you will spend the most time marketing your product or service. Some people say your niche is the type of client you serve.

An example of a niche could be:

- Women going through a divorce.
- Parents struggling to create healthy relationships with their teenagers.
- Men and women looking for creative website design.
- Men and women who are healing from trauma or sexual abuse.
- Parents needing a simple math tutoring program for their middle school–age kids.
- Families who want to eat healthfully.
- Professionals who want to save time and money.

Let's say you want to start a beauty salon. Do you still need a niche? Perhaps the need for a niche isn't so strong for some brick-and-mortar businesses, but it's still a good idea to focus on the people you want to reach with your marketing. Are there other beauty salons in your area? If so, how will you differentiate yours from the others? Is your salon high-end or low-end? If you're targeting clients who are willing to spend a little more, what kind of environment will you create to attract them? What kind of extra TLC will you provide to justify the higher prices? I know a hairdresser who does tarot readings for her customers, and they love it. They refer their friends because it's unique and feminine.

There's a saying about niche that goes something
like this: If you have a niche, you get rich,
but without a niche, life is a bitch!

One of my friends says it this way: "Broad is broke." If your niche is too broad—if you're trying to help everyone with a generic message—nobody will recognize you as a solution to their particular need, and you'll have a difficult time making money. But when you choose to specialize in one area and hang a sign on the door that markets to one type of person, your ability to magnetize clients will skyrocket.

A lot of my clients resist choosing a niche, and so did I—at first. After all, we think we can help everyone, right?

That was me in my first year of business. I was convinced I could help anyone. And in a way, I was right. I could help anyone by putting spare change in their parking meter, for instance, or by baking them a cake. But what if this "anyone" was an irresponsible teenager who needed to be reminded of the parking rules by getting a ticket? What if that ticket would prevent the teen from the next level of disobedience that might lead to something much worse, like jail?

And even if I did have advice and wisdom that could help everyone, there was another problem—"everyone" didn't want my help. I know it can be hard on the ego, but not everyone wants what you can give. Your potential clients and customers *must* have a desire for what you're offering. They have to *want* what you can provide.

SPECIFICITY DOESN'T LIMIT YOU

There's a metaphor I've heard that will explain this even better: If you dig a well for water in your backyard, you don't dig a bunch of shallow holes all over the place. You dig one hole all the way down until water pours into that hole. Only then might you begin digging a second well, in the neighbor's yard.

Yet this is what some of us dabblers do with our businesses. We start one, and before we've built any real momentum, we say yes to side projects and pursue other inspirations. As a result, nothing gains traction. When you treat building your business like you'd dig a well and commit to going deep and seeing your strategies all the way through until the end, resources will begin to flow just like water flows into a well.

Why do we dabble? Perhaps we're secretly afraid of success, so it's safer to skim the surface. Maybe we've needed to try a variety of options on for size to get clear about what's truly right for us. Regardless of why you might have been a dabbler, now's your chance to choose one message and see it through to fruition. Of course, if you're just getting started and need to sample a few metaphorical flavors of ice cream, by all means do that! How would we ever know whether we like rocky road or pistachio best without those little sampler spoons?

But as you try on different business plans and entrepreneurial visions, remember that the success you seek lies in choosing one area of focus, digging one deep "business hole," building your expert status in one area, and exercising your "finishing muscles" so you can see that idea through to ultimate success.

A lot of my clients understand they are *supposed* to choose a niche, but they resist choosing and committing to one group. When I confront them on why they're not making a choice, I've discovered many of them are afraid that having a niche will *limit* them. I'm sure you can relate on some level. You might have a wide variety of interests and want to bring an equally wide variety of experiences, products, or programs to the people you serve. Well, the fastest way to do just that—and to get paid well for those offerings—is to pick a niche. It's counterintuitive, I know, but getting specific with your marketing will allow you to do everything you love to do and serve more people with greater ease.

Even though it might feel limiting at first, choosing a niche will free you. Your niche is just the sign on the door of your business that helps people find you. Once people walk through your door, you can offer all of your products and services to them!

Here's an example from my own business: As I've already mentioned, I love to take women on retreats to Bali, Hawaii, Canada, Africa, Japan, and more. I love to help them gain clarity on their true purpose in life, their career path, and their relationship with money. But I also have another love—singing and dancing with women as a way to help them access their innermost desires. And I'm passionate about helping women self-reflect, journal, and make vision boards. I love doing these things in exotic, faraway places in nature because I find it helps us all discover even more about ourselves.

But my first attempt to sell my retreats was a failure. I promised a myriad of metaphysically based solutions and modalities in the same way I laid them out in the above paragraph. My marketing sounded something like this:

"Join me for a nurturing, regenerative workshop where you'll sing and dance alongside other women, learning to use your voice in courageous ways, focusing on your career and business, diving into intuitive realms to determine your next steps through meditations and visioning."

Sounds like fun, right? But would you really pay thousands of dollars for this? Using this marketing, I went into debt, women constantly asked to take my workshops for free, and I was broke all the time. As a dabbler, I promised journaling and vision boarding, and people were willing to pay me the whopping amount of $25. So I finally decided I should probably listen to one of my trusted mentors who told me to pick a niche. *FINE!*

I had a handful of women clients who were launching businesses, and I really enjoyed working with them, so I claimed it. I remember the day I finally decided they would be my niche. Boom! I have a niche, baby! I wanted to pour my heart into supporting emerging women entrepreneurs.

Shortly after making that decision, I filled that first Bali retreat. I gave the retreat a specific focus. I titled it a "Purpose Retreat for Women Entrepreneurs." It was for women who were launching a business and wanted clarity for their marketing and next steps. I began promoting and marketing the retreat with the focus on a more specific outcome. It was beyond profitable.

My good friend singer/songwriter Heather Houston was gung-ho to help me co-lead the retreat. You know the rest. Aside from meeting with the Balinese women business owners for our sacred cultural exchange, we also helped women get clear on their businesses and marketing. But here's the really super-cool part—we also *sang, danced, moved,* and *reflected.* We journaled, made vision boards, and did all the things I like to do. In fact, we spent the majority of the time doing the things I had loved to do at my retreats when they *weren't* making money.

The difference? I had a niche, and I had *specific* packaging that was marketable. Suddenly I was able to quadruple my prices and sell out my retreats with very little effort. I charged thousands of dollars, and people paid it. I started to take myself seriously, and my clients took me seriously. And the coolest part is that I made a much bigger difference in their lives!

Now, there's a limit to how far outside of your niche you can go. If you have a French restaurant, your customers will be confused if you suddenly add Kung Pao Chicken to the menu. If you're a healer, it probably wouldn't make sense to sell sugar-laden pies at the end of a session. But once you've got your people in the door, you'll have a lot of leeway in terms of what you can do and offer, as long as it's in keeping with solving the problem they need to fix—whether that's building a business or finding a great plate of coq au vin.

Case Study: Entrepreneurial Goddess and Niche-Switcher Cami Ostman

Cami Ostman, a beloved client of mine, became a therapist almost two decades ago because she wanted to ease pain—her own and others'. She loved the work, was great at it, and felt called to it. But her passion has always been writing.

A few years ago, she took up marathon running and got really committed to her writing as well, blogging about training and racing. The result of these two endeavors was her first published book, *Second Wind: One Woman's Midlife Quest to Run Seven Marathons on Seven Continents*. Between running and writing and finding a publisher for her book, the focus of her life shifted from observing past pain to imagining and manifesting what was possible for herself and others in the future. She started to move away from hours and hours a week diving into past hurts in her therapy practice. She wanted to help people lay out the course to their personal victories.

Coaching is a good fit for future-focused manifestation work, and group coaching, in particular, harnesses the power of the "pack" (to use a running metaphor).

When the time came for Cami to expand her business to include group coaching, her inclination was to choose as her niche the population of people who read her book—women in midlife looking to be revitalized, empowered, and inspired. She created and ran 12-week "Second Wind" groups that served incredible women. She enjoyed teaching, but something was still missing for her. She longed for a literary life—encouraging the writing process, editing other writers' material, and having them edit hers.

In her community Cami was considered a resource for other writers and had informally coached dozens of them through developmental edits, platform-building efforts, proposal writing, pitching to agents, and self-publishing. She then realized her true niche—to support writers. She was surprised she hadn't chosen that for herself in the first place, as her niche was right under her nose. Working with writers who wanted to realize their dreams through writing a book fed Cami's own creativity.

After a good deal of soul-searching, she officially switched to her new niche. Everything I had learned about building my own business, getting in front of an audience, and enrolling clients looking for my services was immediately transferrable to her new nine-month program for writers: "Get Your Book Done: Turning Memory into Memoir!"

When I talked with Cami about using her story in this book, she told me about a time she got lost in a footrace. Out in the Arizona desert several years ago, she missed a marker on the course and found herself at the bottom of a dried-out, rocky riverbed all alone— no other runners in sight. She had to backtrack a mile to the last marker she'd seen to figure out her mistake. The detour slowed her down a little but didn't stop her from ultimately crossing the finish line. Sometimes we have to go down a path to find out it isn't where we need to be, and that leads us to the right path.

COMMITTING TO YOUR NICHE

Often those first few weeks or months of doing something are the most exciting and adrenaline-filled. Then the real work begins, and we have to learn to develop what I call our "finishing muscles." That's when we learn to surrender to the people we're being asked to serve and we learn to follow through.

I was a niche-switcher too. In my early years, I tried on the role of empowerment and purpose coach before I realized my heart loved supporting women who were starting businesses. Then came the time for me to fully commit to serving women entrepreneurs. It wasn't always easy. Even after I built a successful company, I would catch myself dreaming of doing something totally different. I've had countless clients land on a niche and then want to make a change, sometimes before they've given their chosen niche a real Girl Scout try. It makes sense, right? We're creative entrepreneurs who have likely been through a lot of transformation in our lives, and we want to incorporate all that we're becoming. We like to reinvent ourselves.

My invitation, if this sounds like you, is to give yourself a set amount of time to try a niche, and once you've had a little time to explore it, commit to it. You will get more wisdom (and serve more people and make more money) when you commit to a niche for a year than you will from years of jumping from one to the next.

WAIT—WHAT ABOUT SUCCESSFUL PEOPLE WITH GENERAL NICHES?

Here's a question I often get from aspiring entrepreneurs in the self-growth field: Can a niche be more *general*? What about Wayne Dyer, Marianne Williamson, or Marci Shimoff? They've been successful while helping all kinds of people, right? Great question.

When you see an author or expert out in the world creating success with a more general message, research their history. How did they get started? How did they build their platform before they became famous? Interestingly enough, Wayne Dyer became "Wayne Dyer" with his first book, *The Oedipus Complex*, which was all about sexuality. (Let's be honest—sex sells!)

As the story goes, Wayne promoted the heck out of his first book. This was before the Internet, so he drove from town to town with the trunk of his car full of books and spoke at local bookstores. As he gained popularity and fame, his message evolved. Remember what I said: Your niche is just the sign on your door. Once you build a tribe and have a reputation, you can evolve your message and serve more than one kind of client very successfully.

Similarly, Marianne Williamson's first book was *Return to Love*. She wrote about love and healing, being wounded, a path to spirituality, and prayer as a means to heal all wounds. Her message, although seemingly general, is consistently oriented toward love, relationships, and returning to a connection with the Divine.

Let me talk about Marci Shimoff in particular, because she's a friend and colleague of mine. Marci has a niche, although most people wouldn't think of it that way. Her niche is happiness and love. Everything she does—all of her interviews, books, articles, and trainings—are designed to bring people happiness. She's consistent. She doesn't switch and suddenly promise her audience that she'll teach them the exact steps to launch a successful business. But within her niche of happiness, she can address lots of different subjects and write incredible books like *Chicken Soup for the Woman's Soul*, *Happy for No Reason*, and *Love for No Reason*.

There are wonderful mentors out there who have the capacity to be very successful, but they resist choosing a niche and stay stuck with a tiny group of clients and an equally tiny income. When clients who haven't chosen a specific area of focus for their business come to me, I help them determine where their passion overlaps with the market so that they can increase their results quickly.

I have a client who's a massage therapist, and her practice tripled once she decided to focus on pre- and postnatal massage. Suddenly she had an area of specificity, so people knew whom to refer her way.

A nutritionist client struggled month after month to make a living until she finally launched a program to help women curb emotional eating. Because she finally began solving a specific problem her future clients could relate to, her business took off.

My client and dear friend Michelle Melendez has been an amazing Pilates fitness instructor and personal trainer since 1996. She had a successful fitness boot camp in the San Francisco Bay Area for local women who wanted a complete workout with core and strength training. After several years, Michelle's boot camp was paying the bills but not growing at the rate she dreamed it would or bringing her the freedom she wanted.

The good news is that Michelle is a student of the Law of Attraction. She has repeatedly used affirmations and Universal laws to make drastic improvements in her life, find her incredible boyfriend, and move to her dream home in Santa Cruz. So Michelle began to apply her passion for affirmations and self-growth to find her next step. She knew she wanted to take her business online, but with so many online fitness programs out there, she needed to stand out. Truth be told, Michelle is so much *more* than just a fitness instructor, and it was time to share that with the world.

She was inspired to film her workouts for her online program called "Women Getting Fit" and weave affirmations and Law of

Attraction teachings into all her routines. With each squat her clients repeat, "I love myself! I trust myself! I am amazing!" Michelle found her niche, and not only did her business grow, but it began to attract her dream clients both online and offline, including clients who travel with Michelle on international fitness trips and hire her as a personal trainer.

Michelle's choice to bring an area of focus to her program helped her build a six-figure business, and she's now traveling around the world doing what she loves!

There's a business in Santa Cruz that's a great example of a successful restaurant with a niche. It's called the Picnic Basket, and it's right across from the beach. Before its chapter as the Picnic Basket, it was just a random beachside café that went belly-up. The owner had the vision of selling healthy, ready-to-go food that people could purchase and take down to the beach. That idea was a huge hit. There's almost always a line out the door, and we're all willing to wait because they have the best darn egg burritos in town.

THE SOLUTION IS THE SOLUTION

The *solution* to figuring out your business marketing is the *solution* you can offer your clients. In your business, what is the *primary* solution you want to offer the world? What is the first problem you want to solve? You'll know you've chosen and claimed a niche when you have a problem you can solve and you know whom you can solve it for. When you're willing to plug your gifts and passions into this problem/solution formula, you'll discover your niche. And that niche has the possibility of making you very rich.

Not sure what solution you can offer? Let's brainstorm: What are the solutions your ideal client most longs for? What are the problems they're complaining about to their friends? What are the solutions they may be willing to invest in?

Make a list of all of the ideas you have for your business message—the potential problems of your niche market and the solutions you can provide for them:

Problems:	Solutions:

Now look back over your list and ask yourself: Are these the problems your potential clients struggle with? Do they have a history of investing in the solutions you can provide?

CLARIFY YOUR NICHE

Are you still uncertain how to choose your niche? Don't worry. I've got you covered. Now that you've brainstormed problems and solutions, there are three steps to clarifying your niche.

- Step 1: Consider whether you're marketing downstream or upstream (I'll explain this in a moment).

- Step 2: Do your market research by talking to real people who are members of the niche you're considering serving.

- Step 3: Define your business mission.

Let's get started!

STEP #1: The Marketing Downstream Checklist

There's a particular marketing problem that plagues beginning entrepreneurs, leaving them clientless and penniless: they offer what they *think* people need—marketing *upstream*—rather than create a solution that people are truly *asking for*—marketing *downstream*.

(Easier)	(Harder)
Marketing Downstream: You give people what they're actually asking for, not what you think they need. Your potential customers know they need you because they're walking around complaining about the very problem you can solve.	Marketing Upstream: You have to educate your potential customers about why they need you. They don't realize yet that they do. Even if you see a solution that they don't see, it requires a lot of effort on both ends to convince people they should hire you. It sets you up for rejection and frustration. You're flowing against the current.

How do you know if you're marketing downstream or upstream? Answer the questions in this checklist:

1. Do your potential customers desire the solution you're offering?

2. Do you know exactly whom your products, programs, or services are for?

3. Do you know what your potential customers long for more than anything?

4. Do your potential clients have a history of investing in the solution you're offering?

5. Can you inspire them with new possibilities that they want?

6. Are you taking a bold stand that sets your work apart?

7. Are your potential clients saying YES to what you offer and investing in your solution?

8. Do you know where to find your potential customers?

9. Do your customers help spread your message and refer people to you?

10. Do you love your potential clients and customers?

NOTE: I don't expect you to know the answers to all of these questions immediately. Consider them food for thought, and refer back to them as you clarify your message throughout the rest of this book and in the coming weeks and months of building your business.

Case Study: Entrepreneurial Goddess Natalie Hill

I have a client named Natalie Hill who originally launched her business by leading with her modality but quickly found that she was making it harder on herself than necessary. She's trained in a method called EFT (Emotional Freedom Techniques), and she facilitates incredible inner work sessions using this tapping technique. When Natalie emphasized EFT in her marketing, she attracted people who already knew about these techniques. This limited her potential client base considerably, because many people didn't understand how she could help them. In order to get most of her clients, she had to explain EFT to people and educate them on why they needed her. She was marketing upstream.

As Natalie and I worked together, I recommended she choose a message for her business that was bigger than her modality. We worked together to identify some of her clients' most common problems. Many of them were struggling financially. Since EFT is a very effective way to shift financial belief systems, Natalie teamed up with other money experts and put together a collaborative Internet course focusing on financial empowerment, using EFT as one of the tools. She attracted thousands of potential clients in a matter of weeks and has gone on to reach more than 26,000 people (mostly business owners) with her message.

Natalie now teaches entrepreneurs that mojo leads to money and money leads to mojo, and that pushing and working hard to make things happen isn't the answer. Natalie hasn't left EFT behind; she uses it regularly in her training programs and coaching sessions. Her clients' results have gone through the roof because she has this inner game tool in her toolbox that helps them get unstuck. Natalie's message is clear: she helps entrepreneurs succeed, and she doesn't need to explain every step of the process in her marketing. That would just confuse her potential customers. Instead, she focuses on the outcome she promises, and once people walk through the door of her business, she's able to do all the things with them that she loves doing.

To find out more about Natalie Hill, visit: www.sacredbusiness adventure.com/.

Attention Chiropractors, Hairdressers, and More!

If you're a chiropractor, acupuncturist, or hairdresser, talking about your modality is actually recommended, because everyone has an idea of what chiropractors and hairdressers do. But don't make the mistake of trying to lead with a modality like EFT or XYC or, let's say, hypno-erotica-epsulum, because the truth is that people's eyes will glaze over and they simply won't understand what you can do for them.

STEP #2: Market Research

After putting together your downstream marketing and answering the questions on the checklist, I invite you to begin gathering market research. Asking potential clients about their struggles is much more powerful than trying to guess. Many business owners want to skip this step, but I can't stress enough how much time and energy you'll save if you get answers directly from the source *in their words.* Trust me when I tell you that using your ideal client's language in your marketing will help you stand out. Your potential clients will be like moths to a flame when you use their *own* words and tap into their innermost struggles.

There are no excuses for skipping this step! This kind of market research doesn't take nearly as much time as you think. A typical interview can be done in about 15 minutes.

I recommend finding at least three to five potential ideal clients to ask the following questions. Bear in mind that people love to feel heard. Keep the interviews succinct, record them or take notes, perhaps buy your interviewees lunch or tea if you're meeting in person, and be sure to acknowledge and appreciate their time.

Sample Potential Customer Interview

1. **Greet them! Acknowledge them. Thank them for their time.**

   Example: "The reason I wanted to interview you today is that I have tremendous respect for you. You might not know this, but I've launched a [insert new business idea]. I'm not trying to sell you. Instead, I'd love your opinion on how to best market and grow this business and serve more people."

2. **Find out what they really want.**

   Example: "As a [insert niche here: single mom, corporate professional, emerging entrepreneur], what are your goals and desires?"

   Example: "I'm in the process of creating a business plan to start an organic café in XYZ location. I'm curious if you would dine there. Do you think people in that area would support such a business? What would you want to see on the menu? What would entice you to choose my café over others?"

3. **What are their challenges, and what is their biggest challenge of all?**

   Ask them: "What has gotten in the way of your goals, desires, or vision? What would you say is the biggest challenge that [insert niche here: pregnant women, single moms, corporate professionals] struggle with?"

   If you feel a personal rapport, you might ask: "What has your biggest challenge been?"

4. **Would they invest? Is this something they would pay money for?**
   Example 1: "Would you invest in a mentorship or training program that promised [insert results: more confidence, more money, greater self-trust, clarity of direction, greater leadership abilities, etc.]? How much would you pay for this? What would it be worth to you to have achieved these results six months from now?"
   Example 2: "Would you bring your pet to a groomer in [your location] and pay [your rate]? How frequently do you groom your pet?"

   Reassure them that you want them to answer as honestly as possible. They're really trying to find out if their market has a history of investing in this kind of product or service.

STEP #3: Your Business Mission

Now that you've done your market research and your Marketing Downstream Checklist, let's pull together all that you know about your clients and consider the ultimate mission of your business. One of the key definitions of *mission* (from Webster's) is "the core purpose and focus of an individual or organization that remains unchanged over time, used to clearly state which markets will be served and how, and to communicate a sense of intended direction to those in inquiry."

When you know what your mission is, you'll define your niche and your friends will know which people to refer to you. Creating a business mission for yourself is like drawing a blueprint for the heart of your business and a reflection of how you want to serve others. A well-thought-out mission statement can give you clarity in a world where you're required to make frequent decisions regarding how you spend your time and energy.

In a moment, I'm going to ask you to conclude this chapter by crafting a first draft of your mission statement. This statement can keep you on track so that you prioritize what's most important to you. It will help you continually move toward your dreams, goals, and vision, even if you're still just in the very beginning stages of your business.

Rules of a Business Mission Statement:

- Make it no more than a single sentence long. Then commit it to memory so that you can easily share it when you talk about what you do.

- Say your mission statement aloud, and make sure it has power and clarity. You don't want to confuse people. A powerful mission statement contains simple words and can be easily understood by a 12-year-old.

- An effective mission statement passes the "face test." This means that when you share it with others, they should be able to identify someone in their life who could benefit from your services. In other words, a referral—someone they may want to send your way to experience what you're offering—should pop immediately into their minds. If not, your mission statement probably isn't specific enough.

Here are some examples of effective mission statements:

- I support women who find themselves single again in midlife to get out into the world and date again, and to get really clear on the kind of relationship they want so that they can find their divine right partner. (Relationship coach)

- I provide people with healthy, fresh food in a peaceful environment so that they can recharge and nurture themselves while enjoying a meal alone or with their loved ones. (Vegetarian café owner)

• I teach executives who struggle with overwhelm and breakdown to claim their leadership and implement structures that free them from being in a bottleneck as they empower their team to become an unstoppable force of efficiency, productivity, and service. (Corporate consultant)

INTEGRATION

Draft Your Business Mission Statement

Now it's your turn! Fill in the blanks below to draft a mission statement. Remember that we're still just experimenting here, so there's no pressure and no right answer. In fact, this template is just to get you thinking and doesn't even need to be followed exactly.

I teach/support/serve/work with/mentor/empower . . .
[List your ideal client here]

_____

who struggles with . . . [Insert their challenges]

_____

but wants to create . . . [Insert what they want]

_____

so that he/she can . . . [Insert results they long for]

_____

Now ask yourself if your mission statement passes
the face test. If you shared it with a friend or colleague,
would they know whom to refer to you?

Extra credit: Take your mission statement for a test
drive, and find out how effective it is!!

*Does your mission statement make you
a little nervous? That's fine!
Remember what Barbra Streisand is often quoted as saying:
"Fear is the energy behind your best work."*

Want more ideas for making your mission statement marketable?

Women Rocking Business VIRTUAL GUIDEBOOK

BREAKTHROUGH BONUS TRAINING #6:

**Sage's Official Mission Statement Business Template
+ 25 Marketable Mission Statements**

To get special access to the in-depth mission statement template
I use with my clients, along with 25 examples of marketable
mission statements my clients have tested and approved,
grab it here: www.womenrockingbusiness.com/guidebook

Chapter 7

THE SECRET TO NOT BURNING OUT

*"Knock on the door of your dreams
and guess who answers? Work!"*

— BRENDON BURCHARD

It was two days before my live, three-day event, and it was my biggest one ever. More than 500 women from all over the world were making plans at that very moment to come see me onstage . . . and I was SICK. I woke up with a mega sore throat. What? No!

In the few weeks prior to the event, I had moved into a new home and rebranded my entire company. I was usually good at spreading out big projects, but this time, the perfect storm hit all at once. So there I was, getting ready for my biggest moment of the year, digging through boxes in my living room to find my Kleenex and echinacea as I sniffled and coughed.

Sister, if you're like me, you like to live big! But living big without boundary-setting, a support system, and conscious self-care practices can set you up for a truckload of stress. Contrary to popular opinion, the purpose of your business is NOT to stress you out or burn you out. The purpose of your business is actually to JUICE you up!

As I learned just before my biggest event ever, if you want your business to thrive so that you can increase your income and your impact, you must start by taking care of YOU! That means taking steps to ensure you have a lifestyle that supports your business and a business that supports your life.

So when I extended myself past my limit, I headed to my acupuncturist's office. As he slowly and gently inserted tiny needles into my back, the tears began to come in a marvelous release. Breath by breath, I allowed myself to really feel, express, and let go of my stress.

It was exactly what the doctor ordered. Leaders need places like this where we can go and be cared for. We need spaces where we don't have to be in charge, where we can set aside our own leadership, and where we can show up as we are. For me that day, it was a much-needed pressure release. If we're going to show up for others, we must learn to let others show up for us.

Now that we've begun to identify what your dream business looks like, let's step back and assess your lifestyle so we can set you up for sustainable success.

Take a moment and ask yourself:

What is my relationship to time?
How does stress affect me?
How do I care for myself under pressure?

As you learn to take immaculate care of yourself, you'll be able to bring the aliveness and vigor you need as a leader. While it can feel like a curse to have to be "on" so much of the time, the vitality required to be a trailblazing entrepreneur is also a great blessing. The stakes are high, and you have to show up. What better excuse is there to indulge yourself in daily relaxation routines and self-care practices?

It has only been through my commitment to taking amazing care of myself that I haven't burned out. This, dear one, is the secret to wo-manifesting all that you desire. We simply can't be "on" *all the time*. We have to learn to engage fully . . . and truly let go.

WHEN TO ENGAGE AND WHEN TO LET GO

So, after all that, how did my three-day event for 500 women entrepreneurs turn out? Well, I'd like to tell you it went without a hitch. But as you know, I was sick, which, simply put, sucked. And it was also the most incredible thing that could have happened to me. Here's why: I had to surrender. I had to trust my team. I had to accept the fact that I was going to have a coughing fit onstage in front of 500 women.

And I did. I coughed hard for several minutes. With all the phlegm in my head, it sounded like a guttural mating call. Then I looked at my participants and said, "That was Czechoslovakian for 'I see the God in you.'" They cracked up. Then I got to have a very real conversation with everyone about what it means to show up when you're not 100 percent. We talked about delegation and letting go. We talked about backup plans and self-care. We talked about the truth that sometimes life just happens, and we get sick and have to show up anyway.

Throughout the weekend, dozens of women approached me and said that was their favorite part of the event. They admitted that the fear of body breakdown stops them from playing big, and engaging in an honest conversation like we did encouraged them to go for it anyway.

On the second day in the afternoon, I made an offer for women to join our yearlong program. This is always the part of the event I'm most nervous about. Thank God I didn't cough when I told my participants about the training program I've worked for so many years to create. After the offer, I was exhausted, and I didn't know how I was going to pull off the evening event. My team rallied together and planned the evening so that they could lead it themselves. Then they pulled me aside and told me to go to bed. They declared that they had it handled and that I was to get my rest. One of my beloved team leaders, Clare, looked me in the eye and said, "This ship is not sinking if I have anything to say about it!"

Tears welled up in my eyes as I realized that I could absolutely trust them. We had trained for that moment. So, after making one of the biggest offers of my life to my attendees, I had dinner, got a massage, and was in bed by 7 P.M. I slept like a baby and woke the next morning ready to face the room of 500 women, who were every bit as enthusiastic and committed as they were the night before, when I'd decided *not* to return to the conference hall.

I had never stepped out of one of my major events. It was a huge breakthrough for me to let go and trust my team. What an epiphany to realize that I don't have to do it all alone and run myself into the ground! The sweetest gift of all was that we had more women from that room (over 100) sign up to study with us that year than from any other event we had ever hosted. Apparently, my compromised health hadn't affected their faith that I could help them successfully rock their businesses. And, as a group, we went on to do just that. We rocked their businesses that weekend.

WHAT IS YOUR BODY TRYING TO TELL YOU?

When I got sick for my big event, I was forced to learn to let go and trust my team. Sometimes our bodies break down because they have a message for us. Listening to your body isn't always straightforward or easy. It's common to misinterpret body breakdown as a sign to stop. But I've found that issues with my body are usually more complex than a simple sign to do less or take a week off. My body speaks up with aches and pains that help me listen at a deeper level to myself as I go about the tasks of growing my business.

It's been my body that has taught me that I needed a standing desk so I'm not sitting at the computer all the time. In listening to my body and tuning in to how my energy flows during the day, I've realized I'm much more efficient in the morning and that I enjoy taking time off in the afternoon.

It's also listening to my body that gets me out for my daily run, weekly yoga, or a swim at the pool. When we step into leadership, we have more energy flowing through us; we are accessing more ideas, taking bigger risks, and running more adrenaline. Therefore, exercise becomes essential to move the energy and tension so it doesn't create stagnation. In other words, as a leader it's even MORE important to get your exercise! Moving your body is one of the secrets to letting go and returning to a more feminine state of presence and being. (If you want to learn more about translating the messages your body might be sending you, I recommend the great book *BodyWise* by my friend Rachel Abrams.)

FEMININE VS. MASCULINE ENERGY IN BUSINESS

Sister, as you're well aware, we women need to know when to let go, but we also need to know when to engage and push forward.

When I surveyed women about what they'd like to learn in this book called *Women Rocking Business*, they asked if I would please teach them how to thrive in business using feminine energy. Here's the thing: we can do business authentically, using our uniquely feminine qualities to our advantage, but I don't believe we can do business *solely* from the feminine. Sorry, ladies.

I believe running a business requires a lot of masculine energy as well. We have both, so it makes sense to use our masculine and feminine energies—the yin and the yang—to grow our businesses. (The most successful men I know are fully aware that they must also use their feminine energy to excel in business!)

Most important, we need to know when to engage the generally masculine qualities of focusing, pushing, going for it, and setting boundaries. And we need to know when to engage the more feminine energies of receiving, resting, and creating. We thrive when we find a healthy balance of doing and being—a balance of pushing and pulling. (Inhaling and exhaling can come in handy too.)

"What??" you may be asking. "Sage, can't I build my business without pushing so hard?" I ask you in return: *What would a pregnant mom do if she weren't able to push the baby out?*

The secret to not burning out has no more to do with *avoiding* work than it does with *pushing* or stressing out. The secret lies in your ability to fully engage and plug in, as well as your equal ability to unplug and unwind at the end of your day.

"The cure for exhaustion isn't rest. It's wholeheartedness."
— David Whyte

Now, I don't agree with the amazing poet David Whyte 100 percent. I'm going to talk about *real rest* in this chapter too. But he's right in that wholeheartedness, passion, and joy are often profoundly restorative. Mastering our stress is about staying deeply connected to our sense of passion and joy.

When we get stressed, most of us quickly begin to fantasize about escaping to a beach in Hawaii or Mexico, piña colada in hand, with endless hours to rest and drape our hot, melting bodies all over the place. But have you ever felt soooo exhausted, only to end up supporting a friend you love and finding yourself with more energy when you were done? David Whyte reminds us that our energy is not finite.

When we can tap into the love we feel when we do good work, we don't feel so exhausted anymore. In fact, doing our best work *gives* us energy. When we're willing to surrender our whole heart to serving the world, the giving stops feeling like an inconvenience, and to-do lists become less overwhelming.

Simply put, when we're wholehearted, passionate, and joyful about our work, we're "on purpose" in our lives.

WHAT DOES IT MEAN TO LIVE "ON PURPOSE"?

Have you ever met someone who seems to be lit up from the inside? Someone who seems to have unlimited energy, who never tires? Someone whose vocabulary doesn't even seem to include the word *exhaustion*? Someone who seems to accomplish three times more in a day than the average competent human?

What do these individuals have going on that other people don't? What lights them up? The answer: *a purpose fueled by passion and wholeheartedness.*

Consider an athlete whose purpose is to run a marathon or complete an IRONMAN competition. (Maybe you've even done that yourself. If so, my hat's off to you!) To complete a race like that is to stretch the capacity of the human body beyond normal potential. These folks are *on fire* to run that extra mile in the blaring heat. They put up with pain, puking, passing out, blisters, burns, and skin rashes to run 26 miles, swim 2.4 miles, and bike 112 miles across the tropical Hawaiian volcano landscape. What propels them to do such a thing? Once again, they're *on purpose.*

PAIN PUSHES UNTIL VISION PULLS

When you feel ecstatically engaged in something with your full being, work stops feeling like work. When you're lit up by passion, the energy just seems to pour through you. These are the moments when you're lifted by life and achieve the unachievable.

After working with thousands of clients, it's clear to me that when we align with our true purpose, we tap into an energy source greater than ourselves. We feel the Universe behind us, and our goals and dreams become bigger than our fears. It isn't about getting rid of the fear; it's about letting our passion pull us through it.

It isn't about getting rid of the butterflies;
it's about getting them to fly in formation!

When you're on purpose, your vision begins to pull you rather than your pain pushing you all the time. Even though your self-doubt will still niggle and details may still drive you crazy at times, your commitment to the contribution you are making becomes bigger than everything else. You feel an overall resonance with what you're doing that energizes and carries you when you most need it. Of course, there may be fear, but as you commit to your vision, you learn to manage the fear. In other words, you're getting your butterflies to fly in formation.

The concept of having a purpose and what it means to be on purpose has been passed down by generations of teachers. One of them—still considered a master to this day—was the one and only Buckminster Fuller. He had a fascinating theory about being on purpose that he called "precession."

THE LAW OF PRECESSION

When I learned the Law of Precession, it was as if someone had lifted a 50-pound weight off each of my shoulders. I realized then that I had always been on purpose and that I was in the exact place I needed to be to carry out my life's mission—although nobody could have convinced me of that through words. I needed to see it for myself through this natural law.

Precession simply means that for every action you take, there will be a side effect arising at 90 degrees to the line of your action.[8] This phenomenon can be witnessed when you drop a rock into water. Ripples go out in all directions. The ripples on the surface of the water are the side effect, happening at a literal 90-degree angle to the path of the rock that you dropped.

Buckminster best illustrated the metaphorical application of precession in a story that goes like this: Imagine for a moment that you're a honeybee. You spend your life flying from flower to flower, gathering pollen to make honey. You're drawn to the next flower, and then the next, and then the next. That's what you do. Gathering pollen comes naturally to you, and the next flower is your goal. It's what you know you must do.

As you go about the process of gathering pollen and making honey, something else is happening at a metaphorical 90-degree angle: you're also pollinating the flowers. You don't know you're doing it, but you are. In following those impulses, you literally bring about the blooming of the flowers in the springtime without even trying. That's your side effect.

Buckminster Fuller said that your purpose is like your side effect to the flowers that bloom when the bees create honey. The goal of the honeybee is to make honey, but the true and more spiritual purpose of a honeybee is to aid in flowers blooming. And what's even more of a relief is that your purpose unfolds without pushing or prying the flowers open; it's a welcomed side effect to you following your desires.

So as you say YES to what's next for you, your purpose unfolds. As you take JUST the next step toward getting your business going, your purpose unfolds. As you plan to attend that next networking event, your purpose unfolds. As you hire that next business mentor, your purpose unfolds.

Often we stress out, feeling that we have to figure out our purpose yesterday. But it's unfolding all the time. The pressure we put on ourselves to hurry up and "arrive" contributes to a great deal of burnout. Yes, I know I said that we shouldn't waste time, and that's true. But we suffer when we try to rush and cut corners. The paradox is that your purpose can't be pushed into being just like you can't pry a flower open before it's ready to bloom. Just like you can't put three pregnant women in a room and get a baby in three months. A baby needs a full nine months to be ready for the world, and your business may need at least that long.

If, as a new entrepreneur, you suddenly had 100 customers tomorrow, that could be a problem, couldn't it? Remember this: Manifesting your dreams, visions, and purpose is more of a metaphorical marathon than a sprint. It will take time to bring your vision into being, so pace yourself.

Breathe deeply and let go, dear sister. You have everything you need to carry out your life's mission. Building a business isn't a swift straight line; it's a path with exciting peaks, frustrating dips, and long slow stretches. So you might as well enjoy the ride, nibble on some toast with honey, and smell some blooming flowers along the way.

BUSINESS ISN'T ALWAYS RAINBOWS AND BUTTERFLIES

It may sound like getting on purpose can be a bit of a magic pill for life, but here's what *doesn't* happen when you get on purpose: a rainbow doesn't appear each morning, songbirds don't accompany you on the way to your computer every day, and your life doesn't all of a sudden get easy forever and always.

Here's a reality check: even if the flowers are blooming and your butterflies are all in a row, you'll still have some problems when you're on purpose. It's just that your problems change. Rather than agonizing about what to do with your life or worrying about the details of your to-do list, you'll likely have the desire to take action and bring that sense of purpose you feel inside you to life.

So when your e-mail account freezes, you forget to back up your files, or you lose the most profound newsletter you've ever written, don't make up stories about it. Don't tell yourself that something's all wrong with your business or your purpose. If you end up with an angry client, please don't mistake it for a sign that you're not supposed to be an entrepreneur.

It's common to live with the misconception that once we align with the business of our dreams, it's all a joyride from there. Not true. And, dear sister, I know you have the capacity and inner strength to walk through the storms when they come.

HOW LONG WILL THE PASSION LAST?

So often, we worry about how much work it will take to grow an enterprise, renovate and open the doors on our dream restaurant, or launch our website. So I'm going to invite you to trust that the energy will always come when you align with the Universe and take deliberate action in the direction of your passion and desire. That isn't to say you won't hit those days when you'd rather not be working! But the passion and enthusiasm you have for starting a business will generate a beautiful adrenaline high that will carry you far in the beginning and will continue to be available at the start of each new project and new chapter of your business that excites you.

Here's another paradox for you: there will probably come a time when that adrenaline high will mellow out. The honeymoon just can't last forever! I'm so sorry, my dear, but I'm going to give it to you straight: just like a marriage, the inspiration and passion will naturally subside after the newness wears off. But just as you continue loving your husband by diving into deeper, more lasting layers of love (even when he farts or gets sick), your relationship with your business will deepen too. You'll develop a new and even more mature relationship with it, and you'll still love your customers even when they're a pain in the butt. (If you've ever been my customer, I'm not talking about you.)

But the further you go down your own road of commitment and dedication to your business, and the more you emanate success, the more those around you will want a little piece of that juice for themselves. Requests will be made on your time and energy.

A new business is much like a toddler who needs boundaries to support healthy growth. So one of the ways you can sustain your inspiration and passion is by saying no to the constant demands on your time that occur as you step into leadership. This includes also sometimes saying no to your own inner worker bee who wants to find just *one* more place to advertise or complete *one* more page of your website.

Keep your mission close to your heart and mind as you consider when to say yes and when to say no. When you've gained clarity on your business direction and your money goals, you can choose to say yes to the opportunities that will move you closer to your mission and no to opportunities that won't. Furthermore, you'll need to stay level-headed to make those decisions effectively. This is one of the reasons healthy self-care practices are so important. Only when you're taking care of yourself can you make effective decisions, and only then can you build your business with sustained enthusiasm and joy.

A NEW DEFINITION FOR *WORK*

At one of my first entrepreneurial events, my clients and I decided to come up with a new definition for the term *work*. We all agreed that the concept of work and all the actions necessary to build a business at times felt like ten-million-pound bricks on our shoulders. At times like those, we wanted to leave it all behind and escape to an ashram in India.

What about you? What comes to mind when you hear the word *work*? Does it feel like a drudge? Do you immediately want a vacation? What if it was defined differently—something like this?

What if we thought of work like this?

W = Willing

O = Open

R = Responsible

K = Kindergarten Mind

In this new definition of work that my clients and I came up with, the *W* stands for cultivating a *willingness* to take action. Nobody likes to work all the time, and of course the word gets a bad rap from most of us in the West, but if we're willing to just take the next step and engage in work that we love, that momentum can bring about miracles.

The *O* stands for being *open* to what needs to be done next, without getting weighed down by our to-do lists. It's also about being *open* to asking for support and receiving help.

The *R* stands for being *responsible* or having the ability to *respond*, which means we're willing to engage with what's in front of us.

Before we move on to the *K*, let's talk about responsibility a bit more. In fact, let's talk about what responsibility is *not*. Responsibility isn't the same as overwhelm, and it isn't the same as stress. Taking responsibility for something is often a reflection of how much you care about it, how committed you are to seeing something through to fruition. In fact, the more responsibility you're willing to take, the more money you'll make. Think about it. The most successful people in the world have said yes to tremendous responsibilities. When you look out in the world, wouldn't you agree that this is true?

But you don't have to give up your life or your schedule in order to be responsible. You should just have the ability to respond when you're needed. And as you grow a team and learn to delegate, you won't have to do everything yourself. But when you're willing to take the risks and the responsibility, you'll experience contribution and financial wealth at an entirely new level.

Finally, the *K* in our new definition of *work* means we adopt a *kindergarten mind* if we want to work at a new moneymaking endeavor. This is a piece that holds my clients back again and again. We get good at our jobs. As we get older, we get comfortable at a certain level of mastery over our lives. Yet when we start a business, we're faced with not being an expert anymore. We have to learn a whole new game in order to succeed.

So the sooner you can adopt a kindergarten mind, the sooner success will bless you. I promise. Don't try to reinvent the wheel. Accept your beginner status, get a mentor to help you, learn, emulate, and imitate.

To make a living, we need to work—regardless of whether we work at a job, work as a parent to raise a child, or work to build a business in alignment with our innermost values, serving clients we love. If you dream of having a business, why not give yourself permission to choose the latter? I invite you to choose a livelihood that will ignite the fire of purpose inside your soul. When you do, no matter how tired you become or how much the honeymoon may have worn off, you'll always be able to return to the sense of aliveness that only comes from being on purpose.

DYNAMIC BALANCE

Guess what researchers have found that Olympic gold medal winners have in common? I'll bet you'll be surprised: *They rested.* That's right. They pushed themselves to train but also allowed themselves rest days to completely unwind and let their bodies recover.

With all due respect to David Whyte, the same is true of entrepreneurs, no matter how fueled we are by our passion and purpose. And you already know I learned this one the hard way! You have to push some of the time, but you don't have to push *all of the time.* Take it from me: the only way to continue to cultivate the aliveness, wholeheartedness, and almost boundless energy that comes from being on purpose is to periodically recharge—whether it means a trip to the acupuncturist or plain old sleep.

By now I'm sure you realize that this is one of those topics that aren't either/or so much as both/and. Yes, you'll have an enormous supply of energy when you're passionately on purpose, but you'll also need moments to regroup and be still.

Years ago, my massage therapist taught me about the concept of dynamic balance, which essentially means that balance is not static. The idea that there's a perfect world where we work exactly eight hours every day, sleep eight hours every night, attend two yoga classes a week, eat our greens, and never get stressed is simply a myth. I believe true balance is a more fluid concept. The real mastery comes in knowing how to restore balance rather than clinging to an ideal of staying perfectly balanced all the time.

The best way I know to find a greater sense of equilibrium as an entrepreneur is to allot blocks of time for rest and recovery when we can let down our guard and melt into a warm nest of support. Women especially, I believe, need ample time for rest and sleep. These are two different activities, and we need both!

"Art washes away from the soul the dust of everyday life."
— Pablo Picasso

When you take the time to clear your mind, whether through meditation, quiet time, or an hour spent in nature, you tap into a timelessness that awakens your inner entrepreneurial artist, and the Universe moves through you. When you're on purpose, you become a divine channel for your work, and you're no longer creating your business on your own. Instead, you're co-creating with the Universe, and there's no better feeling in the world.

MY FREEDOM SCHEDULE

Even if the perfectly balanced life is a myth, you *can* create a lot of freedom for yourself. It may take some time after you start your business, but I've seen many of my clients and colleagues create a great deal of freedom. I've done it, and you can do it too.

I take a week off every month, and I've trained people in my world to know that I'm offline. It's my time to be creative, travel, write, and recharge. My team knows, my clients know, and they all support me in it! I don't like working Fridays, either. My schedule now includes working Monday through Thursday three weeks of the month for a total of just 12 workdays per month. I refer to this as my "freedom schedule."

I love this work flow, and I love that at any given moment I can go full out, knowing that there's always a break waiting for me within a few days or weeks. Many of my clients adopt this schedule or something similar over time. In fact, it's knowing a schedule like this exists that gives many of my clients the energy to start a business in the first place. And yes, my dear, you can have this too!

At first, I admit, I didn't know what to do with the free time. I even kind of freaked out the first couple of times I took an entire week off, afraid that if I didn't work, my entire company would fall apart. Fascinating, right? The fear that drives us to produce, create, and manage can be gripping. It was a gift for me to build the muscle of taking time off, and I recommend you do the same as soon as it's feasible for you. Start small with a three-day weekend, and expand into more as you learn to problem solve and adjust your schedule accordingly.

Here's the best part—and stay with me because I know you'll want to hear this: the best ideas come when you're not "working"! You need to have enough spaciousness in your schedule to access the million-dollar ideas. When you're bogged down and overwhelmed in that "full" state, nothing can get in. If this isn't a reason to work less, I don't know what is! If you come up with an even better plan, please call me.

To see an example of my monthly freedom schedule, a full tutorial on how I've set it up, and a downloadable template to create your own freedom schedule, check out the bonus training from the Women Rocking Business Virtual Guidebook that you'll find at the end of this chapter.

UNPLUGGING IS CRITICAL

My friend Ann is a woman I've always looked up to. She walks with confidence in her step and has a commanding presence. She watched me grow up, and she's so excited about this book.

Ann and her husband, Bruz, are longtime family friends who work for the forest service and live in a small cabin on an island in Lake Vermilion in northern Minnesota. Living this way requires them to pack up and leave their home twice a year for the freeze and thaw cycle. Ann's connection to nature is evident in her words, her walk, and every inch of her being.

She and I recently took a pontoon boat ride together near her home. The sun glimmered on the surface of the lake, which was surrounded by tall white pines, birch trees, and a rocky shoreline. As I explained the concept of this book to her, an eagle swooped down from the sky, hit the water with a splash, and emerged with a fish in its talons. Ann looked at me with a glint in her eye and said, "Don't forget to tell your readers to unplug."

After a week of unplugged time at my cabin every summer, I begin to feel like Ann—at one with the elements around me, calm, and steadfast. I return to my clients and team with a sense of renewal and vitality I couldn't find any other way.

We all need this! So I recommend you find your own way to unplug and put it in your schedule. In fact, you can enter it into your phone calendar right now. (LOL)

"AM I TOO OLD?"

One of my clients, Beth McKinnon, is 74 years old. "It's never too late to start over!" she says. Before she started her business, she was a workaholic living on staff at a meditation retreat center. She didn't know how to say no. She kept getting sick and was diagnosed with breast cancer at age 59.

Beth chose an alternative treatment that cured the cancer, but over the following months, she continued to suffer from exhaustion. When she sought support from her doctor, she faced another diagnosis. This time it was chronic fatigue syndrome. She started to do research into her body breakdown and found that an emotional component of breast cancer is *resentment caused by refusing to nurture yourself and putting others' needs and wants before your own.* Beth knew that was *her* story! So she decided she had to change, or she would get even sicker with chronic fatigue. She also feared the cancer could return.

She took two months off, sought the help of a coach, and took excellent care of herself. The accountability of having a mentor did wonders for Beth. She loved having a coach so much that she did the training to become a coach herself. That's when I met her. As much as she loved coaching, though, she struggled with marketing. So we worked together to create her first signature program, called It's Never Too Late to Recreate: Empowering Women in Midlife.

Now Beth supports women just like herself, and her business has grown. She teaches workshops for women and works with private clients. Beth makes time every single day for yoga and meditation, and she's moving into a schedule that will also allow her to take time off. When I asked her if I could tell you her story, she replied, "Sage, I would *love* to be your poster elder! You tell your women that if I can do it, they can do it! It's never too late!"

Just like me and like Beth, you are the creator of your reality. And, yes, while sometimes you may need to put in a few extra hours to get things off the ground, once you have momentum, you're the one who gets to decide when to say yes and when to say no. *You* get to create it the way *you* want it!

GOOD STRESS AND BAD STRESS

Now that we've established that building a business can be stressful (big news, right?), let's discuss how to best manage the inevitable stress. In addition to our work demands, we all have a personal life and bills to pay, so if there's one thing we can count on, it's stress.

Adding to the business owner's stress is the fact that you're literally selling yourself! Whether you're opening the doors of a gallery you've spent months renovating or working as a consultant, Realtor, or therapist, it's literally *you* on the line.

But here's the good news: A while back, the *Wall Street Journal* reported that a certain amount of stress is good for us. The article said, "The body has a standard reaction when it faces a task where performance really matters to goals or well-being: The sympathetic nervous system . . . pumps stress hormones, adrenaline and cortisol, into the bloodstream. Heartbeat and breathing speed up, and muscles tense . . . The blood vessels dilate, increasing blood flow to help the brain, muscles and limbs meet a challenge, similar to the effects of aerobic exercise."[9]

What happens next is what separates healthy stress from harmful stress. People who experience a feeling of beneficial stress get pumped up by these feelings. People who suffer from the side effects of harmful stress feel beaten down, and the increased heart rate and muscle tension trigger fear.

What would it take for you to allow the feelings of pumped-up excitement to emerge in the face of stress, instead of fear and resistance? If you can reframe the way you think about the stress, it can be beneficial to you just like aerobic exercise.

For those of us following a spiritual path, it's easy to have the misconception that life is supposed to feel calm and peaceful all the time—like a walk among lotus flowers. Nope! Life is a ride, full of ups and downs, peaks and valleys. Your soul didn't come here to sit in peaceful feelings *all* the time. As my chiropractor says, "Successful people eat stress for breakfast!" The stress of the journey can expand your comfort zone and pump you up if you let it. So put that referral partner meeting on the calendar, go to that networking event, get yourself out there in ways that stretch you, and allow yourself to feel the thrill of saying YES to your dream.

Then, upon completion of your bold action steps, go home and meditate, take a hot bath, and slide into your yoga practice. You'll be glad you did, and your body (and psyche) will thank you.

BUILDING YOUR BUSINESS CAN CONTRIBUTE TO YOUR HEALTH

After being in therapy for many years, Chantal Leven decided to end her marriage of 23 years and move out. Two weeks later she was diagnosed with breast cancer. Sometimes life just happens. Chantal had been a foster child and had gone through tough times, but this one really tested her. She made the decision to continue living with her husband for several months while she had her mastectomy and reconstructive surgery.

Although the doctors really pushed for her to have chemotherapy and radiation, she courageously declined. Throughout her breast cancer journey, Chantal chose to maintain her client load in her consulting practice—working with about 10 clients per week and teaching five weekly classes, plus managing the studio/business that she had with her husband.

She chose to work and build her business all the way through her breast cancer journey because, she says, it made her feel good to be in alignment with her soul's purpose. During her intense and painful months of recovery, it was serving her clients, the weekly business training calls with me and my team, and the connections with other inspired women entrepreneurs that pulled her forward and kept her healing quickly throughout a roller-coaster ride of emotions.

Chantal is now happily living on her own and continuing to build her business, more committed than ever to bringing her gifts to women who need it. While she isn't always clear on what the future holds, she walks every day with a prayer—to have the strength to walk her path and to serve her clients as a healer of the heart.

Chantal is here to help women who are living the consequences of adverse childhood experiences but committed to becoming their best selves. She now teaches a workshop for women entrepreneurs called The Burnout Buster Business Blueprint, offering the three keys to leaning into self-care and transforming self-worth into net worth. What an incredible gift Chantal is now able to provide!

It's all energy, Goddess! Remember, your clients *are* waiting for you, but you have to take care of that precious body of yours so they will recognize you and you'll be clearheaded and fully resourced to change their lives for the better when they show up. Trust me—your health, body, and soul will thank you for getting out there and giving your gift. It's a gift that *only* you can give.

INTEGRATION

Your Life-Work Balance Assessment

As we wrap up this chapter on the secret of not burning out, consider the following questions. Keep in mind, though, they're meant to help you set intentions, not to become militant rules you have to live by every single day. Remember that there will be times when you're birthing, launching, and pushing, and there will be other times when you need to pull back and fill up.

1. What does your "ideal" schedule look like?

2. How many days per month do you want to work? (Don't tell yourself that what you want isn't possible. Let that go, and write down what you really want!)

3. How many hours per day do you want to work?

4. What time each day do you want to shut down the computer?

5. What are your favorite ways to decompress at the end of the day?

6. What are your favorite ways to decompress when the weekend arrives?

Your Personal AVOIDING BURNOUT Pledge

I, _____ (insert your name), hereby agree to strive toward my ideal work schedule of _____ days per month, _____ hours per day. During that time, I dedicate my complete heart and mind to the service of my future clients and customers and to bringing forth a gift that is flowing through me on behalf of Universal wisdom. I'm grateful for this opportunity to serve, and I KNOW this responsibility is not on my shoulders alone. I trust that every idea comes with its own infinite supply of energy, and I commit to enjoying and nurturing myself along the way. And SO IT IS!

(This is especially effective when you read it in the mirror.)

Women Rocking Business VIRTUAL GUIDEBOOK

BREAKTHROUGH BONUS TRAINING #7:

**Your Financial Freedom Schedule
Work 12 days per month or less!**

Get a copy of my sample FINANCIAL FREEDOM SCHEDULE and a downloadable template to create your own freedom schedule and design your ideal month!

Grab it here: www.womenrockingbusiness.com/guidebook

PART III

GROWING YOUR DREAM BUSINESS

Chapter 8

SELLING ... WITHOUT SELLING OUT

"What if every act of business could be an act of love?"

— MARK SILVER

When it came time for me to launch my first website, the last thing I wanted was to have my face glued all over the banner, promising a transformation that I knew deep down might not occur for everyone who worked with me. I *loathed* marketing when I started my coaching practice. I wanted some other way to find the people who were looking for me. Deep down, I hoped that I could just find someone else to do the marketing part. Maybe if I just kept smiling at people around town, they'd realize that my wisdom was profound and prolific and hire me on the spot. I'm sure you've NEVER felt this way. (Wink wink!)

Well, as I'm sure you already know, it didn't quite happen like that. And, yes, I now have a website and marketing materials with my face plastered all over the place.

I have to smile when I remember a moment with my friend Michelle on the beach after I had just come from a self-growth weekend workshop. The trainer onstage promised big results and enrolled dozens of people in a yearlong training program that cost thousands of dollars. "I will NEVER do it like that!" I told her. "I'll never lure people into a conference room and hop onstage, pretending that I know everything, and then use the entire event to sell people into programs they might not be able to afford. I just don't resonate with that approach!"

But a year later, I would be eating my words. My first two-day workshop comprised about 70 women, 22 of whom decided to enroll in my nine-month training program that, at the time, cost thousands. And those 22 graduates continue to rave about the program to this day. Of course, I feel just as proud of the 50 or so women who decided not to enroll in my program but who left the workshop feeling like they'd gotten tons of value. In fact, a dozen or more of them joined our yearlong program in the years following the event when the time was right for them.

The feedback before we wrapped up our Sunday night was glowing. And though I had made a decision to never stand onstage and offer a program worth thousands, I eventually realized that my original decision was based in resistance. I wasn't setting myself up to serve as many people as possible. So I gave in and used a business model that has been proven by many to work. *I realized I had to make my commitment to changing lives bigger than my resistance to selling.*

If you ever catch yourself saying "I'll never" or "I can't do it that way" or "There's something wrong with selling," you may want to reconsider. And if you ever draw a line in the sand, which I literally did that day on the beach, there's a chance the Universe might entice you at some point to step over that line.

Now, I didn't do things exactly like that other trainer I saw onstage. I didn't spend my entire program trying to sell people on my longer trainings, and I didn't promise results that I didn't know for sure were possible. And you certainly don't need to market yourself just like me or like any other entrepreneurs you might follow. But allow me to lay out some basic principles for building your business, promoting yourself, and marketing your services that will help you become successful without losing your authentic, essential self. When we learn to sell without "selling out," we learn to offer our services while staying in alignment with our core values and beliefs.

Regardless of how you feel about sales right now, dear Goddess, stay with me, because I'm committed to helping YOU serve a LOT more people.

WOMEN'S BLOCKS TO SELLING

You now have a sense of who your clients and customers are, so the next step is to learn how to offer those customers your services in exchange for money. This is, in essence, what it means to sell. But most of us don't think of selling as a simple energy exchange. Most of us have had encounters with salespeople who were overly aggressive, so much so that we've come to think of selling as downright offensive.

I've noticed that most of my women clients have the same blocks to selling. Can you relate to any of these?

We second-guess ourselves and the value of what we're selling.

Why is it so much easier for men to just ask for the money? Many of us women are convinced deep down that we're not good enough, and because what we create is an extension of who we are, we second-guess the value of what we offer.

If you struggle with self-doubt, it gets transferred onto what you're selling. Maybe you fear that if your customer doesn't like what he or she purchased, you will have failed. It's essential to remember that it's your responsibility to do your best, and it's your potential customer's responsibility to decide whether or not to engage in business with you. When you stay on your side of the exchange, you can be less attached, and it's so much cleaner. Once the sale is set, you can nurture your clients all you want!

We don't want to manipulate people.

Please hear this: Manipulating people and offering them something of value are two very different things!

Here's a story that will show you what I mean. In college, I decided to take a year and travel around the world. When a friend showed interest in joining me, I did everything I could to convince her. I wanted a travel companion, and I adored spending time with her.

When I first approached her with the idea, she said, "I can't afford that! It's crazy and impractical." But I could see us having the experience together, so I pushed on. I didn't want to take no for an answer. I started telling her stories I had read about New Zealand and the Great Barrier Reef, asking her to visualize being there.

Long story short, she came with me! It was one of the best years of both our lives. We backpacked through Venezuela, hiked up glaciers in New Zealand, camped out with yellow-eyed penguins on a remote island, went scuba diving in Australia, sat in Buddhist temples in Japan, and jumped out of a plane over the top of a mountain.

I'll always remember the day she told me with tears in her eyes, "You know, you convinced me to take this trip. I've always valued independent thinking and prided myself on my conviction. I haven't been someone who'd let others sway me toward big decisions in my life. But this time, I allowed myself to be convinced to take a major life risk, and it was the most positive experience I've ever had."

Imagine if I hadn't tried to convince her. What if I had decided not to put pressure on her because she clearly didn't have the money? Well, we've agreed that the two of us wouldn't be where we are today without that experience together. That year changed both of our lives forever. It instilled in us the belief that we can do anything we want in life.

It's important to note that I didn't abuse my powers of persuasion. I didn't manipulate my friend; I *influenced* her. What if, as you embrace this journey of selling, you can see it that way? See it as the power of having something of value to sell someone. People will spend their money on *something*, so there's no reason why you shouldn't throw your hat in the ring as one of their options.

We don't want to do it the way "they" do it.

We've all had at least one experience when we've been bamboozled by a salesperson. We've spent money on something that we thought was one thing, but it turned out to be something else. Maybe you won a great trip to a resort, only to have to sit through a four-hour presentation about a time-share. Maybe you bought diet pills or the latest miracle wrinkle cure and found out they didn't work as promised.

Sneaky sales tactics and bait-and-switch models don't work for us.

Since women are hard-wired physiologically to feel more of the emotional spectrum, aggressive sales techniques just don't sit right with us. We feel the resistance in our potential customers. That just makes us remember all the times we've felt resistant to buying something ourselves, and the whole process starts to feel distasteful, disrespectful, and dishonoring. Am I right? But if we don't embrace selling, we have no business at all, and we can't offer our gifts to the people who need us.

Pure and simple: People need you, and you need to make a living.

That's why I've developed the principles in this chapter that allow you to sell without really "selling" at all. This is how we can sell while still honoring our women's values. It's much more comfortable for us, and the good news is that these principles not only still work, but work better than the hard-selling techniques we've come to loathe.

So now I want to teach you the Five Principles of Feminine Business. I believe these principles will make all the difference in your ability to change your mind-set about sales and fall so deeply in love with marketing that you'll become a feminine sales ninja!

FEMININE BUSINESS PRINCIPLE #1: HONESTY SELLS

The ABSOLUTE SECRET to becoming effective and authentic at selling is to be HONEST. This is where many well-intentioned beginning entrepreneurs stumble. They think they need to be manipulative or secretive about the sale. This is what gives salespeople a bad name.

My dear Goddess sister, you are in business for yourself, or you're about to be. You are a professional. You have products and services for sale. There's nothing wrong with this, so tell the truth about it.

Potential customers don't get offended because you have something for sale. They may get offended if you're pushy, but they also get offended if you're unclear. If you're unsure of yourself, your potential customer could lose trust in you. Minimizing yourself and your services doesn't help. Your potential clients want to know that you believe in your product and you think it's great. They'll respond when you're alive, straightforward, and confident.

This means that you get to tell the truth in your marketing materials, at events, and in selling conversations, fessing up that you have products and services available should people choose to take advantage of them.

And don't try to make that choice for your customer! We get into trouble when we think we're responsible for our customer's decision about whether to work with us or purchase our products. We're not. That's the customer's job. Our only job is to present the opportunity. We women have many beautiful qualities, such as generosity and nurturing abilities, but I've seen woman after woman fall into codependent patterns of thinking they have to rescue or fix their customers.

Goddess, I'm speaking to you woman to woman: Be aware of this tendency inside you if you have it, and make a commitment to yourself that you'll rectify this belief and behavior.

An Affirmation to Release Codependent Tendencies

REPEAT AFTER ME:

"I am not responsible for my potential clients and customers.
It's my job to share the opportunity, serve, and do my absolute best to support my clients. I release responsibility for their results, experience, and outcome NOW. I commit to staying on my side of the fence. I keep my nose on my own face.
I do 'me' and let you do 'you.'"

There's a saying that goes, "An ounce of pre-framing saves you a pound of reframing." In other words, when you position yourself right from the start as a professional who has paid services available, it's respectful to both you and your potential customers. You stay on your side of the transaction, and you trust them to decide for themselves whether or not to invest in what you can provide.

What Honesty Sounds Like

Again, be honest and up front about your sincere intentions to serve your customers generously, both now and in the future when it's a fit for them to invest. Having a selling conversation with them might sound something like this:

> "It's so great to meet with you today, Emily! I want to support you to get as much out of your time today as possible. I'd like to spend about 10 to 15 minutes supporting you with [insert the results you provide; such as "a tool to finish your book" or "a mind-set strategy to help you make more money"]. Then, before we wrap up here, I'd like to see if it's a fit to do more work together, and whether you're interested or not is totally okay. But if you're interested, I'll let you know what that might look like. How does that sound?"

When hosting an event, let your participants know that you have a program or service that will continue supporting them. Here's an example:

> "A few months ago, I worked with a gal who was dating the same guy in a different body over and over again until she realized deep down that she was looking for someone to rescue her. We worked together to clear this pattern, and now, for the first time, she's dating some really nice guys and ending the pattern. If you can relate to this, and if you're interested in working with long-term tools that will help you shift your own limiting relationship patterns, I'll let you know about options for further support before we wrap up."

Being up front about your intentions, as the above examples illustrate, cleans up the energy for you and your potential clients. You let them know ahead of time that an offer is coming and that you're going to be straight with them. Then they can relax and be present in the conversation, and so can you.

Once and for all, let's put an end to the bait-and-switch mentality. We're professional, we need to make a living, and we can sell from a place of transparency and generosity.

FEMININE BUSINESS PRINCIPLE #2: SALES IS ABOUT SERVICE

At night, when we flip TV channels, we see infomercials with people trying to make sales and take our money. We're jaded, and rightfully so. But what if we focused on the times we invested money in something that was of great service to us? The new car that you still love driving, the chiropractor who put your neck back in place so that you could finally walk straight again, the therapist who helped you finally stop blaming your parents and take responsibility for your life, the dress that makes you feel beautiful, or the haircut that gets you compliment after compliment. We tend to forget about all the incredible investments we've made and focus only on the few that left us feeling less than fully served or fulfilled.

So often, my clients come to me with a deep desire to make a difference for their customers. But when we dive into our first lesson on sales, they freeze up, get sick to their stomach, or admit they want to wring my neck with the mala bead necklace I gave them as a gift for joining our program. They're that instinctively opposed to "selling."

The very first thing I do with my clients in our programs is help them see that their limiting beliefs about sales and marketing are probably left over from a bad experience with a used car salesman or an annoying cold caller trying to sell them some time-share condo in Tahiti. Or maybe they have a memory of offending someone somewhere along the line with their own sales tactics.

I ask them, "How are your customers going to find you if you don't embrace sales as a part of the service you bring?" When they really get that sales is an essential ingredient to serving the people they're meant to serve, they begin to not only embrace selling, but enjoy it as a way of changing the world.

Next-generation sales is about service. Conscious selling is an energy exchange between two people who trust each other's inherent goodness. When you approach sales as a service, you can bypass the slimy salesperson story. So anytime you're preparing to share what you do with someone at a party or barbecue, or when you're stepping into a selling conversation or putting together your marketing materials, place your hand on your heart and ask yourself, "How can I be of the highest service to the people on the receiving end of what I'm creating?" Then ask yourself my favorite question: "Would I want to read/receive/listen to this if I were my potential client? If I were considering buying from me, how would I want to be treated?"

Just like when you go to a networking event ready to serve, bringing a spirit of service to your clients will clean up the imaginary "ick" factor and put you in the right frame of mind to show up, give, be generous, and appeal to the people who are waiting to find you. That way, you'll feel good about every penny you earn.

So lead with service and love. Then, when people want more, charge what you're worth. Think of it this way: When someone offers you something wonderful, whether it's a great product or a terrific service, aren't you happy to pay them what they deserve? Sure you are. Remember that as long as what you offer is of value, the people who decide to buy will be more than happy to compensate you for what you give them.

FEMININE BUSINESS PRINCIPLE #3: EMBRACING URGENCY TO SELL MORE AND SERVE MORE

As women, we don't want to force or push people into anything, and as consumers, we don't like having time constraints when making a big financial decision. We like to take our time. Yet how many times have you made a buying decision because there was a deadline, discount, or special of some sort? We've all bought because of special incentives; human nature is simply programmed that way.

If the incentive hadn't been there, you might not have bought at all. That's because none of us like to change or evolve. We're more comfortable with what's familiar. And when we invest a large amount of money in something, it's a big change that takes us out of our comfort zone.

The best salespeople understand that discounts, deadlines, and bonuses are effective because of this psychological habit. We need an excuse to make a decision that's different from what's familiar. So please, hear this:

If you ignore urgency—if you don't give the potential customer a reason to buy now or soon—you'll serve a lot fewer people and you'll sell a lot less.

You won't reach nearly as many people who need you if you refuse to accept this concept. If you want to grow a successful business, you need to embrace urgency. Remember: Urgency isn't the same thing as stress or pressure. It's simply an incentive to try something new.

In my business, there's a sense of urgency because there's a window of time in which it's essential that I get my clients and readers financially self-sustaining. If I don't do that for you, you risk losing time, money, and passion. If I can't make you sustainable within 6 to 18 months, you may never be successful in your business. Therefore, I have to teach you to sell and help you enjoy the process of selling.

Plus, I believe there's an urgency in terms of what's needed on the planet right now. What if the success of your business could make some small difference for people who are suffering? For many women, there's a sense of urgency to make their mark and help to heal the world. Urgency doesn't mean you have to run around frenzied, but it's simply true that the sooner you're making money, the sooner you can do more for others.

Consider how you can add urgency to your first offering. If you open a restaurant, perhaps everyone gets a free cup of coffee during the first month. If you're a chiropractor, clients get three visits for the price of two for the first 30 days. This helps you build momentum. There's nothing manipulative about it.

This is especially important at the start of your business. A rocket uses 90 percent of its fuel just to get off the ground. It's the same in business. Seasoned entrepreneurs will tell you that the first one to three years will require a lot of your attention. Once you have momentum, you can begin to get your life back—but only if you're willing to put in the time and attention during those first one to three years! As my friend Claire Zammit puts it, if you're willing to do that, you'll create something that frees you.

> The fact is, to make a living we have to learn to sell our products or services. So why not make your sales strategies an authentic form of self-expression that you can feel great about?

FEMININE BUSINESS PRINCIPLE #4: SELLING CAN BE A SACRED FORM OF SELF-EXPRESSION

Selling really can be an art form and an opportunity for you to put your creativity into your marketing materials in a nourishing and joyful way. It's your chance to design, choosing colors, fonts, and graphics. Make it fun, and make your marketing a reflection of your soul.

Whether you work with a photographer to create great images of your products or infuse your materials with your favorite inspirational quotes, selling can be a sacred form of sharing more of who we are with the world.

One of my favorite ways of selling myself is through telling stories. In fact, I tell my clients, "Content tells . . . but STORIES are what sell." While it's true our clients come to us for the content of what we're offering, what really sells our services and products are the stories behind our offerings. People are drawn to work with us because of a value alignment that they feel when they know our stories. Our future clients trust us when they perceive the humanness behind the services and products we are offering, and one of the most effective ways of doing that is through stories.

I love telling stories of times I doubted myself and found my way to victory, hilarious stories of falling on my face onstage (yes, it happened), and revealing stories about times I dug deep through grief and tenderness to find the truth within me. When women can feel themselves in my stories, they open up; they realize that if I can do it, so can they. My self-expression gets to be of service to another's growth, which is a deeply fulfilling experience. I want this for you too, sister. Your authentic self-expression, when packaged correctly, is going to magnetize the clients who are waiting for you.

FEMININE BUSINESS PRINCIPLE #5: CONSCIOUS SALESWOMEN ARE DEEPLY PRESENT

What is a "conscious saleswoman"? She's someone who is conscious of her impact and aware of her power as she creates her offerings for the world. She's deeply present and committed to honoring the value of what she has created. Just like nature doesn't hold back its flower petals or its beautiful birdsong, a conscious saleswoman remembers that it's her job to craft something wonderful for the people who need it. She knows there are a variety of ways she could make money, but she's chosen this business path because she genuinely wants to provide the gifts of her heart.

A conscious saleswoman is intuitive and committed to her clients/customers. She's in it for the right reasons, and her customers perceive her integrity. It makes them want to buy from her and refer other people to her.

The conscious saleswoman takes the time to get to know her customers, ask them questions, and find out what they truly want—in their words—so that she can serve them better. Remember, it's essential that you offer what your customers really need, not what you think they need.

Plus, incorporating your customers' own words into your marketing materials—"customer-speak"—is part of marketing downstream. So take the time to interview potential customers. (I'll provide some possible questions shortly.)

Again, we invest our money where we want to see change in our lives, and people can smell whether or not you're committed to what you do. None of us wants to invest with somebody who isn't in it for the long haul. We don't want to sign up for 20 sessions with the chiropractor who's going to disappear to Costa Rica in a few months because she's burned out. (Remember, though, that this commitment doesn't mean you have to give up your personal life. Refer back to scheduling your time in chapter 7.)

In my own experience, I struggled with this a lot because I really like my freedom. I didn't quite know how it would work out if I enrolled people in a yearlong training program. What if an opportunity to hop on a plane and go to Africa came my way? It has been a transformative process for me to learn the skill of committing to my clients and committing to my freedom at the same time. Committing to taking care of my clients has created a commitment on their part as well. I've achieved enormous fulfillment from dedicating my life to my customers. There's a sense of peace in my heart that comes from the knowledge that my life doesn't belong just to me.

As Mother Teresa said, "If we have no peace, it is because we have forgotten that we belong to each other." Life isn't just an egocentric search for pleasure, even though we should experience pleasure along the way. When we're conscious saleswomen, there's pleasure available for everyone. It's a win-win.

THE GROW MODEL

Okay, my dear—we've covered some basic mind-set principles of selling as women. So what does an authentic selling conversation actually look and sound like? The GROW Model can be used to lay a framework for understanding authentic sales. GROW originated in the United Kingdom in the 1980s as a coaching model for goal setting and problem solving. I've found that it also works beautifully as an authentic feminine selling model. Thousands of my clients have used it successfully to create six- and even seven-figure incomes. It helps us identify our customers' needs, desires, goals, and visions. It helps us discover what problems they want to solve. Then we can become the solution to help them close the gap between what they have (or where they are) and what they need. You can use the four steps of this model in a selling conversation, a website, or any other marketing materials.

Now, it's true that the GROW Model does tend to work best with service-based businesses, but you can also adapt aspects of it for product-based and brick-and-mortar businesses.

GROW stands for:

G = Goals—What the client most wants.

R = Reality—The client's current challenge.

O = Options—The mini-plan you will lay out to support your potential client.

W = Wrap-Up—The moment you offer your services or product and take payment.

G = Goals

In this first step, you find out what your clients want the most. What are their goals? If you're preparing to open a brick-and-mortar business, you might conduct market research. You can even interview people on the street in the community or target them through social media, perhaps with a survey.

The owners of a furniture store in my area discovered that a significant number of people wanted handmade, nontoxic, environmentally sustainable furniture. They identified the goals of their target market, such as wanting their kids to grow up in a healthy environment and wanting to avoid furniture that's full of chemicals and odors. These store owners really did their homework, even holding leather furniture in storage for several months before putting it on the selling floor so that it could off-gas the chemicals from its production and be odor-free.

If you have a service business, it's easy to ask these questions in your initial conversation. You might start by saying, "I'm going to ask you some questions, and we'll explore what's been going on for you as well as get you a plan for success. Does that sound okay?" This gets clients to buy into the conversation. Let them know you have, say, 20 to 30 minutes so you'd like to just dive in.

Possible questions might include:

- "What made you decide you wanted to talk with me?"
- "What do you want? What's your goal or vision?"
- "Why is this important to you?"
- "How would it feel if you had that? What would be the best part of it?"
- "How would your business [or health, family life, etc.] be different?"
- "On a scale of 1 to 10, with 10 representing absolutely committed and 1 not willing at all, how committed are you to creating this for yourself?"

R = Reality

The Reality phase of the GROW Model allows you to find out what's in the way of the customer achieving his or her goal. One of my clients is a corporate consultant who works with teams experiencing a communication breakdown. When she first started out, she focused solely on the Goals questions, asking the human resources directors she met what they wanted. Since adding the Reality phase and the rest of the GROW Model, she's noticed that she signs a lot more clients, and her connection with them is deeper and more authentic from the start.

The Reality phase is powerful for her because when she asks her potential clients questions about their biggest challenges right at the beginning, she immediately understands the specific breakdowns within each team. Once she knows the gap between where they are (the reality) and where they want to be (the goal), she can build a vision of the ideal team for the organization. This creates a desire in the potential client to fill the gap, and she then positions herself as someone who can provide a solution. This is, in essence, selling without selling.

Here are some of the questions to uncover the customer's REALITY:

- "What's stopping you?" "What's your reality?" and/or "What have you already tried?"

- "Tell me more about _____ [insert their challenge]."

- "If you don't address this _____ [insert the problem], what will your life look like in a year? Are you willing to wait to address it?" These questions help the customer get in touch with the cost of the problem without painting a picture of disaster.

- "How has this affected your health [or family life, relationships, finances, business, etc.]?"

O = Options

In this step, I recommend that my clients lay out options for their customer that don't necessarily include hiring them. "What?" you might ask. Well, this is the moment when a lot of people make the mistake of becoming overly "salesy." They want to prematurely jump to "Please hire me," which can turn off the customer and derail the whole process.

What I recommend instead is to give your customer some options and ideas *without* making the direct suggestion that they hire you—just yet. Provide some valuable suggestions or a tangible tool that they can go ahead and use. This allows the customer to begin to "act as if" they're already working with you.

During the Options phase, for example, a corporate consultant might say, "What I'm seeing is that you have a breakdown in the leadership team, and you don't have a clear organizational chart. Several people on your team don't know where to go when they need answers, so it all falls back on you. And you don't have the time or capacity to guide everyone effectively. If we were to work together, I'd like to help you establish a more effective organizational chart and structure for your team so that everybody's clear about where to go for support. The lines of communication will get cleaned up, and we'll resolve the conflicts." She doesn't say, "You need to hire me." Instead, she paints a picture of what it might be like to hire her. She also offers a suggestion the customer could implement without hiring anyone. See what I mean?

Old-school selling techniques at this moment in the conversation might involve trying to frame yourself as the *only* option your potential customers have, or painting a picture of how horrible things will be for them if they *don't* hire you. Blech! You can almost smell the desperation, right? And who wants to hire someone who's desperate for their business?

In the GROW conversation, spelling out the Options is more about showing how much you care about helping to solve the customer's problem. You show genuine empathy and understanding. Not only is this in keeping with the way we are as women, but it also establishes trust. And as long as you really do care (and I know you do), the customer's trust in you is well placed.

I often even suggest to the women I work with that they say, "I'm absolutely not the only one who can help you with this problem, but it would be my honor to help you. And here's why . . ."

Here are some other ways that you can lay out the Options:

- Recommend one or two plans you have for them based on their goals.

- Ask: "Would you like me to lay out a mini plan for you right now?"

- Lay out the plan: "Based on what you've shared, I believe that with _____ and _____ [course of action], you could be experiencing _____ [solution] within a few months' time."

- Once you've laid out the plan, ask: "How would that feel?"

Now, if you're selling a product in a store, the Options scenario works a bit differently. If you're selling only one product, you can simply paint a picture of how your item can solve the customer's problem. If you have several products that could solve the problem, such as a furniture store with a number of leather chairs, for example, you can demonstrate how one or two different chairs could do the trick. If you're truly trying to help the customer, though, you don't automatically push the most expensive chair. You listen to what the customer needs and suggest the chair that will most likely fill those needs.

W = Wrap-Up

The Wrap-Up involves asking for the sale, and this is where a lot of my clients hit a wall. They're fabulous at the Goals, Reality, and Options parts. They create beautiful marketing materials and have great conversations with potential customers, but they don't seal the deal because asking for the sale feels so uncomfortable to them.

Why are we so resistant to making an offer and getting that sale? We fear rejection, that awful word *no*, and the even more awful accusation "You're too pushy." With all of those fears in the way, of course you don't want to ask for the sale! Who would?

But here's the thing: All you have to say is "Are you ready to get started?" That's not so bad, is it?

If it still feels difficult, just know that it's a new muscle for many of us—a muscle that you'll simply have to spend some time developing. One way to make it easier is to practice asking for the sale with a trusted friend who role-plays as your potential customer. Keep practicing until it rolls off your tongue as easily as "Please pass the salt" at the dinner table.

What happens when you don't ask for the sale? You miss out on serving many people. It's not only a disservice to you and your business but also a disservice to your potential customer. Essentially, you're making your own fears bigger than your commitment to serve that customer.

Your Conscious Selling Affirmation

My commitment to changing lives is
bigger than my fear of selling!!

As you ask for the sale, remember the sense of urgency we talked about earlier in the chapter!

Here are some ways you can handle your Wrap-Up:

- Offer your solution if it's a fit.

- Ask: "How were you hoping I might be able to support you further?" Or say: "I'd like to make a recommendation . . ."

- As you describe your service or product, tie back each component to their problem and what they said they wanted. For example: "My program provides simple, healthy meal plans to women like you who have struggled with understanding what to eat in order to feel better" or "Our office chairs are ergonomic, and for many of our customers, they've prevented the kind of back pain you've been experiencing."

- Emphasize the results you'll provide: "Here's why this is so valuable . . ."

- Add an incentive to buy now or soon.

Another way to smooth over your Wrap-Up is to address the potential client's objections before they even arise. The most masterful salespeople take a thorough inventory of the biggest objections their customers have and address them on the front end. Here are some ways you can do that in a variety of business types:

- The hairstylist guarantees her haircuts. "If you wake up the next day and decide it isn't what you want, come back for a complimentary reshaping."

- The massage therapist reminds her clients that the cost of a massage is much more affordable than the cost of getting sick.

- The clothing designer guarantees that her clothes are all prewashed and won't shrink.

- The coach offers a free introductory session or workshop so that clients can be sure it's what they want.

- The ice-cream shop offers free samples.

- These are just a few of the hundreds of possible ideas.

- The book editor suggests working on just the first chapter as a trial.

These are just a few of the hundreds of possible ideas.

Here are some more ways that you can address a prospective client's concerns right from the start:

- If the client is concerned about money, address it directly. Say something like "I completely understand the risk or discomfort of investing at this level. Can I ask you a question? What would you want to get out of this in order for it to be worth it for you?"

- Help them get in touch with the cost of not investing. "I'm curious: What is the cost of your waiting? What will your life look like in one year if you don't address this soon?"

When the client says yes, explain how to get started: "The first step is to process your deposit [or payment] and schedule your first session [or delivery]. I'll get you a copy of our agreement [when appropriate]. What credit card would you like to use?" Then, of course, be ready to accept payment!

I tell my clients that knowing how to facilitate a powerful enroll-ment conversation is really the "Mother Skill" . . . in other words, it's the most critical skill in being able to convert someone who's just *interested* in your services to someone who is actually ready to *invest in* your services. A lot of people want to skip learning this step and just slap a button on their website, but unfortunately, it doesn't work that way! We all need to know how to sell when we're talking to a poten-tial client, and we can do it without feeling salesy or inauthentic.

Case Study: Entrepreneurial Goddess Clarissa Medeiros

Clarissa Medeiros worked for 16 years in the corporate world in Brazil, mostly reporting to men. The pressure was always on to sell, and she struggled with stress and anxiety daily. Her health began to suffer. She knew something had to change, so she launched her consulting business, hoping to create more freedom and autonomy for herself.

But her first four years as an entrepreneur weren't much eas-ier than her life in the corporate world. The problem was that her mostly male role models had used traditional selling tactics, includ-ing cold-calling and long-form, scripted selling conversations that left her feeling inauthentic and pushy when she used them. She longed for true freedom with a business model that would allow her to be all of herself.

When Clarissa joined our training programs, she discovered a feminine model for doing business without the pressure and manip-ulation. She now focuses on using the GROW Model for her selling and on creating a safe container for her potential clients. She reports that thanks to this model, she feels more like herself. She's attracting amazing women, and she loves working with them. She also val-ues herself enough to set boundaries and has learned to determine whether she's talking with an ideal client within the first 15 minutes of a conversation. If it isn't a good fit, she lets them go with no regrets. As a result, enrollment and selling flow naturally.

Clarissa has also begun to see her clients in groups so that she can earn more for fewer hours worked. She's found this model to be good for her clients too, and she says it feels more feminine to have time to rest and dream again. Most important, Clarissa no longer feels she has to separate the professional consultant from the personal, authentic woman inside. She's finally on purpose and at peace every day.

Her growing company, Brilliance Veritas (which translates to "brightness of truth"), focuses mainly on supporting women CEOs to create meaningful businesses so they can have more success, serve more clients, and change the world.

Clarissa admits that there are moments when building a business can be overwhelming, but she loves her clients and her business so much that she lives in joy most of the time. What's more, since putting feminine sales principles into place, she has more than tripled her income and brought in the equivalent of more than $130,000. Most important, she feels like she's giving the world her full contribution. Boom! You can find out more about Clarissa at www.clarissa-medeiros.com.br.

CONNECTION EQUALS CURRENCY

Connection is the special ingredient that makes businesses grow, and everything I've outlined in this chapter is about making a connection with your clients or customers. In this way, conscious selling becomes about connecting, not selling. The truth is that even with the rise of technology and the Internet, it's still relationships that persuade people to buy, even when they do so online. As entrepreneurs, we can't shortcut the value of developing relationships with potential customers and referral partners.

It's the quality of those relationships rather than the quantity that makes for a successful business, however. You've probably heard that studies show it takes an average of seven touch points to get a customer to buy. So we have to be willing to establish that currency of connection with people, whether it's through conversations, ads, open houses, or marketing materials. All of these provide opportunities for our prospective clients to experience the value of what we do. It's why you see Internet marketers in your inbox and on Facebook, Twitter, Instagram, and other sites. You'll see them everywhere, and that's often what makes you tip over into trust and see someone as the obvious solution to what you need. We can't afford to feel entitled and assume that people should buy from us after the first encounter. Conscious selling is a marathon, not a sprint!

People approach me all the time with complaints: "I've put up a website, but I'm not getting clients. I'm not making any money."

I always ask, "How many people are you talking to about your business?"

The answer is usually something along these lines: "I've been too busy working on my website"—or Facebook page, Instagram profile, or some other hot new social media tool or online marketing widget.

It's a common misconception that you can throw a website online with a "Buy Now" button, and money will just show up in your account. Any seasoned online marketer will tell you it doesn't work like that! Unfortunately, you can't launch a business on the Internet and hide behind your laptop screen. Sometimes we seem to forget that there's actually a live human being on the receiving end of our website or Facebook posts. So we have to be willing to open our hearts, build intimacy, and show we care. Remember the old adage: "People don't care how much you know until they know how much you care."

The most successful online marketers don't do all their sales online. They train salespeople to pick up the phone and make that real connection, human to human, with the person on the other end of the line. Turning a potential client into a paying client requires this kind of connection. Bottom line? The most magical and mysterious Internet marketing strategy won't work unless you've genuinely connected in some way with the real live people you want to reach with your product or service. E-mails alone just aren't going to cut it. Be willing to pick up the phone, get out in the world, and have real-life business conversations. You're probably better at this than you think!

What Kind of Customer Are You?

How do you attract better customers who are the kinds of buyers you want? Become a better buyer yourself! What would it look like for you to cultivate good, clean buying habits? Notice your own patterns. Are you the kind of customer you'd like to have? Or do you often regret purchases and return things? Are you late for appointments? Are you late making payments? Do you try to talk someone out of charging you if you cancel within 24 hours?

Respect the sales process, and embrace what it means to be a good, joyful consumer. Then you'll find it easier to embrace what it means to be a good, joyful salesperson.

WOMEN ARE THE ECONOMIC ENGINE OF THE PLANET

According to *Harvard Business Review,* "women now drive the world economy."[10] Simply put, we are the economic engine of the planet. So why wouldn't we be uniquely positioned to be great at sales—especially since we're probably going to be selling a great deal (if not primarily) to other women? We can look at our own psychology about buying and apply that to our customers. We can intuitively perceive what creates a beautiful buying/selling relationship.

Remember that when we buy something, we do it to improve our lives or create some kind of change, whether it's organic herbal shampoo that makes our hair feel and look amazing or a coaching program that helps us finally turn around those niggling bad money habits and grow our wealth. When we sell something of value, it's an opportunity to improve the lives of our clients or customers.

Goddess, think of it this way: To hold back on selling your own services or products is a selfish act. Adopt this mind-set shift: To sell is to change lives.

INTEGRATION

Clear Your Inner Clutter around Sales

1. Make a list of the times you can remember feeling "sold" or turned off by a pushy salesperson.

2. Now make a list of the times someone encouraged you to purchase something that changed or improved your life. For example: a favorite piece of jewelry, a life-changing vacation, an inspiring book, or a transformational workshop. Reflect on how you felt when you experienced or used these purchases and how they made a difference in your life.

3. Next, reflect on how you want your clients or customers to feel when they purchase your products or services. What difference do you want to make as a conscious saleswoman?

4. Practice asking for the sale with a trusted friend. Keep going until it rolls off your tongue and you feel comfortable offering what you have to give.

Women Rocking Business VIRTUAL GUIDEBOOK

BREAKTHROUGH BONUS TRAINING #8:

The Feminine Enrollment Client Attraction Template

Discover how to use the GROW Model to have an authentic Enrollment Conversation . . . the Woman's WAY!

Grab it here: www.womenrockingbusiness.com/guidebook

Chapter 9

YOUR COOPERATIVE ADVANTAGE AS A WOMAN

*"There's a woman's way of doing business,
and when we embrace it, business becomes
expansive, joyful, and full of possibility."*

— BARBARA MARX HUBBARD

With a baby on one knee and a laptop on the other, she found the courage to launch her business. It was slow going, so she struggled to pay the bills. And without the supportive community she needed, loneliness set in. Yet she couldn't find the time to create the community she needed to support her. There were many days when she simply lost hope.

What did she do? Something ingenious. Something feminine. She created an imaginary community with an imaginary board of inspirational directors that included Maya Angelou, Melissa Manchester, Audre Lorde, and Joni Mitchell. When fear and worry threatened to get hold of her, she'd play a Melissa or Joni song, or she'd listen to a recording of Maya Angelou's poetry: about being a "phenomenal woman." Maya, Joni, Audre, and Melissa were always there for her, letting her know that she could do it. She could be successful as a woman, the woman's way.

Who am I talking about? My mentor and friend Mama Gena, aka Regena Thomashauer. Sixteen years ago, Regena was a single mom to an infant daughter, but she also had a vision. She dreamed of starting a school of "Womanly Arts," where she would teach women to be women and also be successful.

And the rest, as they say, is history. Despite her rough start, Regena now runs a multimillion-dollar organization with thousands of graduates from more than 36 countries around the globe. The first time I heard her speak, she said, "We women have 8,000 nerve endings all dedicated to pleasure! The physiology of a woman gives us a clue as to how we work. Women hold the consciousness of pleasure for humanity."

Mama Gena discovered early on that her business was just like her infant—it needed to be "fed" every hour or two. That's when she discovered the need to bring pleasure into the workday to balance out the stress of business. Today you can find her rocking out with her team in her New York City offices during short dance breaks on a daily basis. What happens during these dance breaks, she says, is that our cells are bathed in neurotransmitters that bring feelings of relaxation, focus, regeneration, and inspiration. It doesn't matter what you listen to or how you move—just get up and dance. "It's as if your cells have been taken to the spa!" says Mama Gena.

Ready for a dance break? Let's GO!

Turn on the music . . .
and rock out for a few minutes!!

When we dance, eat chocolate, have sex, or just take a break, our pleasure nerve endings also turn on neurotransmitters and hormones associated with bonding and heart opening. And when our hearts are open, we're more effective, juicy, and inspired entrepreneurs!

Women are simply hard-wired to be more sensitive than men and to connect with others. As I mentioned in chapter 4, women produce more oxytocin than men, which predisposes us to "tend and befriend."

Yet our patriarchal world isn't set up to honor women's values of pleasure, play, expression, and connection. Therefore it's up to us to restore and prioritize these values within our busy workdays. But honoring these values isn't just for our own sanity while we plug away at our businesses like men. Staying connected to our feminine nature is exactly what gives us an advantage in the business world—a *cooperative* advantage, though some people might call it a *competitive* advantage. In other words, when you embrace your natural tendencies toward *service, generosity, nurturing, honesty, collaboration,* and *alignment with Universal Laws,* you give yourself an advantage in business. In fact, these are the very six principles we're about to explore to help you ROCK your business this year.

Remember what I said in chapter 1: It's *because* of our uniquely feminine qualities—not in spite of them—that women are excelling in business today. And your clients don't all have to be women for that to be the case. Your femininity is a strength regardless of what you're doing or whom you're serving. In other words, everything that you've been told is a liability to women in business is actually an asset. Yes, that includes your people-pleasing tendencies and your emotionality.

As women, we thrive when we build businesses
that *empower* others rather than have *power over* them.
Businesses based in *collaboration* rather than *competition*
and in *contribution* rather than *greed.*

Because of our concern for the people around us, we're able to win
hearts and enroll followers in our vision.

What a beautiful thing to be a WOMAN!!!

There's simply never been a more exciting time to be a woman, and you don't have to change the essence of who you are to be successful. Yes, as I previously said, you'll still use some of your masculine side, but you won't have to negate your femininity in the process.

Femininity is not only a great way to be successful, but maybe even the best way. As the Barbara Marx Hubbard quote at the beginning of this chapter says, it's definitely the most expansive and joyful way to do business.

So let's talk about the qualities you can embrace NOW that will give you a *cooperative advantage.*

Goddess, you are going to LOVE these!

YOU HAVE A COOPERATIVE ADVANTAGE WHEN YOU LEAD WITH GENEROSITY

We women are good at giving. We all know it's true. Sure, there might be some women who aren't, but if we're in tune with our innate femininity, giving is what comes most naturally to us. We thrive and shine when we're generous. So *lead with generosity.* If what you do complements another person's business, offer your services.

The great news is that when you give someone great advice, great content, a free workshop, or free guidance, they will likely want more from you.

The free event or open house model is one of the best ways I know to get a business off the ground. When I started out, I hosted a free, informal, two-hour class called Three Keys to Clarify Your Purpose and Make Money Living It at local bookstores, community centers, and libraries. The first time I did it, the bookstore helped promote me, and 24 people came. Half of those people bought a $1,000 package from me that included some coaching sessions and a class. By leading with generosity and giving two hours' worth of my services, I ended up making $12,000 from that one night.

What if you have a brick-and-mortar store? One of my clients owns a lingerie boutique that was barely hanging on until she started holding open houses. Then she planned Free Panty Friday, giving free panties to the first 20 customers who walked in the door. The next thing she knew, her business was growing with lots of loyal customers.

If you have a day spa, you could offer a free add-on service or half-price treatments for a couple of hours one day a week. If you have a restaurant or bar, you could start a happy hour. There are so many possibilities no matter what kind of business you have!

Later in the book, I'll give you lots more ideas for planning a free event, including how to get people in the door.

Your Ability to Nurture Gives You a Cooperative Advantage

Many women entrepreneurs are advised by business mentors to toughen up and set better boundaries. While this advice can serve in some ways, it's important to note that what's being craved in the marketplace is a more nurturing approach. All you have to do is look at the articles in publications like *Entrepreneur* and *Forbes*, and you'll see titles like "How to Create an Emotional Bond with Your Customers." Who's better equipped to do that than women?

NURTURING AS A COMMODITY

Let's face it: We all need more nurturing. In chapter 4 I talked about how much technology has isolated us from one another. We're on the computer or texting on the phone without actually talking to people. These days many of us don't even know our neighbors. I made a point to meet my neighbors, and now my neighbor Laura stops by with her kids just to say hi and give me hugs. Since I don't have children of my own, these moments are a bright light in my day!

Women's nurturing qualities are needed to help us reconnect and heal from the isolation of our plugged-in society. We innately know how to nurture and take care of one another, counteracting the effects of our modern-day loneliness. This talent that we uniquely have as women can be regenerative, as we bring to our customers and clients the love and attention that they crave—whether it's as a coach or as a computer salesperson.

We don't tend to think of nurturing as a commodity, but trust me—it is! For a while, I drove all the way across town to a particular market just because the owner had a smile that lit up the place. We don't choose our Realtor or our hairdresser just because of their talents. We choose them because of how they treat us. This is why staff members at the finest hotels refer to you by name, even though they might have 300 guests at any given time. It feels good when someone is friendly and welcoming, doesn't it? And it makes you want to continue to do business with them.

Author Martín Prechtel uses milk as an apt metaphor for nurturing. No matter how hard our parents tried, he says, none of us got the milk we needed as children, and we're still operating at a milk (nurturing) deficit as adults. So, at some point in our lives, we have to dig deep and start giving milk to others because the world is so hungry for love and nurturing. Then, as we do it, we're nurtured in return because we receive appreciation, repeat business, and referrals from our clients. And some of them even want to nurture us in return.

But what if you're already an over-nurturing type? Well, releasing that energy toward your clients in your business is actually a healthier way to use it than over-giving to your family and friends. So nurture away! Help your clients or customers feel good, whether you're serving them a meal, handing them their dry cleaning, or leading them in a workshop.

Now, this doesn't mean that you have to climb into the booth with your restaurant patron when she starts sobbing in the middle of her cheesecake (although maybe you'll want to do exactly that), or give away 100 percent of your products or services for free (*never* do that). Nurturing can take many forms. It's a customer-focused way of being, and it's where your old people-pleasing habit can be your greatest asset.

For example, one coffee shop owner saw that a lot of her customers showed up with dogs, so the shop started providing water bowls for the dogs while the people drank their java. It can be something as simple as feeding the local four-leggeds!

Think about the little touches of nurturing you've received from businesses now and then and how it made you feel. When a business owner cares about you as a customer, you come back, don't you? See, I told you a woman's nature is a cooperative and competitive advantage! (Told you so! Told you so!) Your ability to nurture can actually put money in your pocket and bring love to all involved.

Why do we build our businesses in the first place? It's really just about love wanting to express itself through us. Building a business, in its simplest form, is creating a container to express more love on the planet. Our businesses become vessels for giving and receiving love. And we LOVE to LOVE, don't we?

FEMININE VALUES IN NETWORK MARKETING

I'm partnering with Bella Shing and Joy Bernstein and consulting for them on the launch of the next level of their multilevel marketing (MLM) business. They are true powerhouses in a company called dōTERRA essential oils. At the time of this writing, they're already making more than $30,000 per month (combined) after only a few years in the business.

When I asked Bella about her success, she admitted to me that she feels the lack of female CEOs and other executives in the corporate world isn't because there's a glass ceiling. Instead, after working with thousands of women, Bella feels the nature of traditional corporate models can cannibalize the cooperative spirit and thus repel women.

On the other hand, network marketing is a very feminine business model in which leaders are successful only if the people below them are successful. That incentivizes everyone to nurture those they bring onboard. People below you can outpace you, and you get your bonuses only if you can help them to be successful. This contrasts with the traditional corporate model, where you have one CEO at the top, then executives and workers underneath with only one person who ever gets to make the lion's share of the income.

It's no surprise that the majority of the top earners in dōTERRA are women. It also helps that network marketers tend to be more supportive of mothers, allowing them more flexibility. Bella and Joy's product line, which consists of high-quality essential oils, actually helps kids have a more restful sleep so that moms can get their work done. It's said to boost immunity, too. For more information on Bella, Joy, and dōTERRA, visit Essential Intention, a resource site housing groundbreaking content on the healing power of essential oils: www.essentialintention.com.

FOR WOMEN, COLLABORATION IS KEY

Historically, my clients try to go it alone. *"I can do this! I got this! I can do it BY MYSELF!!"* More often than not, because most of us have stepped onto a path of women's empowerment and we value our independence, we forget to ask for help. Or asking for help just plain makes us uncomfortable because it wasn't modeled for us. But as I said in chapter 4, we aren't built to do it alone!

Furthermore, most of us are much more comfortable promoting somebody else than promoting ourselves. There's no question that it's a vulnerable feeling to publicize your own business. So why not use one of the qualities that's a distinctly feminine asset—collaboration? It's help, but you reciprocate. Discomfort problem solved!

The best way I know how to collaborate is by finding referral partners. It's a classic example of word-of-mouth marketing, and here's how it works: you and your referral partner make a commitment to go out of your way to send each other business. Voilà!

9 Hot Ways to Find the BEST Referral Partners

1. Attend events hosted by your potential referral partners.

2. Go to Meetup group events.

3. Make connections on social media. For example, visit the

Facebook, Twitter, or Instagram pages of folks whose work you love, and begin to interact with them.

4. Ask your community and network for referral partner ideas.

5. Become a guest blogger for a target referral partner.

6. Tap nonprofit and humanitarian organizations with large databases. You may want to consider hosting an event that will benefit the organization; they'll probably be happy to send promotional material about you to their mailing list. I'll talk about this idea in more detail in chapter 12.

7. Enroll guest teachers in your programs in exchange for their promotional support.

8. Connect with chiropractors, yoga teachers, day spas, and wellness business owners in your area—they often make great referral partners.

9. Be a leader! When you put together events, people look to you as a leader, and referral partners will find *you* as a result.

My favorite way to find referral partners is at networking events. Now, if you're like me, you've been to plenty of networking groups, business mingles, and chamber of commerce luncheons that left you feeling like you'd rather be watching Netflix on the couch with your favorite pillow. Maybe you pumped yourself up to attend that big networking event. You may have had big hopes for business break-throughs, answers to some of your questions, and even a new client or two, only to come home frustrated. You walked through the crowd, trying to meet as many people as possible and gather as many business cards as you could. But then nothing ever came of your efforts. Or maybe everybody at the event was desperate for business, working hard to sell everybody else . . . but nobody was actually interested in buying. In other words, there was no *collaboration* happening at all.

If that's been your experience, or if you've avoided networking groups because they sound like some version of modern-day torture, I have the answer for you! You probably won't experience networking events the same way—ever again. Once I discovered this secret, it made all the difference for me.

Hottest Networking TIP of the YEAR:
Stop going with the intention of finding clients.
(You heard me!)
Go with the intention of meeting referral partners instead!

Yes, I know, they say that networking groups are all about finding clients, but here's the thing: if you go with that intention, the desperation will actually repel the very people you're trying to attract. Tell the truth—hasn't desperation in other people repelled you at these events?

Instead, *go with the intention of just serving people.* As John F. Kennedy famously said, "Ask not what your country can do for you; ask what you can do for your country." Translating that for our purposes, "Ask not what the people you meet at networking events can do for you; ask what you can do for *them.*" Again, lead with generosity.

That might sound like the wrong way to build your business, but the secret is to show up in service with the goal of establishing actual, deep, core relationships with just a couple of people. Yep—just one or two. When you walk into the event, place your hand on your heart and scan the crowd. Who pops out at you? We women are intuitive, so trust that you can read the energy. Who seems to have natural charisma and enthusiasm? Who are the three or four people who draw you toward them? Then approach only those people with the intention of finding out how you can serve them, become friends, and create core referral partnerships.

You could start the conversation this way: "What are you most excited about in your business? How can I be of support to you?"

If you question what support you can offer someone and whether you have anything to give, remember that most of us have at least a little bit of free time. We can all carve out an hour or two in our week for something important. Maybe you'll meet someone who's hosting an event. You could simply show up and help in some way, or you could gather some people to fill the seats.

At my very first networking event after I discovered the golden secret, I made an amazing connection with a hairstylist from Santa Cruz named Melanie. We were both new to the city and interested in building our businesses. Our personalities were a good match, so we hit it off and scheduled a lunch. She offered me a free haircut, and I gave her a free business coaching session in return.

Now, I think I can safely say that I have great hair! I have a cute, short, pixie haircut that I got from this hairstylist. People constantly complimented my hair, so I sent them straight to Melanie. Meanwhile, at least once or twice a day in her chair at the salon, she had women who complained about their jobs and told her how much they dreamed of starting their own businesses. She sent them straight to me! In our first six weeks of knowing each other, we sent each other $5,000 to $10,000 worth of business. No kidding!

That's what collaboration can do. And it feels great. It's a feminine thing to do, and it *also* builds your business. But because we're so accustomed to seeing business in traditionally masculine terms, walking into a network event with a mind-set of service has become counterintuitive. If I had walked into that event and just tried to collect everybody's business cards, I wouldn't have had a long enough conversation with Melanie to discover what our collaboration could do for both of us (not to mention the great friendship and support we each received).

And guess what? By walking in with the spirit of collaboration and cooperation, rather than desperation to gain new clients, you actually become *more* magnetic to the people there who might buy your product or services.

But surely, this method works only if you team up with women who are in a different business from yours, right? You can't collaborate with direct competitors without shooting yourself in the foot, can you? Sure you can! Your foot will remain intact, I promise. It takes an abundance mind-set, but that's a natural state of mind for women.

We know intuitively that the world works better for all of us when everybody wins. So read on, dear Goddess . . .

COLLABORATING WITH "NICHE MATES"

I know a woman in Portland, Oregon, who has a coffee shop. Next door to her is another woman who owns a competing coffee shop. Rather than be at odds with each other, they collaborated as "niche mates," and they both won. They agreed to run different kinds of promotions that wouldn't compete, and each agreed to market the other. So while one of the coffee shops held an open mike night on Fridays, the other held a special farmer's market breakfast on Sundays. At the first coffee shop's open mike night was a notice on the tables promoting the other shop's Sunday breakfast, and the breakfast had a notice about the open mike night. That's what I call a win-win!

My amazing editor, Melanie (a different Melanie from the hair-stylist), told me about her friends in England who own a fish and chips shop. They don't have a liquor license, so they started a collaboration with the pub across the street (well, it's only about eight steps across the cobblestones). At first the pub encouraged its patrons to get their fish and chips from the shop and bring the food over to the pub. But customers loved the idea so much that the fish and chips shop started delivering the food to customers at the bar. Then it became even more popular, and it's been a moneymaker for both businesses. The pub even changed its seating arrangement to look more like a bistro.

Melanie also tells me that her huge network of writers and editors help one another out all the time. They send one another overflow work or clients who would be better suited to someone else. I do the same. If a client comes to me needing something I don't do, 9 times out of 10, I know exactly who can help them.

Collaboration instead of competition—it's one of the best ways I know to build a business, and it comes naturally to women. Now you can see what I mean by a cooperative advantage, right? May your own cooperative advantage support you to create a much bigger impact . . . and income!

WORD-OF-MOUTH MARKETING IS GOLD

Never underestimate good, old-fashioned word-of-mouth marketing. When one of my referral partners sends an e-mail about me to her list, it can net me as many as 2,500 new names of potential customers to add to my own database. From a single referral partner promotion! A Facebook ad might cost $2 per lead, which means if I wanted to add 2,500 names through Facebook, it could cost me $5,000 or more. (In marketing language, a "lead" is a potential customer.)

But what do you pay your referral partners? My partners promote me in exchange for a commission on sales, rather than up-front money. So, while they might earn great money through me on the back end, it costs me nothing to start. Furthermore, leads generated through sources like Facebook are "cold," which means that they don't know me at all and are less likely to buy what I'm selling. Referral partner promotions generate much "warmer" leads—people who are more likely to buy from me because they've been referred by someone they trust.

So I can't emphasize enough how important it is to align yourself with referral partners and organizations with an online database of the kinds of clients you want. It can be one of the most effective ways to create a marketing funnel for yourself.

"Your network is your net worth."
— Shanda Sumpter

THE GENIUS OF COLLABORATIVE EVENTS

My friend and mentor Shanda Sumpter is absolutely right that your network really *is* your net worth. I borrowed a format from Shanda that proved her point. Four other women entrepreneurs and I got on the phone together once a week for five weeks and decided that rather than just promote one another, we would design a collaborative event. The other women were none other than Christina Morassi, Alexis Neely, Lisa Sasevich, and Kendall SummerHawk. If you don't know these women, you should! They are amazing.

The five of us decided to create a daylong virtual video training for women entrepreneurs that was all about collaboration, and we called it UNITE. Two months after the seed was originally planted for our vision, Christina, Alexis, Kendall, and I flew to San Diego, stayed in the same hotel, gathered in Lisa's living room overlooking the mountains, glasses of wine in our hands, and brainstormed about supporting thousands of women. Before we knew it, we had designed the curriculum for our training while getting to know one another more intimately. We all agreed that it was the first time we had experienced a true entrepreneurial collaboration in the worlds of joint venture partnerships and Internet marketing. The next day, we all drove to a video studio and shot our individual sections of the training.

The UNITE Virtual Training was a huge success, with more than 14,000 participants! And we added another twist by making it a fundraiser that brought in about $22,000 for women in the Amazon rain forest who were starting their own businesses to try to keep oil companies out of their communities.

What's more, when the training was over, we took turns promoting our own services to the thousands of women who had participated. Collectively, we generated more than $250K of income from women who signed up for our programs and products as a result.

Most important, we had the opportunity to impact thousands of lives, between the women who signed up and the women in the rain forest. Still, the most fruitful part of the experience was that the friendships among the five of us have continued to evolve. The love I have for these women and vice versa lives in our hearts, and we continue to lean on one another for support.

CHOOSE REFERRAL PARTNERS CAREFULLY

As you develop relationships with referral partners, it's important to remember that quality matters more than quantity. So, dear sister, here's what I recommend: "date" before you "get married," and use caution before you form business partnerships—even with your friends. Some of my clients dream of starting businesses with all of their friends, but if things go south, it could mean the end of your friendship. Start with a small project that has a specific start and end date, and see how it goes first.

The Legalities of Partnering in Business

I've had referral partnerships that required legal contracts, and I've also had my fair share of verbal agreements along the way. Here's my advice, keeping in mind that I'm not a lawyer: what's most important is that you keep your agreements crystal clear. I've learned the hard way not to make assumptions. Be sure you've laid out exactly what you're hoping your partner is going to do for you and what you plan to do in return.

If you don't have the budget or time to draw up a formal legal contract, still get your agreement in writing, and make sure each of you signs it! At the very least, send an e-mail outlining the terms you've both agreed to, and have your partner shoot you an e-mail back letting you know he or she agrees. Save the e-mails in your files.

If you enter into a more formal or long-term partnership with someone, get legal counsel, and draw up an agreement with an end in mind so that each of you has a way out of it. You certainly don't want to be stuck in a partnership that isn't good for you, and you don't want anyone to be stuck with you, either!

And don't think you can avoid a legal contract because you're working with a friend. That legal contract may be the only thing that protects your friendship.

Early on, I had an experience that led me to become disheartened with one of my referral partner relationships. I had gone out of my way, spending time and money to promote and endorse this part-ner, and when it came time for her to support me, she didn't fulfill her promise. Despite the verbal agreements we had made, she didn't follow through. I was left feeling unsupported and frustrated. Experiences like these can really dampen the sweetness of collaboration.

Some partners seem to promote each other as more of a "tit for tat" exchange or simply because they want to make a few dollars. Their hearts aren't in it.

Big lessons: your referral partnership agreements should be clearly laid out in writing to protect both parties. Referral partners should resonate with your message or product, and vice versa. It's also important to sample each other's programs, services, or products. Get to know each other! Then you can promote the other from an authentic, experiential place.

Having just a few committed partners is far superior to having dozens or hundreds of alliances with people who aren't committed to you. Again, your partnership should be a win-win for you both!

Here's a message for women who tend to over-give: Stay mindful of offering more than you receive. While you don't want to keep a balance sheet (no "tit for tat"!) with your referral partners and be nitpicky about always staying 100 percent equal, you also don't want the alliance to become too one-sided. As soon as you start to feel resentful, it's a warning sign. If that happens, ask your partner to do something specific for you. If she refuses, you might need to reconsider that particular relationship.

Types of Referral Partners

When choosing allies, it's important to know what kind of partnership would be best with that particular person. There are three basic types of referral partners:

1. **Cross-Promotion/Referral Partners:** This is the most common type of referral partner. You promote them, and they promote you. Again, be sure to choose complementary partners whose work you love. Be sure to make it easy for your referral partners to promote you by writing e-mails and marketing materials on their behalf so it's easy for them to get the word out.

2. **Joint Venture Partners:** This is the arrangement I had with the UNITE team. You team up to lead a program or create a product together, and you promote it together. While you might see other definitions of this arrangement, in the traditional sense, joint venture partners are two or more people who team up to create a product or lead a program together.

3. **Affiliate Partners:** Affiliates are people who promote your programs for a percentage of profits on sales. You may not create as strong a connection with affiliate partners, but I urge you to still choose people and businesses that resonate with what you do. The same is true for businesses you choose to promote. Do so only if you can endorse them wholeheartedly.

Strategies for Working with Referral Partners

If you aren't sure what to do after you find a referral partner who interests you, here are my 10 most important steps for making that connection and cultivating the relationship:

1. **Don't be afraid to reach out.** When you find someone who inspires you, reach out to him or her. If writing or calling someone cold makes you uncomfortable, go to one of your potential referral partners' events, and introduce yourself in person.

2. **Pursue warm connections.** When reaching out to established experts or big names, it helps if you have a friend who knows the person you want to contact. Ask your mutual friend to e-mail a warm introduction to your potential referral partner. Here's an example of one I sent:

   "Dear Ryan, meet Alison. I wanted to introduce the two of you. You are both thriving, amazing entrepreneurs with consciousness and integrity. Alison is excited about what

you're up to with your Social Entrepreneur Series! I'll bet you both could find some great ways to support each other in your businesses. I've worked with Alison before, and she takes great care of her clients. I think your folks would love her. I'll let the two of you take it from here. Love, Sage"

3. **Follow up and get together.** After you've been introduced to your potential referral partner, ask for a lunch or phone meeting to get to know each other better.

4. **Lead with generosity, and show up in service.** Offer to give first, asking what your potential partner has planned and how you can help. You might ask for materials that you can send to your list or offer 10 minutes of stage time at your event.

5. **Be specific when you ask for promotion help.** Big players are busy, so make a specific request. Always provide the materials they need for the promotion, whether it's an e-mail, blog post, flyers, or sample products. Make it easy for them! It's also easier to promote an event than a product. So if you're launching a new food item, for example, perhaps host a free event that your referral partner can announce to her list.

6. **Don't ask their age, but feel free to ask the size of their database!** It's okay to ask the size of a potential partner's community or customer database, but do it with class. You could say: "So, tell me about your customers and your community. Who are they? What are they looking for? I'm curious about your goals for your business, and I'm curious how big your database is." This way, it becomes part of a larger conversation that allows you to learn how best you can support one another.

7. **Ask for other referrals.** This is huge! Before you get off the phone or leave a meeting with a referral partner, ALWAYS ask, "Who else do you know that you think I should know?" Then offer your resources in return.

8. **Always follow up.** Take great care of your referral partners, and always follow through on your promises. Organization is key. Use online promotion calendars, Google Docs, or spreadsheets with your team to make sure you don't lose track of what you've said you'll do and when. Stay in touch with your partners, and use the forms of communication that work best for them.

9. **Think long term, and if you don't rock it for a referral partner, make it right.** Keep in mind that the most lucrative referral partnerships are long-term, not short-term. Investing in a relationship can prove to be incredibly valuable over time. Some of my referral partners and I have generated six figures or more of income for each other over the years. That didn't happen overnight, but over the course of our relationship as we got to know each other's products and audiences. We've grown to think of each other as family and get behind each other both emotionally and strategically. What happens if you don't get the same results for a partner that she got for you? Simply reach out and recommit to another promotion for her: "What else do you have planned in the coming months that I can help you with?"

10. **Be careful not to waste your time.** It can be tempting to fill your calendar with collaborative lunch meetings with cool entrepreneurs. You might spend your lunch hour talking about your business so that you feel closer to making money, but if it gets in the way of generating anything tangible, it's just a procrastination enabler. I recommend meeting with one (maybe two) new referral partners per week at the most when you're first getting started. You can add more if you have a big launch of some kind, like a grand opening, and you're trying to gather a bunch of referral partners at once.

> Remember: When it comes to rocking it out with
> referral partners,it's about the QUALITY of the
> relationships, not the QUANTITY of connections!

So go out there and find a few great partners. And when they support you, just like your mama said, always say thank you! This is critical! Always express your gratitude to your referral partners *and* your customers. I've given my most profitable referral partners all kinds of thank-you gifts, ranging from flowers to a $2,500 electric bicycle to massages for their entire family and team. No matter the size of the gift, people love being appreciated, and the gesture will deepen the relationship and support future win-wins.

Can You Attract Rock Star Referral Partners When You're Just Beginning?

You bet! Befriending and forming alliances with just a few of the right people who are up to big things is potentially the smartest single strategy for growing your business quickly. But what if you're starting from zero and want to attract the kinds of partners who've already developed a strong following?

When I was just starting out, I hired a coach named Ryan Eliason to help me build my coaching practice. I met him at a conference and trusted him immediately. You can feel Ryan's heart from about 20 feet away. He supported me as I enrolled my first 10 clients, and he was there to hold my hand as I got my business off the ground. Hiring him really changed the direction of my life and business forever. But more important, we formed a deep bond.

Ryan and I have a similar niche. We're both socially conscious business mentors, so we understand each other's business on an intimate level. Not long after our coaching contract was complete, Ryan began reaching out to me for support with an online event he was hosting. I had some experience with the kind of online training he was launching, so I offered him everything I had—checklists and advice on how to ensure his success. I even promoted him to the people in my database.

Ryan's first virtual event was a massive success, and he built his database to about 15,000 potential clients as a result. He soared past me in the virtual world.

To a blind eye, one might wonder why Ryan and I would support each other when our niches are so similar. Wouldn't sending potential customers to each other cost us money? On the contrary, Ryan valued the advice I gave him for his online event so much that shortly thereafter, he promoted me to his database (which was at least four times bigger than mine). His promotion generated more than $30,000 in revenue for me by allowing me to serve more than 30 customers from his database. Further, he earned more than $10,000 in commissions on his promotion of me.

But what's more profound is the lifelong relationship that's developed between us. Over the years we've sent each other hundreds of clients and generated tens of thousands of dollars in commissions from each other's successful online training programs. The best part of all is that I know I have a loyal partner in Ryan. Being in business for yourself isn't always easy, and knowing you have partners to turn to who understand the game is more valuable than any amount of income generated.

Many entrepreneurs in my situation wouldn't have approached their own coach with a request for promotion, but Ryan could see that I was up to big things. Our mutual generosity toward each other has paid off tenfold.

So even if you're just starting out or don't have a following of your own yet, you can still offer a more experienced referral partner something of value. One of the best ways to gain the attention and dedication of partners is to simply show up for them. When I started my practice, I showed up big-time for a bunch of coaches and consultants whom I met through networking events and at conferences. I would support them at their events and share whatever resources I had with them. In that willingness to lead with generosity, I gained the respect of valuable referral partners who were further along, and they were all able to reciprocate in one way or another throughout the first months of my business.

How else can you support someone who is further along than you are? How can you help get the word out if you don't even have a database yet? Pick up the phone! We're all connected to a community. If you want to support a potential referral partner, ask yourself who would be a great client for them and call that person. Send your referral partners a few potential clients. Your recommendation will speak volumes.

"But, Sage, I need people to promote ME!" I hear you. If you want promotion to come your way, you have to start by getting off your butt and being willing to promote others. It's karma, sister, and that's the good news. You show up for others, and they'll show up for you. It isn't rocket science! And trust me, I know you're worth showing up for, or you wouldn't have gotten so far along in this book.

If you feel that the inequity between you and your target referral partner is just too great, offer to promote her in a year after you've grown your business and client base. You could say, "I'm committed to really making this happen, and I'm confident I'll be reaching 10,000 to 50,000 people in a year or so. If you can help me now, I'll absolutely promote you at that time because I know I'll be able to produce similar results for you."

Whatever you do, respect how much work successful people have put in over a period of years. I can't tell you how many impersonal and one-sided requests I get to promote people I don't even know. So honor people who are further along than you, and always stay aware that being a leader can be challenging. When you approach potential partners, especially those who have achieved more than you so far, acknowledge how much their work has contributed to you. Show how you see a partnership as a win-win for both of you.

And if someone turns you down, don't take it personally. Some leaders receive so many requests that they can't possibly say yes to everyone. If someone doesn't resonate with what you do, it means she isn't a good referral partner for you anyway. Understand that she's done you a favor by not wasting your time.

Likewise, if someone asks you for a partnership and you don't feel you resonate with what they offer, don't say yes to avoid conflict. Be kind, but simply say that you don't feel the partnership would be in alignment with your business. If you know someone else who might be a better fit, by all means offer a warm introduction to that person.

Most important, when approaching possible referral partners, be yourself, follow the energy, and don't hesitate to ask for what you want!

It Takes a Team

No chapter on the cooperative advantage of women would be complete without mentioning my incredible team and the teams that support brilliant entrepreneurs all over the planet. The truth is that it isn't about the business logo, the celebrity brand, or the face of any movement you see. Behind any great leader lies a legion of committed, heartfelt humans who are dedicated to making the world a better place. At a certain point, for many of us who are entrepreneurs, the reason to grow a business is because of our team. We see the gift of creating opportunities for the incredible women and men who show up to support us. In chapter 10, I'll give you tips on how to hire, when to hire, and how to train a team that you can count on.

WOMEN THRIVE WHEN WE ALIGN WITH NATURE'S LAWS

Besides our connection to other people, part of our cooperative advantage as women is our ability to sync up with nature's laws and universal energies. Many of us find our connection to our divine source and to what's meaningful in our lives when we're in the natural world—on a hike in the woods, climbing a mountain, swimming in the ocean, or kayaking down a river. For years, scientists thought nature was inherently competitive, but ecologists and other researchers have recently identified that nature is actually inherently cooperative. Does competition exist in nature? Of course. But that competition exists within a cooperative system.

Humans are fundamentally cooperative. We want to help one another, as do other species. For example, mother humpback whales, lions, and elephants teach their young to hunt. Likewise, wolves, penguins, and eagles all are examples of species that mate for life.

Women's bodies are literally synced up to the earth's cycles. Our menstrual cycles even align with the 28-day cycle of the moon. There's no arguing that when we honor this connection between ourselves and the Universe, we can use these energies to our benefit. The Universe will love us for it!

What if the Universe and all its energies want you to succeed?

Judy Wicks is an example of an extraordinary business owner who's built her business in alignment with natural laws. Author of *Good Morning, Beautiful Business*, Judy launched White Dog Cafe in 1983 in Philadelphia and realized that what was most important to her were the personal relationships she created through her restaurant. Whether it was a local storytelling event or a gathering on behalf of immigration or lesbian issues, she invited the community into the café as a gathering place for growth, connection, and awareness. When Judy had the opportunity to expand and launch a business in surrounding states, she decided against it. She realized that if it expanded too quickly, White Dog Cafe would begin to lose its uniqueness. By focusing on one restaurant, she would allow her café to grow as nature does, rather than becoming an invasive species that goes into other communities to compete with the local economy. She wanted White Dog Cafe to first grow roots more deeply in its local environment. Like a native species, the café could then grow more diverse in terms of its local events and more in service to its natural ecosystem.

Of course, White Dog Cafe is a green business: 100 percent of its electricity comes from renewable sources, and all of its food waste is composted. Just like in nature, nothing is wasted. Not only has White Dog Cafe been composting its own food, but it now has a composting center where all the restaurants in the area can bring their food scraps.

Judy's goal was to have as many responsible practices in her business as possible. She realized that there's no such thing as one sustainable business. To really make a difference, she wanted to create an entire local food economy. I was especially impressed when she told me that most businesses keep their supplier sources private in the hopes of keeping a competitive advantage, but she publishes her resources. In fact, she connected her organic farmers, suppliers, and fellow restaurant owners and chefs by creating a nonprofit network called Fair Food. Judy encourages her competitors to buy from the very farmers she uses, so White Dog Cafe is building an entire system that will help all the local restaurants and farmers to thrive.

Naturally, there's still friendly competition within the cooperative system. For instance, chefs still compete to make the best dishes from similar ingredients. But there's an entire community of people now benefiting from Judy's commitment to sustainable, natural, cooperative business practices. How cool is that?

Business in Alignment with Nature's Laws

All the core business lessons that I teach my clients align with nature and the elements. In fact, you can see this in the Elemental Wheel that uses the Native American principles of the four directions and four key elements of air, fire, water, and earth. The graphic on the next page shows us how business principles that work well are actually aligned with nature's laws. It isn't just about making a buck! We realize, then, that our businesses are divine work and the highest form of service.

As you can see from the graphic, the East is associated with Air, which is about having a vision. The universal principle used in business for this direction and element is: *your vision is bigger than your to-do list.*

The South is associated with Fire, which is all about taking action and going for it! The universal principle used in business for this direction and element is: *taking action is alchemy.* We've already talked about how you'll learn more from taking action than from thinking about it.

The West is associated with Water, which is all about flow and resources. The universal principle used in business for the direction of the West and this element is: *making money is a spiritual path.* (Money represents resources, like water is a resource.) We've already discussed this one too.

The North is associated with Earth, which is all about being grounded and held in a structure like the root system of a tree or the veins of a leaf. The universal principle used in business for this direction and element is: *being a free spirit takes great discipline.* It's all about embracing structure and organization to support the growth and freedom of your business. (You'll learn more about that soon! Just keep reading.) Again, working with the laws of nature can help put your business on the fast track to success by growing in alignment with universal laws rather than trying to fight against natural order.

I'm excited to see what's possible for you as you grow into alignment with the expansiveness of the East, the transmission of the South, the wisdom of the West, and the restoration and organization of the North. Let's do this thing, Goddess!!

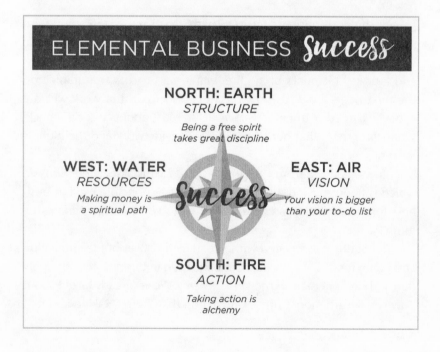

ELEMENTAL BUSINESS *Success*

NORTH: EARTH
STRUCTURE

*Being a free spirit
takes great discipline*

WEST: WATER
RESOURCES

*Making money is
a spiritual path*

EAST: AIR
VISION

*Your vision is bigger
than your to-do list*

SOUTH: FIRE
ACTION

*Taking action is
alchemy*

INTEGRATION

Exercise: Take Stock of Your Feminine Assets

As women, we've all been told we're too much this or not enough that, and most of us have been told that our feminine qualities will hold us back from success in the business world. Well, I'm here to say that's ridiculous propaganda. So let's make a list of what you've felt was a liability and reframe it into the asset it truly is.

In the first column, write down all the qualities you're least proud of as a woman. What have you been accused of being too much or too little of? Too emotional? People-pleasing? Too generous? Not strong or ruthless enough? List them all.

Then, in the second column, write about how each quality has served you. Check out the example below for ideas.

What qualities have you been least proud of as a woman?	How have these same qualities served you?
Example: I've been told I'm "too emotional."	Because I'm in touch with my emotions, I can right away identify when one of my clients is struggling with something. Last week I was able to show up for one of my clients in a way that she said no one had shown up for her ever before. It can pay off to be emotional!
_____	_____
_____	_____
_____	_____
_____	_____

COOPERATIVE ADVANTAGE EXERCISES

1. Make a list of three to five potential referral partners whose products or services are complementary with your business.

_____

_____

_____

2. Create a checklist of what you have to offer right now to each of the above referral partners or other rock stars in your community or around the world. Ideas include giving your time, promoting their events on social media, offering your skills, putting them in touch with people you know who could help them, or sending them a book they might like. Contact your potential referral partners with proposals for supporting each other.

3. Do some research and find three to five networking groups or local business events in your area that might have good referral partners for you. Then make plans to attend. Just remember: *concentrate on quality, not quantity!*

Check out the Elemental Wheel graphic, which illustrates nature's laws, in my Women Rocking Business Virtual Guidebook. You can print it out and put it on the wall in your office as a constant reminder.

Women Rocking Business VIRTUAL GUIDEBOOK

BREAKTHROUGH BONUS TRAINING #9:
Sample Referral Partner Promotion Materials

Get exclusive access to the Promotion Partner Packet we've created for our online Niche Clarity Training Program. Then use it to model your own referral partner materials!

Grab it here: www.womenrockingbusiness.com/guidebook

Chapter 10

STRUCTURES FOR GROWING YOUR BUSINESS

"Being a free spirit takes great discipline."

— Paramahansa Yogananda

I used to have a major *(MAJOR)* revulsion to structure. I was a free spirit, baby! I was growing my business based on cunning instinct and mysterious feminine impulse.

Well, that didn't get me very far as my visions got bigger. In fact, had I not learned to embrace structure, my big visions would have come crashing down on me. Building a business without structure is kind of like building a house without a foundation.

One of my big visions in the early days of my business was to launch an online interview series, which helped me quickly grow a 5,000-person mailing list. In the series, I interviewed several women entrepreneurs who were making six- and seven-figure incomes, and not surprisingly, lots of people were interested in learning from these business goddesses.

Then, seeing an opportunity, it dawned on me that a few people might like to know how they too could interview luminaries in their own field and grow a big database of potential clients as a result.

So I started a program to teach people how to do just that, charging $997 per person. I expected to get 20 students to sign up—tops. Instead I got 100! It gave me a nice $100,000 income boost (for those of you who are tracking with me, I'm referring to the same $100K income boost I mentioned in chapter 1)—an amount that used to take me three years to make. But it also thrust me into work overload.

With 100 people signed up for the program, I was almost instantly buried in e-mails and customer service requests. I was up every night, late into the evening, *personally* answering e-mails. As soon as everyone realized they were directly in touch with the instructor of the course, they wrote back and asked even more questions! So the e-mail onslaught was endless. Boy, did I need an assistant!

At the time I was living in a little house at the base of a mountain in Santa Cruz with my amazing roommate, Maggie Ellis, who had also just moved to town. She had spent three years as a tour manager and business manager for a well-known band, so she had plenty of marketing experience. She looked over my shoulder one day while I was answering the endless e-mails and said, "We can create a system to handle this, you know."

She grabbed my computer and started organizing the e-mails. Then she helped me put together a system for copying and pasting e-mail responses. We also created a "Frequently Asked Questions" page for my website so that people could get most of their answers from there. All of this helped me think through how to actually have a business, not just a hobby. For the first time, I was sold on the importance of structures, and I'm grateful to Maggie to this day.

Whether you love structure or resist it like me, you'll want to enlist the help of structure lovers to support you along the way. It took my roommate to convert me into a structure-worshipping CEO. Now I've been able to work with my team to implement systems and foundations for our company that allow us to do things it used to take hours to do . . . in minutes.

Most of my clients are like I used to be. They resist structure because they're visionaries—highly creative women who want short-cuts for running their businesses. But what I've learned is that it's the very structures I have in place that free me to be the leader and woman I'm meant to be in the world.

Now, it's true, dear Entrepreneurial Goddess, that when you first start a business, you end up doing almost everything yourself until you have the capital and budget to hire some help. But even on your own, structures and systems can help you. In the beginning, I kept my own bookkeeping records in a three-ring binder, writing everything on notebook paper. I used a pencil so that I could erase when necessary. That notebook got me to the point where I was generating more than $12,500 a month in revenue. Then I was able to hire a professional bookkeeper!

Systems can not only get you to the place where it's possible to delegate to others but also make it easy to teach an assistant how to do the task you're delegating properly. Then voilà! Guess who doesn't have to spend her time taking care of that task anymore?

THE MAKING-MONEY-WHILE-YOU-SLEEP MYTH

My friend Marisa Murgatroyd likes to say, "If you want to learn to make money while you sleep, you first need to learn to make money while you're awake." When you're learning to be self-generative, it's crucial to understand how customers and money flow into your business, and in my experience, the only way to get orders or clients is to set up structures and systems. Some of those structures will be automated, and some won't be.

In chapter 1, I said it was a bit miraculous to me when money "showed up in my inbox" after launching an online program. But don't get me wrong—a lot of work went into making that money "show up." No matter how many structures you put in place, none of them will be fully automated. So the idea that you can make money in your sleep is a bit of a myth. Any system you use will need regular maintenance.

Still, structure is a trusted friend that, when embraced, will save you hours of precious time and build the kind of support that allows you to function effectively. Then you have room to expand and grow—and make money while you're sipping a piña colada in a hammock on the beach. Automated structures have allowed me to get the attention of potential clients while I take a nap, have lunch with a friend, or enjoy the ocean on my surfboard. My idea of a blissful moment is when I check my phone after catching some great waves and discover I've just made a sale!

The goal of most entrepreneurs is to get to the point where they're in their zone of creative genius 60 to 90 percent of the time, rather than taking care of the mundane aspects of business. You simply cannot accomplish that without structures.

Remember my freedom schedule that I told you about in chapter 7? Having a structured daily and weekly schedule will allow you to rest and enjoy your workdays and spend regular time off with the confidence that everything will still get done.

THE THREE MOST IMPORTANT BUSINESS-GROWING STRUCTURES

Most types of businesses use three primary structures to promote growth and expansion. They are:

1. **Marketing**—How you communicate the value of your products and services to potential customers.

2. **Selling**—The moment your customer is willing to receive your products or services in exchange for money.

3. **Fulfillment**—The delivery of your products or services in an effective way that (hopefully) makes your customers happy.

Most business owners are good at one or two of these, but not all three. You may be good at marketing, for example, but you might have a difficult time keeping your customers. That leaves you on a constant hamster wheel of marketing. Talk about exhausting! Great salespeople might have a product that's low in quality, which leaves them making great sales but lacking in the fulfillment department. Not to mention the refund requests that drown them. As business owners, we all need to "skill up" in various aspects of these three areas as our businesses grow.

Remember what I've emphasized in the last couple of chapters: It's the quality of the relationships you develop with your customers that will make your business successful.

Let's start with marketing. If you notice your stomach turning when I say the "M" word, stay with me, sister, I'm going to break this down for you nice and easy.

Marketing Structures

E-mail Marketing. Like I said, it's tempting to design a gorgeous website and hope clients magically show up, but that's like building an incredible restaurant in the middle of the desert with no roads that lead to it! You need strategies to get people to your website, and there are *many* options you can choose from, such as Facebook ads, Google ads, social media, or those live events we've been talking about, where you can ask people to write down their e-mail addresses on an old-fashioned clipboard. You can also become a guest blogger on other people's websites, or advertise through Groupon or Yelp.

Once you get people to your website, you need to keep them there long enough to engage with you. And the most effective website structure I know—whether you have a service-oriented business or a brick-and-mortar store—is capturing your potential and existing customers' e-mail addresses.

One great way to do this is with an irresistible free gift that you'll provide when your site visitors trust you with their e-mail address.

The key word is *irresistible*. If it's something they can get elsewhere, they might not click that "Get your free gift now" button.

Find out what your clients and customers want, and provide one of those things! For example, every time we offer a free quiz, we get more than 60 percent of site visitors to trust me with their e-mail addresses. That's a very high number! Checklists, templates, and downloadable meditations are often effective. I've had clients offer things like a visualization for not overeating, a "trust your intuition" 10-step checklist, a 3-step guide for creating an online dating profile, or a 2-minute decision-making tool to help people trust their inner wisdom.

What if your business is a day spa or a law office? You could offer a "5-step guide to flawless skin" or "10 ways to protect yourself from lawsuits."

Keep your free gift simple and digestible. If it seems like it's going to take an hour or longer to consume, many people won't take you up on it. Remember that they want it to be easy! Once you've gained their trust, you can offer something more complex if necessary.

The best part of the free gift strategy is that it's automated. There are many systems you can choose for capturing e-mail addresses and automatically sending your free gift to prospective customers. This lead-generation strategy of making contacts that could lead to a sale is how you'll be able to stay in touch with potential customers in an active way that keeps them engaged with you.

Think how passive it is to just put up a website and hope people come. When you send someone an e-mail, you're *actively* marketing. You can send a series of e-mails or newsletters that contain valuable information your targeted customers want, along with regular offers, if appropriate. You might invite them to a free presentation or send them a coupon for a discount. These e-mails will (1) establish you as an authority, (2) build trust in you, and (3) create relationships. Sometimes they're enough to give your potential clients the touch points they need to feel ready to buy from you. And all these e-mails can be placed into your system so that they're sent automatically at specific times you designate. This is how you switch from a hobby business to a highly successful business.

Word-of-Mouth Marketing. I've already written about the importance of referral partners, but there are even more word-of-mouth marketing strategies you can try. One particular word-of-mouth structure I adopted easily resulted in $240,000 in income in less than a month! *And* it attracted some of the best clients I've ever worked with.

When I host my Women's Leadership Summit every year, I have a Bring a Friend campaign. My current clients can bring up to five of their friends to the event for free. All their friends have to do is pay a $100 deposit that's refunded to them at the door. This way, I don't end up with no-shows. It makes it super easy for my clients to bring people, and I have a full room of fired-up women ready to be inspired.

You love your customers, right? That means you'll probably love their friends too. Plus, for your clients there's accountability to keep using the tools or a shared value when their friends are consuming the same product or service.

What's the incentive for your clients? Here's what I do: If they bring three friends, they get extra coaching. If they bring five friends, they get a $2,000 training course with me, as well as the extra coaching.

Positioning is key here, however. You don't want your clients to feel used, so remember to be transparent and give them something truly valuable in appreciation. I tell my clients that when they bring their friends, it supports me, them, and their friends. To make things more fun, the person who brings the most friends each year gets a $10,000 VIP day with me. We've had women bring 17 to 21 friends because they're competing for that VIP day. They're promoting a program they believe in, they're doing me a favor, and I like to reward them generously for it. It's a WIN-WIN-WIN.

So how did this structure earn me as much as $240,000? On average, 25 to 30 of the friends who show up each year enroll in one of my annual online training programs at a cost of $8,000 to $12,000. Again, I'm completely transparent about offering these programs, and it's up to each individual to choose to sign up or not.

This is the power of word-of-mouth structure and contests that can make a big difference in a short amount of time. How can you use word-of-mouth marketing to help you attract more of your ideal customers?

Sales Structures

Remember, the difference between marketing and sales is that marketing is about reaching your potential clients, and the sale represents the moment they buy from you. We already covered a lot of sales strategies in chapter 8—mostly in the form of free events that introduce people to your products or services and, of course, the selling conversation using our GROW Model. Other examples of sales structures in online marketing include shopping carts that accept credit cards, videos that make offers on your website, and return policies that allow your customers to feel safe when they make an investment. You'll want to do some research and study people's websites whenever you see someone selling something online. Make a note of sites, systems, and verbiage that resonate with you so you can refer back to them when you're creating your online sales materials.

The selling conversation, whether in person, on the phone, or in writing, is the most effective selling tool in most industries, especially in the beginning. If you've ever listened to a presentation by a Realtor or the guy who tries to get you to buy a timeshare in Costa Rica, you could probably tell that a lot of thought and planning went into it (whether or not it was effective). These sales presentations are far from random, and yours shouldn't be either. It doesn't mean you have to sound like the time-share guy or like a used car salesman. You don't need to customize your conversation for a particular client, but you do need to spend the time to plan what you'll say. This ensures that you don't stumble or forget to say anything important.

Again, it isn't about manipulation! It's about being professional and well prepared.

Structures in Writing

For those of you who will require contracts with your clients and customers, I recommend you honor feminine values by making sure those contracts are two-sided. Take into account what the other party needs, and guard against making your written documents too skewed in your own direction.

If you don't understand legalese, work with a lawyer, and educate yourself so that you can be sure your lawyer follows your wishes. Most attorneys will start with an agreement that's more in your favor to find out what you can get away with. But your clients may read a contract like that and wonder if they can really trust you.

I urge you to invest the time and money to create a fair contract. It will say a lot to your clients about who you are—someone who wants your business dealings to be a win-win for both you and your clients.

Fulfillment Structures

Stand Out by Nurturing. Keeping an existing customer is nearly always easier than finding a new one, and fulfillment is all about client retention. So, first and foremost, make sure the product or service you offer is excellent and valuable. But you need to do even more than that to stand out from all the other marketers. Luckily, it's something women are singularly qualified to do—nurturing our clients and doing special things for them.

It doesn't have to be complicated or expensive. An example would be my nutritionist client who gives her clients a call after their first session to see how they're doing with their new meal plan. I also have a Realtor friend who always stops at her favorite coffee shop to buy her clients a cappuccino.

Offering first-session discounts is a great system to get clients to continue to use your product or service. For example, maybe the first yoga class is free and the second is 20 percent off. Or have you ever been given a free tote bag the first time you shop in a store? It can even mean simply sending your new clients a welcome packet.

In my business, all my new clients get access to five to seven free training modules as soon as they jump into one of my programs. This allows them to begin working with me immediately. They also all get a welcome call with one of my coaches. These calls are gold! In a time when everything happens online, it feels so nurturing to have someone call you. It builds a lot of trust, commitment, and safety into the relationship. During that welcome call, it's important to help your client feel that you're going to take great care of them. Always take the time to listen to what your client wants to achieve in working with you, and get them excited about taking the next step.

As I do, you can have a team member make the welcome calls. If you don't yet have a "team," you might buddy up with another entrepreneur and make each other's welcome calls. In other words, become part of the other's team. It adds a layer of professionalism.

Another way to nurture is to create a structure for keeping tabs on your clients. If you're a yoga teacher, make notes so you remember which student has a sore shoulder or a weak knee. Have you ever had a practitioner remember something important about you? I'll bet it made you feel loyal and faithful toward that person.

It's very important for me to know the specific struggles of my individual clients. I have a system in place to store notes that I take during my calls so I can refresh my memory and always offer my clients the best possible support. If one of them is resistant to authority, for example, I can work with her on that issue with a lot of love and support to help her embrace her own inner authority. Then she can step into that power in order to run her business.

Future-Pacing. This is another "mother skill." When you do a great job at what I call "future-pacing," you'll be able to serve clients over the long term, support them to create even bigger results in their lives, and create recurring revenue. This involves helping a client anticipate the benefits of your offering. It can be as simple as letting your new yoga students know that returning students have reported far less neck pain after attending six months of classes. Now they can pick up their young children without hurting their backs. Letting your students know the benefits of long-term engagement with your service or product will help you create lifelong customers, or at least customers who stick around for a good while!

Future-pacing can also involve specific strategies for renewing your clients' engagement with your product or service. If you're selling a product, you can make it easy for the customer to set up automatic purchases every few months to replenish her supply. Pay attention to how the businesses you frequent focus on future-pacing. How often do you get a coupon from a store that offers a discount for specific dates in an upcoming "limited time only" sale?

Success Mapping. If you have a coaching or mentorship-based business like mine, you can show your clients the next step you recommend they take to experience great results. You'll need a specific structure for keeping track of where each client is on your "map" or "blueprint." If you're a nutritionist, for example, you might start your clients with a diet plan. Then, in month two or three, you begin working with them on emotional eating to make it easy to stick to the diet and commit to a healthier lifestyle. Remind your clients where they are on your blueprint, and teach them from the beginning what they'll need to do to be wildly successful in your program. The best thing? They will love you for it, and you'll get to build real, lasting relationships with clients you adore and who adore you in return. THIS, my friend, is heart-full business at its finest.

Accountability Structures. Part of my fulfillment system is designed to address blocks that might cause my clients to quit. I warn them that resistance can come up in the process of making change. Building a business forces us to build new muscles, and it's common to want to give up. So I offer mind-set tools and strategies that help them get through the rough spots. I'm genuinely committed to helping my clients (and you readers) become successful. If you take yourself out of the game, I don't get to make a difference for you!

In my business training program, we have a periodic accountability day. Once a month we get on the phone together at the beginning of the day, and everybody shares the action step that will make the biggest difference in their business. (It's usually something they've procrastinated about because it makes them feel vulnerable.) They also report on their action step on our Facebook page, and we support one another to get it done. At the end of the day, we have another call and talk about our progress.

If someone didn't manage to complete her action step, our team lovingly talks to her about what got in her way. People love these kinds of accountability structures! They want to be pulled out of their comfort zone by mentors or guides they respect.

Assessment Structures. If you're an educator or trainer of any kind, finding a way to measure your clients' progress can be a powerful part of your fulfillment system. You can start with an initial inventory and then do another measurement after you've worked with a client for three to six months so that they can see their growth. We tend to underestimate or discount our growth because it happens so gradually that we don't recognize internal, or even physical, changes. When your clients can see on paper how far they've come, they'll never underestimate the benefits of working with you!

Here's a sample assessment that you could adapt for your business:

Introductory Business Coaching Assessment

Fulfillment Scales: Indicate below how satisfied you feel in each life area using a scale of 1 (not satisfied) to 10 (extremely satisfied). For the life areas you wish to improve, please describe the improvements you seek. *Rate from 1 to 10.*

Life area	Rate from 1 to 10
Family	
Significant Other	
Social Life	
Career/Business	
Physical Health and Well-Being	
Emotional Health and Well-Being	
Physical Environment	
Finances	

Spirituality/Religion	
Education/Personal Growth	
Fun and Leisure	
Life Balance	

- What is your website?

- Do you have a mailing list, and how big is it?

- How many customers do you have?

- How many would you like to have?

- What's your biggest challenge in business?

- What are your business goals?

- How much money do you want to make in your business monthly and annually?

Thank you for your honest answers. They will be held confidentially. Please attach this form in an e-mail to my team at: support@ sagelavine.com, and keep a copy for yourself. I look forward to helping you rock out your business!

This strategy won't apply to everyone who sells a product, but it can work for any service or product that offers clients some sort of progression, whether you're a coach, personal trainer, yoga teacher, or chiropractor.

Building a Community. One of the best fulfillment tools I know to add to your system is building a community. You can do this with almost any kind of business. Create a Facebook page, and give people an excuse to visit it. If you're running a fitness center, get people to post their workout goals when they arrive at the gym. As an incentive, enter them in a contest to win something cool like new running shoes or an exercise bike. You can even partner with other businesses that might give you the prize for free in order to advertise their product.

Another great way to build connection, engagement, and community is to run contests with your clients. In the Entrepreneurial Leadership Academy that I run every year, my clients play a game the first 60 days of the program, and they earn points for implementing the basic business-building tools I teach them. The most points can earn them support sessions with me and my coaches, or free prizes like a website design. It's very sweet to watch your clients engage fully and support one another on your Facebook or member page, sharing their wins and reporting on the progress they've made. You can encourage clients to team up with one another and support one another outside of the program . . . and a little friendly competition never hurt anyone either!

WHY YOU NEED A TEAM

I don't like hitting the ground running on Monday mornings. While millions of people around the globe spend them commuting on trains or in cars on multilane highways, I'm often working out at the beach. Then, before hopping on the phone with my team, I stop for my favorite green smoothie at Whole Foods in my yoga clothes, wander through downtown Santa Cruz, then head up to my little office overlooking our city center. Or if I feel like working from home, I might be lounging on my back deck in my outdoor work area underneath my redwood trees a couple of blocks from the ocean.

I get started most Mondays by checking on my clients on Facebook. As I read what they've been up to—speaking at conferences, launching their online programs, or supporting one another to get their message out into the world—a wide smile always spreads across my face.

My call with my awesome team begins at 11 A.M. We usually start by checking in about our weekend or sharing one thing we're grateful for. We make a conscious effort to stay personally and professionally connected because we know that when we feel connected, we can stretch time and triple our efficiency. (Connection = Currency!)

Jenn Sebastian, my online business manager, lets us know what's on the calendar for the week. Shannon Fisher, head of our coaching department, jumps in with updates about our upcoming events and client care questions. Tonia Kalafut chimes in with any updates from the payment department. Next, my coaches join us and share what's been going on in their individual sessions with our clients. This lets us know what's happening in our groups.

I always leave our Monday calls feeling grateful for the tribe we've built around our common vision of helping women globally launch purpose-based businesses that make a difference.

So why is a team important? It lets you stop feeling like you're carrying the entire weight of the business on your own shoulders. This allows you to reach and serve more and more people while maintaining quality results. Simply put, your team will help you make a bigger impact and scale your business. It starts from the moment you hire your first assistant and grows from there.

When Do You Need a Team?

How do you know when to begin hiring others? I believe that most women need a team *yesterday,* so in my opinion, you should hire *before you're ready.* I know that might sound crazy, but there are ways to get help in the beginning of your business before you have a budget for it.

When I started, I didn't have the money to hire a team either, but what I *did* have was a friend who wanted my coaching. And that friend couldn't afford to hire *me.* So we traded. We mutually decided that each hour of my coaching was valuable enough for her to invest three hours of business support in exchange. (Bear in mind that when I coach my clients, there's more that goes into it than just the hour we spend talking.) So once a week, we'd have a coaching session. Then she'd help me organize my client content, do my bookkeeping, invoice my clients, and call potential clients. It felt so professional to have someone in my office making phone calls on my behalf.

As I mentioned, you can also find entrepreneurial buddies and make reminder calls to one another's customers. Having the perception of a team or even an assistant in the early days will "uplevel" you and help you grow into the best leader you can be.

There are many creative ways to finance support. One of my clients was overwhelmed by technology, so at a minimal hourly rate, she hired her 12-year-old neighbor to set up her Facebook page, update her website, and teach her about social media. Many of us can relate to feeling overwhelmed by technology—am I right?

So think creatively. Maybe your son or daughter is capable of helping you with technology. (You taught them to use a spoon, after all; it's their turn to pay you back!) Or it might be your retired mother who can help with administrative or bookkeeping tasks.

Having someone in your office for even a short time every week will give you accountability and teach you to think like a CEO right off the bat. If you come from a do-it-yourself mind-set, the danger is that you'll try to handle everything. The problem with that is you might spend five hours launching a website when you could pay an expert to do it in one or two hours at $30 an hour—a total of $60.

So calculate what your time is worth, and decide if it makes sense to complete a task yourself. Let's say you're a consultant who can handle 10 clients per month, and you need to make $5,000 each month. That means each of your clients must pay $500 a month for your services. If you spend two hours of your time per month with each of those clients, your time is worth $250 per hour. At that rate, why would you perform a task that you could pay someone else to do for $25 an hour or even $100 an hour? For $10 to $15 per hour, an assistant can spend 10 hours per week taking a *lot* off your plate. That's just $500 to $600 per month. While that might still be a stretch for you (it was for me at first), it won't be forever. When you get to the point where you're making $250 an hour with enough clients to cover your expenses, those few hundred dollars will be well spent!

Now, I'm not saying your time is inherently more valuable than a website designer's time or a housekeeper's time, but remember that as an entrepreneur, you're spending 50 to 90 percent of your time getting your business up and running. Marketing and organizational tasks are unpaid time, so you must account for that when setting your hourly rate. Plus, you spent thousands of dollars to build the skills necessary to do what you do, not to mention the fact that market rates simply vary for different kinds of professionals.

I've seen women go farther faster with a lot less stress when they surrender to the truth that they need help and become willing to ask for it. As soon as my clients hire assistants, their business grows, and they don't look back.

Build Your Team—but by How Much?

The first team member you hire should be a jack-of-all-trades who's willing to do whatever it takes to help you. She (or he) needs to understand that you're at the start of your business, and you'll need her to do a wide variety of things.

Being part of a startup is both exciting and challenging. I recommend warning potential team members that in a small organization, everyone will be called upon to step up and just take care of whatever needs to be done, and this can mean long hours at times. During an interview, I always tell potential hires that I will often be throwing tasks at them, sometimes faster than they can keep up. This could entail bookkeeping and high-level client calls one day, followed by errands like picking up dry cleaning the next day. Everyone who works for you needs to be on board with these realities.

The bright side is that your employees have an opportunity to help you bring something new to the marketplace. They will be working with amazing leaders like you, and they will likely have some flexibility in their schedule and variety in their duties. Your team members may also have more responsibility than if they worked at a large corporation. Don't overpromise, but let your assistants know there's potential for growth. They won't be doing grunt work forever.

How do you know when to hire more people? My belief is that you grow your organization as you need more people and as you have the budget. There's an organic process to how quickly any company will grow based on how motivated you are as the CEO. I've watched some of my colleagues grow million-dollar companies almost all by themselves (with only one or two part-time assistants), and I've watched others hire 18 people after their first successful project. I've seen both of these recipes work, and I've seen both of them fail. But I don't usually recommend hiring a large number of people in one fell swoop. If you do, the pressure to keep up with that level of growth is enormous. Suddenly you have a lot of employees whose livelihoods depend on you. That kind of stress might give you an ulcer and even cause the business to go under.

So be honest with yourself about how quickly you want to grow and still maintain that level of emotional stretching and learning on a day-to-day, week-to-week, and month-to-month basis. (Not to mention keeping up with the costs of the business growth!)

If you have the budget to hire more help, do it, but be conservative about it. The people on your team should be bursting at the seams before you bring in a new hire. I let my team know that we will hire only when we have a very real need because as an organization, we don't want to compromise our paychecks. That way, we're all willing to do some of our least favorite tasks to avoid diminishing our profit margin too much.

Of course, I believe the ultimate goal is to have everyone on your team spending 60 to 90 percent of their time in their personal area of genius so that they're mostly doing what they enjoy. But everyone will have to do a few tasks they don't like as much.

Hot Tip: As you grow, you can turn your primary people into department heads and hire assistants for them.

From day one, you can cultivate leadership in your team and prepare your assistants to become department heads. Be willing to trust your team members to take responsibility. Let them know that they're in charge and should report to you weekly on their progress.

This serves more than one purpose. First of all, it empowers your early employees to own their sets of responsibilities. They can also manage any team members who work underneath them and take on the role of decision making within their divisions. This way, as the

CEO, you can avoid managing a large number of employees directly. I suggest that you have no more than three or four direct reports. Otherwise, you'll be inundated with questions all day, and you won't be able to stay in your area of genius and vision!

Imagine how much further you can go when you're not the only one committed to that vision. As management expert Ken Blanchard put it: "None of us is as smart as all of us."

A Hot Entrepreneurial Tip for Tracking the Money

I can't tell you how many entrepreneurs I know who are out of touch with the amount of money going in and out of their business. Now, as your business grows, it's impossible to keep track of all that's coming in and going out. But the thing you'll want to pay attention to is your PROFIT MARGIN. And you want that profit margin to be POSITIVE, which means you have more money coming in than going out.

To calculate your profit margin, divide your gross profit by your total revenue generated. Example: If you collected $15,000 in total revenue but ended up with $3,000 after expenses, you would divide $3,000 by $15,000 to get 0.2. Multiply the result by 100 to find your gross profit margin percentage. Finishing this example, you would find that your gross profit margin equals 20 percent.

What's a good profit margin? It depends on your income level and industry, but obviously you want your profit margin to be positive, at a level that covers your expenses and allows you to save some money.

Don't be too worried if your profit margin fluctuates. I've had months when my profit margin was negative for the month, but I've finished the year in good standing. This is the ride of being an entrepreneur. Hire a bookkeeper and financial manager to help you, and don't be afraid of the numbers!

Heart-Full Hiring

The process of hiring employees can be stressful if you haven't done it before. How do you find viable candidates? How do you know if someone is right for your company?

Here's a three-step hiring process that you can use to take some of the anxiety out of the experience.

Step 1: Place an ad on a site such as Craigslist.org or Upwork.com, advertise the opening on your own website or Facebook page, and/or ask your database or network for leads.

If you hire an assistant who's going to work remotely, should you hire someone overseas? There are both benefits and drawbacks to hiring people outside the United States. There are some wonderful assistants available in other countries, and they're often happy to work for lower pay ($5 to $12 per hour) because their cost of living is lower. Just be cautious, as English-language difficulties can cause problems when you need to convey instructions or when the assistant talks with customers.

I prefer starting with someone local for another reason: It will help to curb the feeling of isolation that's common when you're starting a business. There's a greater sense of security and camaraderie, and having someone in your office allows you to give him or her physical tasks that you can't pass off to someone who's remote.

> *Hot Tip: Ask applicants who respond to your ad to put a certain sentence in the subject line of their e-mail response (something like "I'm your next marketing manager"), and set up your e-mail account to dump those who didn't follow the instruction. This helps save you valuable time and screen out people who are likely not a fit for the position.*

Step 2: Perform a written interview first, before an in-person interview. This is an enormous time-saver that allows you to filter your applicants. Those who put the right sentence in their subject line can receive an auto response with the written interview questions.

In the written interview, ask candidates to perform a task that's similar to what they would do on the job. Don't provide too much instruction because you want to see how well each applicant can think independently and figure out their own solutions. You could ask, for example, that they plan a hypothetical trip for you to a business training across the country, or they could write a letter to a potential referral partner. Tell them there's no right or wrong way to perform the task but that you're looking for resourcefulness and problem-solving skills. (At the end of the chapter, I'll provide a link to my Hiring Process Templates, which include examples of advertisements and interview questions.)

Step 3: Hold a group interview with the top two or three candidates. This will save you a TON of time and allow you to compare and contrast your candidates on the spot. If you aren't hiring locals, you can hold the interview via Skype. When you get to this point, you know they have the skills, so you're trying to determine who has a positive, can-do attitude and is a good cultural fit for your company. Attitude is vital! Skills can be taught, but attitude is innate.

Let them all know what would be expected of them in the job, find out their schedule availability and flexibility, and ask what they *aren't* willing to do.

After the interview, call their references! Some people skip this step, but it's very important and could save you from hiring someone who doesn't work out. Ask about the individual's dependability, temperament, strengths and weaknesses, biggest accomplishment, and ability to handle conflicts and pressure.

When you make your final choice, negotiate pay and dive in. If you're excited about one of the candidates you didn't choose, let them know and keep their information on file for future possibilities.

Managing Your Team

Okay, so you're thinking seriously of hiring some team members, but you have no idea what to do once they're there. Here are some tips for you from my own experience and the experiences of my clients:

Independent Contractors. I always recommend starting with a 90-day trial and hiring people as independent contractors at the outset, perhaps to take on a single project to start. Find out the legal requirements in your state regarding independent contractors, however, as you can get into trouble for hiring them full-time.

When people are independent, they have the autonomy to make their own decisions, they operate more as entrepreneurs in their own right than as employees, they're responsible for their own health insurance and other things employees might receive as benefits, and they can deduct their expenses on their tax returns. Obviously, this scenario doesn't work for everyone, but many people prefer it. In return they get to maintain some control over their schedules and hours.

It can also be advantageous if the people who work for you become income-producing. For example, you might offer an hourly rate plus a commission for every client they sign up. Then they have some skin in the game.

It's a good idea to have contracts with anyone you hire, not just independent contractors. Now, as I've said, I'm not a lawyer, so I can't advise you in detail on the legalities of starting or running a business. I strongly suggest that you hire a business lawyer or use an online legal service if what you require isn't too complex.

One thing I can tell you is that your contracts should include confidentiality/nondisclosure provisions that protect all of your content and the materials you create so that your employees can't leak your intellectual property before it's accessible to the public.

Hot Tip: Include a commitment to future training in your contracts with freelance contractors.

Once you've finished the 90-day trial period, have your freelancers sign a contract that says when they choose to leave the position, they'll stay on for at least four to six weeks to train the next person. Since you're a small company, you're uniquely dependent upon your team members, and the loss of one person can have a significant impact on your business. This provision protects you when someone needs to leave.

Don't Train Your Team! This is counterintuitive, but I've found it makes more sense to hire great people who are motivated to train themselves. And of course, if you already have an established team or teammates transitioning out of your business, as I mentioned previously, enlist their support to bring guidance as well. But the take-home message here is that finding self-motivated individuals is key. During the interview, explain that you're looking for people who are self-directed and resourceful. Training themselves might mean finding and watching training videos online, for example, or picking up the phone to call customer support to solve a problem. Obviously, some instruction from you will be required, but when possible, let them figure it out on their own.

Operations Manuals. Every time your assistant completes a task in your business, have him or her document the steps and build a training manual for you. As they streamline their work, they can revise the manual to reflect best practices. It will make it much easier when it's time to train the next person, and it means you won't have to create the manual before you hire your first assistant. Isn't that genius? Build your business with the mind-set that your assistants will create their own structures as you go!

Meetings. I believe in morning meetings to get a company off the ground. I like to hold two or three meetings per week to keep people connected, productive, and on purpose. Ideally, you'll want to gather at the beginning of the week and set goals for the week. Then, toward the end of the week, you'll check in about what everyone accomplished. If your team is in different locations, hold the meeting on the phone or via Skype.

Ask your team members to hold their questions and ask them at the meetings. This gives them the responsibility of setting the meeting agendas, and it saves you a long list of e-mail requests during the week.

Incentivize Your Team. Ask your team members what motivates them, and do your best to provide it. For example, I've taken mine to the spa a few times a year. My assistant, Shannon, told me more than two years ago that she wanted to go to Hawaii, so we set a team goal based on that. When they hit the goal, they earned their trip, so

I recently took them all to Hawaii! Volcano hike, dolphins, and snorkeling! That kind of incentive creates a team that's more motivated, committed, productive, and efficient than anything else you can do because they're working for something they actually want.

21st-Century Delegating

How do you know what tasks to do yourself and which ones to give away to an assistant? Here's a rule of thumb: anything you hate to do or that's going to take you longer than 5 to 10 minutes to learn *how* to do can probably be given to someone else. In the beginning, try to spend 50 percent of your time on marketing, 40 percent on client fulfillment, and 10 percent on administrative tasks.

Some of the tasks that you might give to an assistant include technology support for your website, administrative tasks like bookkeeping and invoicing, client care, and marketing.

If you're uncomfortable with delegation, you're not alone. In the beginning I struggled. I caught myself one day saying, "Um . . . could you do me a favor and, um . . . help me track these new prospects so that, um . . ." By the third um, I finally stopped and admitted to my team that I was uncomfortable telling them what to do. We all had a good giggle. I also told them I was committed to working on delegating and becoming more straightforward about it. When you're honest with your team and let yourself be human, they'll be even happier to support you.

Furthermore, while delegation is important, your number one job as a CEO is to hold a vision, not to delegate. You don't have to become a detail-oriented taskmaster. Rise above that, and show your team the end result that you see is possible. Then get them involved in the process of creating that result.

In my business, we have a local entrepreneurial Meetup group that's become a significant part of our income. I LOVE serving local women entrepreneurs, but I was torn because of the opportunities that were coming my way online. I finally went to my team and admitted I was running out of time to grow this important local group. I asked them: "What do you think we need to do so that I can devote no more than one hour a week to it?" They decided they wanted to take ownership of the Meetup group. They put up a website and developed ideas for growing and profiting from the group. They take great pride in it, and I now spend an hour or less a week on that particular division of the company.

I could only hand it over, though, because I didn't micromanage. I held a vision of what that division could become. When I laid out the vision, the team got excited about what they could do, and what they did was amazing! This is what every CEO secretly longs for, but we have to be willing to let go in order to receive that kind of support.

STRUCTURE IS YOUR SAVIOR

Okay, Goddess, how are you feeling about structure now? Perhaps by now you're seeing that no matter how resistant you might have been to structure in the past, your future willingness to embrace systems like the ones I've outlined in this chapter will save you a ton of money and time. And we all like money and extra time, don't we?

Whatever systems you add to your business,
remember: Infusing everything with your own sense of joy
is the whole point of doing business the woman's way!

And when you provide incredible services and products, your customers will fall in love with you and tell their friends, taking you off the marketing hamster wheel as word-of-mouth referrals pour in. I can't emphasize enough the power of creating a critical mass of happy clients. And the way you get there is by embracing the power of structures. The free spirit inside you is going to love how much time you save once you have aspects of your business totally dialed in. Let's do this, sister—together!

INTEGRATION

Embracing Structures and Systems

Business-Growing Structure Exercise #1

During the next week, *pick one business-growing structure*, and do more research on it. This might involve finding three websites that you'd like to use as models for your own site or brainstorming several word-of-mouth marketing strategies you could put into place, like coupons or bring-a-friend specials.

Business-Growing Structure Exercise #2

Make a list of the top three tasks you'd like to give away to an assistant. If your business is already in place and you have employees, decide to give away those tasks within the next three weeks. Possibilities include creating e-mail or letter templates, developing an invoicing system, or writing a systems manual.

Women Rocking Business VIRTUAL GUIDEBOOK

BREAKTHROUGH BONUS TRAINING #10:

Hiring Process Templates

You'll get:

1. Detailed ads that I've run to hire customer service managers, online business managers, bookkeepers, financial advisers, marketing managers, etc.

2. An extensive list of interview questions I've used for both written and in-person interviews.

3. Scripts for checking references.

Grab it here: www.womenrockingbusiness.com/guidebook

Chapter 11

SPEAKING FOR SUCCESS

"According to most studies, people's number one fear is public speaking. Number two is death. Death is number two. Does that seem right? That means to the average person, if you have to go to a funeral, you're better off in the casket than doing the eulogy."

— JERRY SEINFELD

For years, I wanted to be the one onstage. I dreamed about being in front of large crowds as words of wisdom and profound inspiration just flew out of my mouth. But I was also terrified of public speaking. Every time I got in front of a group of adults to speak my truth, my voice would shake and my knees would knock together.

Since I knew deep down that I wanted to speak and run trainings, I took a part-time job with a seminar company working in the back of the room. I was happy to be of service, but I didn't want to be there forever. I wanted to somehow make my way to the front.

Whenever one of the trainers took the stage, I could feel my own desire to be up there overtake me like a volcano. I fantasized about one of them keeling over so that I'd have to take charge of the work-shop. (Of course, I didn't want anyone to be in great pain. Maybe just a small case of the flu that needed a few hours of recuperation.)

I longed to be the MC who got everybody fired up before the main speakers. The MC got to hop up onstage, lead dance breaks, and make announcements—SO COOL! "I can do that!" I thought.

So I asked the head trainer if I could have a chance at MC. "That's the hardest job in the room," he said. "You'll have to stand onstage and get people's attention at the end of the break when they'd rather be talking to each other. Are you prepared for that?"

He made me think. Was I prepared for it? I realized there was a gap between where I was and where I wanted to be—on that stage. I came to terms with the fact that there had been points in my life when I didn't take the time and go that extra mile to get what I wanted. So my task was clear: my *attention* had to match my *intention*.

Hot Tip: Attention + Intention = Success

I made it my personal mission to study everything the MC did. It definitely took a certain level of mastery. I watched how she gathered the energy in the room, one person at a time. She had to be more interesting than the conversations people were having or the tea and cookies they were enjoying in the back of the room.

She'd start by engaging a few people at the front, getting them on their feet dancing with her. Then others would notice until she had the entire room engaged.

Well, one fateful day, the MC was sick. It was finally my chance. So I went back to the head trainer and showed him my notes from my studies. He got a funny look on his face but said, "Okay, you're on!" My heart dropped into my gut. I was terrified but made my way to the stage.

The DJ asked, "What song do you want to use to warm every-body up?" With a growing sense of dread, I realized I was suddenly in charge. I had no idea what to tell him, but I heard myself say, "Waka Waka" by Shakira.

As I walked onstage, the song pumped over the sound system, Shakira singing about the pressure you feel when all eyes are on you . . . wow, looking back, I realize how appropriate those lyrics were!

None of the people in the room had ever really noticed me before. I was just an invisible presence in the back. I think one girl up front even rolled her eyes when she saw me onstage. (Or maybe I imagined it.) I asked a few people in the first rows to dance with me. It was slow at first. There was one, then three, then five. Finally, within about five minutes, I had the whole room engaged.

What I learned from that experience is that opportunity often comes in the most surprising moments. Because I had put in the time in the back of the room and set a clear intention to learn to be onstage, I was able to step into that moment. And I'm grateful to my trainer for preparing me and trusting me.

That short time onstage gave me a natural high for 72 hours and a growing confidence that no amount of visualization or meditation could have given me. My visions for my own business and my own speaking engagements began to take root.

Too often we sit back and secretly believe someone is just going to "discover" us. But the truth is that we have to be prepared to jump when an opportunity presents itself. That's how we write our own fate. Nothing just happens magically. It's up to us to *unite* the vision inside us with the courage to step into our future success.

Are you like me? Do you long to get onstage and convey your message? Or do you dread the thought but know that your business would thrive if you presented talks to the public? Even though it can be uncomfortable, speaking stretches us. It's a hurdle that, once surpassed, can help you feel more confident in a host of situations.

JUMP IN!

As I've mentioned before, when you lead with generosity and offer a speaking engagement to your potential clients as a gift to them, it honors your feminine nature of giving. For many women, speaking is a natural way to build a business and grow a client base very quickly.

Of course, it's normal to feel nervous about being onstage. But I assure you that it gets easier every time you do it. It's true that you need to do some marketing and planning before you get up and speak in front of an audience. As I said, attention + intention = success. But you don't have to be perfect or polished right out of the gate. You only have to be a couple of steps ahead of your potential clients in your particular area of business focus. If you wait until you're perfect or have the best possible script, you'll end up procrastinating and never get yourself out there.

Here's a tip: The more nervous you are, the more prepared you'll want to be. But don't let your inner perfectionist hold you back! People want you to be authentic when you speak, so just be you! Start small, and gradually gain experience and confidence. As you do that, you'll gather a following at the same time.

Of course, once you're at ease onstage, it can be an enormous amount of fun. Plus, it's simply the single fastest way to promote yourself and your business.

WHAT ABOUT SPEAKING ONLINE?

Clients come to me all the time and ask me why they can't just put together a teleclass or webinar on the Internet instead of speaking live. Teaching into the phone lines as you sit behind your computer seems far less intimidating and exposed, doesn't it? The truth is, speaking online as a beginner takes far more work, strategizing, and time than speaking live in order to get the same results. And setting up online classes can be costly!

Let me give you some numbers to back up my case. Let's say you want five new clients. In order to get them from a live speaking engagement, you'll need to recruit 15 to 20 people to attend a free event. That's because it's common to convert 25 to 35 percent of a live room of people into paying clients if your event is set up correctly (which we'll cover later in this chapter). If you wanted to sign up those 5 clients online, you'd need far more than 20 people in a webinar. Online classes, teleclasses, and webinars usually convert around 1 percent when you're first getting started, which translates to 500 people in your teleclass! Plus, in order to get 500 people, you'd likely need 1,000+ registered because not everyone shows up. Conversion rates can vary, of course, but these numbers are based on my experience and the experiences of my clients and colleagues.

HAVE I CONVINCED YOU TO GO LIVE?

So how can you prepare for your big moment? Join Toastmasters or a speaking circle, or attend an open mike night or storytelling gathering like "The Moth." Observe others onstage, and take notes.

Then don't wait long before you get your feet wet onstage. You have a couple of options for speaking in your community or surrounding areas.

Options for Planning Your Speaking Engagement

OPTION #1: Offer to speak for free to an existing group.

Possibilities include the library, clubs, membership organizations, Meetup groups, community centers, the eWomenNetwork, the Chamber of Commerce, Rotary Clubs, Leads Groups, telesummits, local collectives, day spas, gyms, practitioners' offices (perhaps your chiropractor or your doctor), networking events, and conferences. Research what groups might be interested in your message, and contact them with a specific description of your talk and how it will benefit their members/attendees.

OPTION #2: Host a free event, open house, or workshop of your own.

As we've discussed in previous chapters, you can host an event in your local library or community center, a wellness center, or a day spa. You can even use your living room or the home of a friend.

Get ready for some HOT information about how to market and fill your events, Goddess, as we move through this chapter together!

HOW TO APPROACH A VENUE OR GROUP ABOUT YOUR EVENT

How do you approach a group leader or venue owner about offering a free talk? If you can get a warm introduction from someone else, that's ideal. If not, you can still approach them. Here are some tips:

State the intention of your talk. For example: "I'm a career clarity mentor, and I help my students and clients get clear on creating a successful and rewarding career path. I've created a workshop called '3 Keys to Career Clarity' that I'd love to deliver as a gift for the community as a 100 percent free training."

- *Ask if it would be a fit to host a talk or workshop at their venue.* For example: "I'm wondering if you accept outside speakers for free talks and whether it would be a fit to host a free training some evening at your center."

- *Offer a sample of your work so that they can experience your awesomeness.* Share a 10-minute audio or video, or provide a flyer with your best stuff. Be sure to include testimonials if you have them!

- *Look for win-wins in terms of promotion and compensation.* Let the venue owner or group know that you'll be marketing the event and would like to promote them as well. If you're going to monetize the talk as we've discussed in previous chapters, you could also offer sales commissions to the group or venue. Of course, ask them to promote the event to their list too.

- *Be straightforward and concise, and make it easy for them to say yes.* Let them know you'll provide everything they need: "I'm willing to do all the work to make this successful. I'll provide flyers or an e-mail announcement for you to post or send to your list."

- *Suggest ideal dates and times to hold the event, but be flexible.*

- *If you're turned down, don't take it personally.* Always be gracious and grateful because they might say yes in the future or know someone else who would say yes to you. Ask if you can check back with them in a few months.

Case Study: Entrepreneurial Goddess Lisa McCardle

When Lisa first came to me, she had been running a wellness center for seven years, seeing 20-plus clients a week as a healer. Although she considered herself "successful" because of the sheer volume of people she served, she felt burned out inside and stuck in an old model of trading hours for dollars while not charging what she was worth. She knew something needed to change, and she ached to serve more people, but she had no idea what that might look like.

In our programs, Lisa learned a formula for creating a signature talk to attract and serve clients and customers through a group mentorship model. She later told me that formula was like the golden ticket for transforming her business. From the talk, she would offer a free 30-minute breakthrough session for potential clients who wanted to work with her further. Afterward, when she was on the phone with those clients, they already respected and trusted her, so it was easy to convert them into paying clients.

Lisa started out by hosting her signature talk as a workshop predominantly in her wellness center, but as people realized what she was doing, she was soon invited to speak at other places. She led a workshop for women about manifestation and how to heal their relationship with money, and she found it rather easy to attract an audience of anywhere from 5 to 50 people.

Now Lisa says yes to opportunities to speak all over the San Francisco Bay Area. What she loves most is getting to work with her clients for much longer periods of time to change their relationship with money, which in turn changes their lives. In fact, she's in the process of preparing the spa for sale because she loves her mentorship business so much more. Lisa gives gratitude daily for being able to help these women transform, and this gives her a bounty of hope for the future of womankind and the future of her business.

ARE YOU AN ARTIST OR PERFORMER?

Sirena Andrea (another Entrepreneurial Goddess) came to me as a performer, storyteller, and artist who loved to tell stories onstage, and she was good at it. Magnetic and charismatic, Sirena won the hearts of everyone in the room the first time I saw her onstage. But when she came to our training programs, she had no idea how to make a living as a performer. She had been studying with several success-ful performers around the Bay Area but found that the formula for making money and selling out a show, especially as a beginner, was mysterious. She witnessed dozens of struggling, talented performers and was on a mission to figure out how to fill a performance hall and make a living that she could count on.

She attended a local Fringe Festival to study which shows were selling out and how the performers were doing it. What she found was surprising. Only two shows sold out—a one-woman show about her personal journey with her sexuality, and an all-female burlesque show. Here was evidence that something Sirena had learned in my training programs was true: when you focus on a specific topic, espe-cially an edgy topic like sex, people are attracted like bees to nectar.

Now, I'm not saying you have to teach or speak about sex to be successful. It's true that sex does sell. But so do love, money, intimacy, health, and other topics. The trick is choosing a topic to create a name for yourself. This doesn't mean you have to stick to that topic forever, but having an area of expertise will attract people to you and give you traction as you build a platform.

Sirena was drawn to a message of sexuality, but she wanted a more soulful, meaningful message that wasn't degrading to women.

She wanted to empower women to find their voices and share their life experiences with sexuality. When she saw *The Vagina Monologues* by Eve Ensler for the first time, she knew she had found her calling—to do her own version of the monologues where women tell their *own* stories. At that moment, *Yoni Monologues* was born. Sirena invited women to a couple of free workshops, where she had personal conversations with those who wanted to apply to tell their story onstage. Sirena spent nine weeks coaching the group and grooming their performances.

I'm proud to say that when *Yoni Monologues* launched, Sirena sold out in three cities. Today these performances continue to impact thousands of women in the Bay Area and raise money for teenage girls through the Artemis Project.

If Lisa, Sirena, and thousands of my other clients can do it, so can you. It isn't rocket science! It just takes the willingness to put yourself out there.

How to Get Butts in the Seats

Do you have the "What if nobody comes to my party" fears? Me too. Most of us do! I advise my clients to spend four times as many hours marketing their speaking engagement as creating the content for the talk. You can be the best speaker on the planet, but if the room is empty, what does it matter? Fill the seats first, and plan your talk later. Knowing people have signed up or you've got a venue booked will hold you accountable. No more excuses—you'll have to show up and do it!

Here are some ways to market your
event and get people in the seats:

1. Call or e-mail your current clients, colleagues, coworkers, friends, and family. Ask them to tell people who might be interested.

2. Post an ad for a community event on Craigslist.

3. Post a notice with appropriate Meetup groups, of if you plan far enough in advance, start your own Meetup group.

4. Advertise in your local newspaper. Sometimes you can advertise for free if it's a free event.

5. Post flyers or postcards everywhere—hair salons, wellness centers, doctor's offices, grocery store bulletin boards, college bulletin boards, your church, lampposts, etc.

6. Ask colleagues, referral partners, and local businesses to e-mail their clients about the event.

7. Post on all your social networking sites (Facebook, Twitter, LinkedIn, Instagram, etc.) and groups on Facebook that are frequented by your target customers. Ask local organizations or leaders if you can post the event on their walls.

8. Advertise on local e-mail lists or community resource websites.

9. If you're hosting an event at a venue like a spa, wellness center, or bookstore, ask the management to promote you to their list. Let them know you'll promote them in return.

10. Invite a guest speaker, performer, or sponsor to help you fill the room.

11. When people register, invite them to bring a friend, and e-mail them two or three times to remind them about the event.

Here's a sample ad:

FREE WORKSHOP: Unlock Your Life
Purpose & Make Money Living It.
Tuesday, January 17, 7–9:30 P.M. at the Chi Center in Santa Cruz.

Learn this powerful five-step method to uncover your gift
so that you can have clarity, confidence, and fulfillment
regarding your authentic life purpose. Discover a
blueprint to make money doing something you love to do!!
And learn the #1 reason people aren't manifesting
the life they want. Limited seats. Register early.
E-mail: support@sagelavine.com to register.

PREPARING FOR YOUR TALK

Okay, Sage, I have my talk booked. What do I do next?
Here's a handy checklist:

- Use the ideas for getting butts in seats, and market, market, market! As I mentioned, when you're just getting started and don't have a following, spend about four times as much time promoting the talk as you spend preparing what you're going to say. I tell my clients to start promoting about 2 to 4 weeks ahead of time for an evening or afternoon event, and about 4 to 16 weeks ahead of time for a full-day or multiday event.

- Choose a HOT title for your talk. Use the template at the end of this chapter to help you create a title that will pique interest.

- Don't over-script yourself. Create an outline of what you want to say so that you stay on point, but don't just read it to your audience! You'll sound stiff and insincere, and you'll lose all credibility. Be authentic, and talk as though you're giving *one* person advice. If you're worried about getting off track, creating a slide show can help you stay on topic.

Hot TIP: The two parts of your talk to practice several times are the introduction and the offer—the part where you talk about your service or product. Those are the sections you'll probably be the most nervous about.

- Time your talk beforehand to make sure you can get your points across in the allotted minutes. Remember to leave time for questions.

- Visualize yourself speaking and being successful!

- Always bring a friend, assistant, or family member to the event—someone who will have your back and give you moral support.

- Visit the venue ahead of time so that you can plan how to set up the room and inform your participants ahead of time about parking.

- Choose music, if possible, to play as you walk onstage in order to set the tone and get you (and everyone else) either fired up or in a calm state.

- Have water, your notes/script, and a timer or clock with you.

- Have a handout or slides for visual learners, have attendees repeat a key point or two back to you to help auditory learners, and/or include a gesture of some kind for kinesthetic learners.

Start with Your Offer

Before you think about *what* to say, you need to think about *how much* to say. Most speakers try to cram too much in. You'll be surprised how quickly the time goes once you're onstage. The danger of this is that if you're making an offer for your services, which I recommend, you may run out of time to describe it. And your offer is essential if you want to get business from your talk!

So when you plan your speech, I recommend *starting* with your offer when considering the content. You're probably thinking, "Start with the offer? Isn't that SALESY?" On the contrary, dear Entrepreneurial Goddess, if we don't get you making money as a result of this talk, you may not be in business for very long. So let's embrace the fact that you're a professional, you're giving the talk to serve, *and* you're going to offer your services.

When you begin with the end in mind, you can reverse engineer your content so that your participants are prepared to understand what you're selling, and the right people who want more of you and your incredible wisdom will raise their hands. Remember that you're not trying to turn everyone into a client, just the ones who are ready.

Then ask yourself this question: "What do my participants need to know in order to be prepared to take the next step with me?" Here's an example: Let's say you're a dating coach who helps people find their next long-term partner. You would ask yourself, "What do people need to know in order to feel confident about investing in my dating coaching?"

They might need to know that there are strategies for setting up an online dating profile to sort through potential candidates before the dreaded dinner date happens. They might also need to feel as if they can affect their love life, like they are not a victim to whomever the Universe sends them next. When they begin to feel empowered about dating and hear about your services, they will be more prepared to invest.

Ask yourself . . .
What do your participants need to know
in order to take the next step with you?

Seed Your Offer

Any chapter on speaking as a way to grow your business wouldn't be complete without a mention of seeding, which means planting "seeds" throughout your event that let people know there's support available if they're interested. Seeding prepares people for your offer by letting them know you're not out to pull a bait-and-switch; instead, you're up front about the offer that's coming.

For example, you might say this near the beginning of your talk: "By the way, for those of you who are interested in getting support or who would like to possibly work with me more closely, a little later I'll share with you what that can look like."

Seeding also allows people to feel what it would be like to be your client or customer. If you're a mentor, allow people to imagine themselves in your loving presence twice a month or taking the scary actions they want to take, knowing you'll be by their side. If you're a Realtor, walk people through what it would feel like to move into their dream house.

You can also plant seeds of successes you've had with past clients. For example: "I worked with a woman who was considering going back to a dead marriage due to the fear of being alone. After she completed the Reclaim Your Independence process, not only did she file for divorce and begin her new life, but during a really painful time, she began to feel hope and excitement. She moved into a new bungalow with a girlfriend and took herself on a trip to India."

Finally, practice standing firmly in your beliefs and why you created your programs or products in the first place. If you're a natural foods chef, it might sound like this: "I created these products because I understand the hectic lifestyles so many of us lead. When you have healthy snacks to reach for in the refrigerator every day, you're not going to keep reaching for the junk. You'll feel better, and you'll probably lose weight too."

How Much Should You Say?

For a two-hour event, I recommend that you have two or three primary speaking points. As I mentioned, rather than inundating your audience with everything you know, give them just a few key concepts or tools. If you overstuff them with information, they'll likely feel they don't need anything else from you, and they won't be willing to pay for your services. But wait! I'm not suggesting you hold back your best stuff! Absolutely not. Give them some great content, including some of your best stuff so that they leave inspired, with new knowledge, and *wanting more.*

My favorite way to design an event is to alternate between great teaching points and integration exercises. There's a saying that goes *"Impression without Expression leads to Depression."* If we fill people with too much information (impression) without an opportunity to integrate that information (through some form of expression), they'll probably become too "full" or zone out and stop paying attention (depression). So after you've taught some great stuff, put your participants with partners and have them share with each other. Or invite a group discussion. Then, once your audience has had a chance to interact with the information, teach them some more great stuff.

A lot of beginning speakers worry they won't have enough content to fill the time available. In this instance, you can create an outline with a couple of backup activities or teaching points that you can throw into your presentation *if* you need them. That way, you can relax in the knowledge that you have more than enough wisdom to share.

At the end of the chapter, I'll direct you to my downloadable template for what I call a Signature Talk, which will help you attract lots of customers and clients.

Another Hot Speaking Tip: Talk to One Person

Talk to one person in the room. Choose a smiling, friendly, safe person, and make eye contact with him or her as you're speaking. Create intimacy between the two of you, rather than scanning back and forth throughout the crowd. Others in the room will be drawn to the connection and want to be a part of it.

YOUR AUDIENCE WANTS THE *REAL* YOU

However you incorporate speaking into your business, I want to remind you once again: Always be authentically yourself! We're living in a time when there's a growing force of awake people on the planet who are losing respect for formulaic, falsely confident, and manipulative leaders who wear masks. We hear leaders making impossible claims, like "Just take this magic pill, and your life will be better." I believe we're ready for a more authentic approach, aren't we?

Brené Brown is an awesome, feminine example of the authenticity we crave in leaders. Thank you, Brené!! She's paved the way for her audience to be raw and vulnerable in its self-expression. I believe she's on the cutting edge and has captured the zeitgeist of where business and leadership are headed.

Becoming a Pro Speaker

Once you've established yourself as a speaker, besides holding your own events that people pay to attend, you can get paid for speaking to other groups. It takes some time to reach the ranks of paid speakers, but even lower-level speakers make an average of $5,000 per event.

Then there's the other end of the spectrum that includes people like Hillary Clinton, who has commanded $200,000 to speak to a group for a day, or Richard Branson, who earns $100,000 for a speech. The average salary of a motivational speaker starts at $88,000 and increases to $277,000 if there are books and CDs to accompany the talk.[11]

Sounds pretty good, right?

Goddess, you've got this! Whether you're just getting started and are only a few steps ahead of your audience, or you're a seasoned businesswoman standing before a crowd, it doesn't have to be as intimidating as you may think.

Remember: Attracting your ideal clients to your speaking engagement BEGINS with a hot title. So let's help you create one, shall we?

INTEGRATION

Crafting a Magnetic Talk Title

When you develop the title for your talk, use clear, simple language; don't get caught up with trying to be clever! People need to know what they're getting. If you're too clever, they'll just be confused.

Using numbers and benefits in your title will help your audience perceive the value of attending. The formula below will help you come up with possible titles.

Possible Title Formulas:

- # Keys / Proven Steps / Strategies to _____ _____

- How to _____ so you can _____ _____

- How you can _____ in the next _____ (# of weeks/months)

Example titles:

- Six Simple Steps to Reclaim Your Health

- 9-Week Lose-Weight-without-Dieting Program

- Five Months to a Stress-Free Life

Use Benefit Words:

Simple	Learn How	Proven	Decrease	Lose
How to	Discover	Reduce	Increase	Quick
Maximize	Accelerate	Avoid	Strength	Restore
Balance	Strategies	Maximize	Experience	Fast
Avoid	Personal	Individualized	Customized	System
Done-for-You	High-End	Renew	Techniques	Easy

Now list at least three sample ideas for a talk you'd like to give on behalf of your business!

1.

2.

3.

Your talk is going to ROCK, Goddess!!

Women Rocking Business VIRTUAL GUIDEBOOK

BREAKTHROUGH BONUS TRAINING #11

Downloadable Done-for-You Signature Talk Template

Plug your content into this pre-crafted outline to create your next speaking engagement that's designed to gain the attention of clients and customers.

When you grab the template, you can also take the **QUIZ:**

What TYPE OF SPEAKER ARE YOU?

Knowing your style will help you tap into your inner genius as you create and profit from speaking to build your business.

Grab it here: www.womenrockingbusiness.com/guidebook

Chapter 12

GIVING AND GETTING

"In all the blessings I've experienced throughout my life, the more I give away, the more that comes back. That is the energy of money."

— REV. DEBORAH JOHNSON

I'm in the middle of the Amazon rain forest—the heart of the jungle. It took us three days to get here. First we flew to Quito, the capital city of Ecuador. Then we drove through the Andes to arrive at the small town of Baños. From there we took small planes 500 miles beyond where all roads end to a small landing strip near a village of indigenous people.

When we come to a stop on the landing strip, a group of Achuar people with painted faces emerge from the dense brush. They usher us like special guests down a forested path into long, handmade dugout canoes, and we ride downriver to our temporary jungle home.

We'll stay in a lodge in the most biodiverse forest on the planet for the next 10 days, getting to know the Achuar people and their shamans during ceremonies, meals, hikes, and canoe trips. We'll experience a tropical world alive with monkeys, parrots, river dolphins, and more rain forest beetles and crickets than the imagination can conceive of.

Why am I in this amazing place? When I first started my business, I vowed to guard against losing myself to the urgency of reaching more people or making more money. So as I stand in this place in Ecuador, I'm following an impulse deep in my soul to leave the frantic, bigger-better-faster-stronger society behind me . . . at least for a while.

When my friend Lynne Twist told me about her work in the rain forest and the Jungle Mamas program, I knew in an instant that I wanted to be a part of it. These women are building businesses as a way to protect their rain forest home and preserve indigenous ways of life. They do this by using rain forest seeds and sustainable materials to create stunning jewelry, baskets, musical instruments, and other artisanal goods to sell to tourists.

My company has raised hundreds of thousands of dollars for the Jungle Mamas' mission, and we'll continue to support these women in the rain forest for as long as we're able. As I mentioned before, when we as women entrepreneurs hitch ourselves to a cause that's greater than ourselves, we're able to find immense strength and inspiration to keep going through the day-to-day challenges of growing a business.

The Jungle Mamas are grateful for our support, but as far as I'm concerned, we're the winners in this exchange. Because of my alliance with them, I get to bond with a group of women who are deeply connected to the earth and to a raw and primal impulse that moves through them, driving their daily actions and connections. I want to always remember this pure way of returning to nature for my answers as I grow my company and become the kind of leader I've envisioned.

Remember my epiphany at the beginning of the book? I made a pact with my Higher Self to support women in financially disempowering situations if the Universe would help me find my own abundance. Well, I have found abundance. So supporting these women in the jungle to raise the money to protect their forested home fulfills a mission from deep within my soul.

The Jungle Mamas program is part of the larger nonprofit organization I mentioned before called the Pachamama Alliance; *Pachamama* means "Mother Earth." This organization works with indigenous people to preserve our precious rain forest lands—the lungs of the planet—doing everything it can to keep the oil companies at bay. Lynne and the founders of Pachamama also bring indigenous wisdom back to modern Western culture. In fact, the indigenous people of Ecuador have a saying:

"If you're coming to help us, don't waste your time.
But if you're coming because you know
that your liberation is bound up with ours,
then let's work together."

The Pachamama Alliance and the indigenous people want to change the dream of the West from power, consumption, and materialism to social justice, sustainability, and spiritual fulfillment.

When you arrive in the jungle with Pachamama, you're not a tourist, an outsider, or a Westerner. You're a friend of the jungle, and you're invited into the most sacred and treasured home of these beautiful people.

The Achuar people live lives opposite from ours. They have no electricity, but living off the river, they have everything they need. And as long as Westerners don't infringe on their territory, they're happier than we are.

These people are known as the dreamers of the planet. They give incredible weight to their nighttime dreams. They begin every day early in the morning by drinking a kind of highly caffeinated tea that helps them remember their dreams. They gather around the fire in their rain forest huts and recount those dreams to one another and to their shaman. They interpret the imagery and make key decisions about their lives from this inner guidance—decisions about where to hunt, whom to marry, and—among the rain forest activists—how to navigate their communications with the government to counter the political demand to extract oil from the jungle.

The rain forest trees provide an enormous percentage of fresh oxygen to the planet, not to mention that there are hundreds of species of insects and animals, as well as medicines found in the soil and plant life. This is not the place to be drilling for oil.

It's day four of our trip, and I'm sitting with a group of the Jungle Mamas, these indigenous women who have an amazing strength that shines right out through their eyes. This group of Goddesses has banded together to keep the oil companies out of their forest home. When they find out I'm the donor who raised money to support them last year, they thank me with a gorgeous necklace made of eight strands of rain forest beads.

Our guide asks if I'll take home a story from them to *my* tribe of women. There are two translators who turn the story from Achuar to Spanish, then Spanish to English.

The women tell me there are masculine roles and feminine roles in the Achuar culture. The feminine role is to create, make babies, and make *chicha*, their special drink that supplies carbohydrates. The women are also the community builders. The masculine role is to hunt, fish, be a warrior, bring home protein, cut down trees to make shelter, and be the required destroyers who keep the village alive. Both roles, the feminine and the masculine, are essential.

The woman telling me the story checks to see if I'm truly listening. Looking in my eyes, she sees that I'm riveted. Her voice then drops as she says something very important: The Achuar women have one more role—*they tell the men when to stop.* Women tell the men when there are enough trees for shelter: "You don't need to cut down any more trees," they exclaim. Women tell them when they've brought home enough fish and the village has enough to eat: "Don't kill any more fish," they say.

When the Achuar see pictures of our cities in the West, they have only one question: *"Why haven't the women stood up and said, 'Stop'? There are enough skyscrapers and highways and cars and oil rigs."* My heart drops down into my stomach. They're so right. *Why can't we see when enough is truly enough?*

As a culture, it's time to stop focusing on accumulating, to start connecting with those we love, and to bring back a balance that's gone missing from the modern-day dream of the West. Of course, this isn't just a message for women. It's the feminine energy inside all of us that can recognize when we've done enough, that there's plenty to enjoy, that we can create more consciously, and that we can stop and rest.

The Achuar women asked me to please bring this message back to *you*. They ask that those of us who are called to build a business keep in mind the feminine values of sustainability, love, and respect for future generations.

For some of us, this message comes as a relief rather than a prescription. Many of us know deep inside our souls that there's a materialistic imbalance on the planet, and we don't want to be a part of it. As conscious women leaders, we often look out at our fast-paced, technological world on steroids and we're left with a bad taste in our mouth. We don't want to contribute to the problem. So I challenge you to hear what my Achuar friends are really asking of us. These indigenous people aren't asking us to stop growing our businesses; those businesses are needed! They're just asking us to grow with balance in mind.

> Your business is needed to usher in a
> social and societal balance that promotes
> sustainability, kindness, and respect.

BUILDING A BALANCED BUSINESS

Okay, my dearest Entrepreneurial Goddess, now that you've begun to clarify the purpose of *your* business, I'd like to introduce you to a final but essential mind-set shift that will allow you to support more people while leaving a legacy on this planet that so badly needs our attention.

You may think you have to wait until your business is thriving with a surplus before you can begin to give back. But I'm here to tell you that's a wrong assumption. What if I told you that you could build giving back into your business on the front end, and it would help your company grow?

Building a business in balance means that we recognize the eternal flow of money as energy—money into and out of the business. When we consider giving back as part of our business flow, we tap into a universal supply that can move us toward wealth even faster.

As I've said in these pages, we women have a history of devaluing ourselves and giving our time and skills away for free or for less than we deserve. We often put other people's needs ahead of our own. Although this can lead to pain, illness, and resentment, it can also have the extremely positive benefit of assisting us in serving the world in a bigger way.

As I've also said, after working with thousands of female clients, I've found that we often have a personal financial ceiling that's lower than the average man's. Once we meet our basic and family needs, we tend to be less motivated to grow our income. So why not take advantage of the truth that we have a desire to nurture and care for our world? Why not build into our business structure from the beginning a way of giving back to others, so that the primal urge to *give* can actually grow our financial success? It's full-circle abundance! The feminine way of doing business is a win-win for all involved, and I believe it's next-generation enterprise. It's the way we're headed because it's necessary and heart-full.

As the Rev. Deborah Johnson says, "When we give back ten percent of our income, it comes back to us tenfold." When we give back a certain percentage of everything we earn to causes greater than our clients and ourselves, we give back to the Divine, which opens a channel of spiritual partnership and co-creatorship in our businesses. We step into being an even greater conduit of the divine source energy that flows through us. Plus, when we open the channel for Source to come in and do divine work through us, it can take the pressure off and save us from stressing about the little details.

Isn't the goal of most artists and creatives around the world to be plugged into the Universal supply so that something wondrous can come through? Operating from that energetic vortex is the ultimate human gift, and it simply works.

People are waking up on the planet, and they want to spend their hard-earned dollars on services and products that support humanitarian and environmental causes. As I've aligned with the women of the Amazon jungle, I've grown a million-dollar company, and those women are a part of it.

When you partner with a cause that's aligned with who you are, your vision becomes bigger than you, and your business is no longer just about you. Bear in mind, though, that it isn't about the *quantity* you give back; it's the *quality* of the donation and how it affects you energetically. Whether you donate $25 a month to feed a child in Africa or $250 a month to help end modern-day slavery, it's the energy of aligning with that cause that helps you view your business as bigger than yourself or your customers. To put it simply, giving back is motivating for women, and for a lot of today's men too.

Case Study: Entrepreneurial Goddess Eileen Fisher

I recently met Eileen Fisher, the founder and chairwoman of Eileen Fisher, Inc., at a women's conference. Her clothes are worn and celebrated by women around the globe. When she first launched her business, more than 30 years ago, she envisioned a company that would support and empower women. Through her consistent commitment to her values, her company grew quickly and consistently and is now worth hundreds of millions of dollars. She has more than 1,200 employees and makes choices for the well-being of the planet. For example, in the Spring 2016 collection, 92 percent of the cotton was organic, which is a record for the company.

Eileen understands what it means to do business in alignment with women's values. When we spoke, she expressed a deep devotion to service in creating clothes that represent the feminine essence of a woman with elegant simplicity. She spoke about clothing that feels good against the skin, that breathes, and that allows what's inside to be expressed fully as we walk through the world. Her alignment with her mission inspired me to add a few key Eileen Fisher originals to my wardrobe!

Even more inspiring is her dedication to giving back. Over the years, she has given away millions globally through a recycling project. In 2004, she launched the Business Grant Program for Women Entrepreneurs that has given more than $730,000 via 55 grants to women-owned businesses.

Eileen and her company recognize that entrepreneurship isn't always easy, and having a community for encouragement along the way can make a big difference. She hopes that collectively these efforts will contribute toward systemic change. She wants to see a world where every woman and girl is a leader, every person enjoys human rights, and human health and well-being are protected through environmental initiatives.

Goddess, this is what we can all aspire to when we hold what's most important close to our hearts. Am I right?

HOW TO FUND-RAISE AND GIVE BACK IN THE EARLY YEARS

But how can you give back if you're just getting started? Early on, I discovered an event model for simultaneously growing a business and fund-raising for awesome social causes. Each year, at my annual Live Women's Leadership Summit on the California coast, I invite humanitarian leaders to speak on my stage and do a fund-raiser. Most years I've chosen the Pachamama Alliance as our featured cause, and I invite Lynne Twist and Sara Vetter, Pachamama's fund-raising director and keynote speaker, to speak onstage and bring an element of giving back to the event. They tell stories of women empowerment projects from all over the world and ask my audience to donate. We always raise at least $35,000 at each event, and Lynne and Sara have helped me fill my event by sharing news of the summit with their community.

As I've mentioned already, this kind of collaboration can get you past the fear that no one will attend your event in the first place.

Besides hosting a live event like the one above, here are two more of my favorite ways to partner with a nonprofit:

- Align with a nonprofit that already hosts its own events. You help fill or support the event, and you and your products are featured at a booth, as a silent auction item, or during a presentation onstage.

- Give back a percentage of your profits to a nonprofit in exchange for access to its database or the opportunity to include the organization's logo on your website. This lets your clients or customers know that you have a bigger vision and that your values align with theirs.

All you have to do to get started is research nonprofit organizations and make a list of the ones that inspire and motivate you. Then find out the right person to approach about exploring partnerships of this nature.

Voilà! You're on your way. It really is that simple. You build your business and give back at the same time. It's brilliant, right?

GIVING BACK THROUGH LENDING

Another way to make a big difference with your business is to use a percentage of profits to lend money to entrepreneurs in less fortunate circumstances. In fact, I believe so strongly in micro-lending that when women entrepreneurs join our year-long training programs, for every new member of our training academy Women Rocking Business invests in a woman entrepreneur in need. (Micro-lending is the lending of small amounts of money at low interest, usually to a start-up company or self-employed person.)

We do this through an organization called Kiva, a nonprofit on a mission to connect people through lending to alleviate poverty. Kiva supports people, especially women, looking to create a better future for themselves, their families and their communities through starting businesses. Kiva has found that on average, loans have a repayment rate of about 97 percent and women who borrow through Kiva reinvest 80 percent of their income in the well-being of their children and families.

We've had the honor of lending thousands of dollars to women in developing countries. We recently helped a 25-year-old woman in

West Africa named Awa Julienne purchase African cloth to make and sell children's clothes in her local markets—using the profits to pay for school for her kids. We also supported a 31-year-old mother of five in Zimbabwe named Miriam, who wakes every day in the wee hours of the morning and heads to the fish market to sell fish so she can improve the life of her family.

What a thrill to watch Western women launch their online businesses through our programs, and alongside them, watch women in developing countries begin to thrive because of our contribution. This is truly what it means to be a WOMAN ROCKING BUSINESS!

I have personally found the process of lending money alongside thousands of others to feel like an incredible contribution, and as Kiva puts it on their website, it's one of the most powerful and sustainable ways to create economic and social good. When a Kiva loan enables someone to grow a business and create opportunity for themselves, it creates opportunities for others as well. That ripple effect can shape the future for a family or an entire community. Find out more and make your first loan through Kiva at www.kiva.org.

YOUR CLIENTS ARE WAITING FOR YOU

At our women's events, we host a bonfire for our clients on the closing night. There's a particular moment from one of these that will be engraved on my memory forever. One of my clients stood up and declared her commitment not only to her clients but also to the planet. "I'm putting a stake in the ground to never give up on my dream, to never give up on my commitment to contribution and a larger vision," she proclaimed.

Another woman committed to making her business contribute to future generations—the children of the planet, our children's children, and our grandchildren's children. One by one, each of the women stood up and made similar commitments to support their clients through healing modalities, practical consultations, or products and services that benefit the planet, are ecologically responsible, and are socially just. What would you have proclaimed had you been at that campfire, surrounded by women launching the businesses of their dreams?

What would you like to proclaim about the future of your business right here, right now? What if it was no accident that you picked up this book? What if every moment you've lived has been preparing you for the next chapter of your contribution? What if you are at a crossroads, and in this moment you can choose the road leading you toward the ultimate contribution, financial freedom, and support system you ever imagined? What if you being who you are is exactly what the world needs?

**I've said it already, but don't just read this—KNOW this:
your clients are waiting for you—
not for someone like you, but literally, uniquely, YOU
and only you.**

We've been on a journey together, you and I, since chapter 1. You've had the opportunity to reflect on your true business desires and heal the places where you've been hurt by money. You have learned to take action as the means to finding clarity.

Furthermore, you now understand the importance of having Entrepreneurial Sister allies with you on your journey. Hopefully, you'll want to join our tribe of Entrepreneurial Goddesses at one of our live events so that you can count us among your inner circle.

Throughout the book, we have assessed your life as a Ph.D. program preparing you to bring your gift in an even bigger way and further clarify who your clients are. You've begun to put the self-care practices and freedom scheduling into place in order to create a sustainable, thriving life to support you as an entrepreneur.

You've learned an authentic selling system that lets you offer your services to the world without feeling salesy, and you've identified the strategies for building your business in collaboration rather than isolation. You're even prepared to speak on behalf of this incredible business of yours. You have a full toolbox, and you have a map to give back to the world through your business—and even to allow that giving back to be a mechanism for reaching more people.

You're ready! You've heard a call from deep inside your soul to let your gift fly free in the world.

And so it is, my friend. The business of your dreams is waiting. All you have to do is walk toward it, one step at a time. Keep the faith, stay focused, and get the support you need to keep your vision alive. Your clients and customers are waiting, and the planet is a better place to live just because . . . YOU SAID YES!!!

It isn't just your future clients who will thank you for building your business—your future self will too. Whether it's a year from now or 10 years from now, you have the opportunity to wake up in an entirely different life—a life in which you rise out of bed each day, pulled forward into your vision. You'll have freedom to express yourself fully, contribute, travel, reflect, write, create, and bring what's most true in your heart to clients you adore.

I look forward to staying in touch with you via the online Women Rocking Business Virtual Guidebook and supplemental materials or even seeing you at one of my events. Keep going! You can do this. You have everything you need to make a huge contribution through launching your business. Take it one step, one day at a time. Take care of *you*—your business will thank you for it. I'm proud to be on the path with you, sister. I am with you. You aren't alone on this journey. The world needs you, just as you are. You've got this. Now GO!

Women Rocking Business VIRTUAL GUIDEBOOK

BREAKTHROUGH BONUS TRAINING #12

**Attend a WOMEN ROCKING BUSINESS Live Event—
Claim Your Discounted Ticket!**

Experience the Biggest Business Breakthrough of Your LIFE. . . and Make Lifelong Friends with a Tribe of Women Entrepreneurs Who Will Hold You to Your Greatness!!

Grab it here: www.womenrockingbusiness.com/guidebook

WOMEN ROCKING BUSINESS IS . . .

An invitation to women everywhere who feel they have something to say and/or give and want that contribution to come from their true self. We train our clients to embrace their own unique, feminine expression and leadership style as the essence of their business while committing to playing an integral role in the planet's evolution . . . and we can do it together.

Find out details about ALL our programs here:

www.womenrockingbusiness.com/programs

GIVING BACK

We love giving back and express deep gratitude for the support we've received from the Pachamama Alliance, Lynne Twist, and Kiva, a nonprofit dedicated to micro-lending to women business owners in developing areas. Therefore we are thrilled to donate a percentage of author proceeds from *Women Rocking Business* to:

The Pachamama Alliance. The Pachamama Alliance is dedicated to empowering indigenous people to preserve their territories and way of life, and thereby protect the natural world for the entire human family. Their main strategy includes supplying rain forest peoples with the tools and resources necessary to support the continued strength and vitality of their communities and culture. The indigenous people offer new ways of seeing and living in the world that is inherently interconnected and sustainable. Together, this reciprocal partnership is working to bring forth an environmentally sustainable, spiritually fulfilling, and socially just human presence on this planet.

The Pachamama Alliance
1009 General Kennedy Avenue, PO Box 29191
San Francisco, CA 94129
Phone: (415) 561-4522
Website: www.pachamama.org

Kiva. An international nonprofit, founded in 2005 and based in San Francisco, with a mission to connect people through lending to alleviate poverty, Kiva celebrates and supports people looking to create a better future for themselves, their families, and their communities. By lending as little as $25 on Kiva, anyone can help a borrower start or grow a business, go to school, access clean energy, or realize their potential. For some it's a matter of survival, for others it's the fuel for a lifelong ambition.

Kiva believes lending alongside thousands of others is one of the most powerful and sustainable ways to create economic and social good. Lending on Kiva creates a partnership of mutual dignity and makes it easy to touch more lives with the same dollar. Fund a loan, get repaid, fund another. When a Kiva loan enables someone to grow a business and create opportunity for themselves, it creates opportunities for others as well. That ripple effect can shape the future for a family or an entire community.

Kiva Headquarters
875 Howard Street, Suite 340
San Francisco, CA 94103
Phone: (828) 479-5482
Website: www.kiva.org

ENDNOTES

1. Amy Haimerl, "The Fastest-Growing Group of Entrepreneurs in America," *Fortune,* June 29, 2015, accessed Sept. 1, 2016, http://fortune.com/2015/06/29/black-women-entrepreneurs/.

2. U.S. Department of Commerce, Economics and Statistics Administration, "Women-Owned Businesses in the 21st Century," Oct. 7, 2010, http://www.esa.doc.gov/reports/women-owned-businesses-21st-century.

3. David Prosser, "Five Reasons Why Women Make Better Entrepreneurs Than Men," *Forbes,* April 20, 2015, accessed Sept. 3, 2016, http://www.forbes.com/sites/davidprosser/2015/04/20/five-reasons-why-women-make-better-entrepreneurs-than-men/#6164420a10f7.

4. Melissa McGlensey, "64% of Donations Are Made by Women . . . and Other Facts about How We Give," infographic, April 29, 2014, accessed Sept. 3, 2016, http://www.huffingtonpost.com/2014/04/29/infographic-shows-charity-is-more-than-money_n_5233390.html.

5. Dr. Randy Kamen, "A Compelling Argument about Why Women Need Friendships," *Huffington Post,* Nov. 29, 2012, accessed Sept. 3, 2016, http://www.huffingtonpost.com/randy-kamen-gredinger-edd/female-friendship_b_2193062.html.

6. "How to Increase the Odds of Reaching Your Goals by 85%," Shay Goulding Meurer, Jan. 8, 2015, accessed Sept. 3, 2016, https://uponly.co/2015/01/08/how-to-increase-the-odds-of-reaching-your-goals-by-85-2/.

7. Dominique Mossbergen, "Organic Food Has More Antioxidants, Less Pesticide Residue: Study," *Huffington Post,* July 12, 2014, accessed Sept. 3, 2016, http://www.huffingtonpost.com/2014/07/12/organic-food-study_n_5579174.html.

8. "The Law of Precession," Success Resources, accessed Aug. 15, 2016, https://www.srpl.net/the-law-of-precession/.

9. Sue Shellenbarger, "When Stress Is Good for You," *Wall Street Journal,* Jan. 24, 2012, accessed Sept. 3, 2016, http://www.wsj.com/news/articles/SB1000142405 29702043014045771711927040053250.

10. Michael J. Silverstein and Kate Sayre, "The Female Economy," *Harvard Business Review,* Sept. 2009, https://hbr.org/2009/09/the-female-economy.

11. Rick Suttle, "The Salaries of Motivational Speakers," *Houston Chronicle,* accessed Sept. 4, 2016, http://work.chron.com/salaries-motivational-speakers-26243.html.

ACKNOWLEDGMENTS

Once a book decides it wants to live in the world, it will begin to tap on the consciousness of those most suited to write it until . . . finally . . . some naïve author or aspiring writer surrenders to letting the text flow through, sentence by sentence. And therein lies the magic. Books bring with them their own magic. This book did just that.

It began when I confided the idea for this book to Gregg Braden. Instead of giving me the polite nod that I've experienced in other circumstances, he looked me in the eyes and said, "Sage, women need this book. You need to write it. Get me a draft of the proposal and I'll connect you with my editor." Eeeek! Now I was actually going to have to do something to bring forth what I knew was going to be a huge project.

Being the CEO of my quickly growing women's training company, my time was limited, and I knew nothing about putting together a book proposal. There was one book proposal expert in my life, but I was hesitant to reach out—my friend Doug Abrams. In addition to my choice to recently break up with Doug's best guy friend, I knew Doug was very preoccupied putting the finishing touches on his book he had just finished with the Dalai Lama, *The Book of Joy.*

Let me back up for a moment. I have girl wounds. The wounds that take place when people in your past kick you out of the club. You've read about this in chapter 4. For those of us who have been painfully excluded, we carry with us an "ouch" that at some point in life will come to the surface for healing. This was one of those moments. Carrying my tender book idea in my heart, I reached out to Doug despite my fear of rejection. Doug would have had every excuse to be too busy to help me. Instead of putting me off, Doug invited me over for dinner with his three children. His wife, Rachel, was out of town. During his one free hour of the day, while chopping onions and carrots from the farmer's market, Doug talked me through my proposal. His guidance in helping this book be born was immeasurable and his generosity deeply healing. The entire process of writing this book has been magical, in every way.

Last night I sat at my birthday party looking into the eyes of 24 of my best friends, teammates, colleagues, and mentors and told them that *Women Rocking Business* wouldn't exist without them. Even to say this sounds trite. I can't put into words the feeling of having such incredible leaders, friends, and family members believing in me and, of course, believing in this mission to empower women business owners.

To start with, I have an entire team alongside me who have all given a significant portion of their life force energy to the women we serve. Shannon Fisher, thank you for the work you've done to acquire the superhuman skills that have allowed you to wrangle resistance into recommitment in both our team and our clients. Jenn Sebastian, thank you for your incredible ability to manage details and technology, implement, and run the company while your visionary leader CEO finds her way. Sirena Andrea, thank you for being a sister, friend, and story-extracting genius for the women we serve. Shana James, thank you for holding our level-two clients with so much wisdom and strength. Clare Cui, thank you for your fire and for holding our clients' success even when they forget who they are. Tonia Kalafut, thank you for seeing where we are going with the clarity of a wizard. Lisa Scott and Alana Jordan, thank you for your deep commitment to our financial well-being. Kat Kim, thank you for capturing my ideas in graphic form and for standing for our brand with such grace.

Thank you to every client who has ever walked through the threshold of the Women Rocking Business program, Entrepreneurial

Leadership Academy, Leverage Training program, or any of our online courses. Thank you for trusting me and for believing in yourself enough to bring your gift to the world. It takes courage. I love you dearly. I'm so proud to be doing this work together.

I especially need to thank Melissa Russell, Nathalie Hill, Emily Utter, Beth McKinnon, Willow Brown, Clarissa Medeiros, Cami Ostman, and Lisa McCardle for being so brave, for including your stories in this book for women entrepreneurs around the globe to learn from, and for being angels on my path. Thank you, Meghan Neeley, for being the kind of client who raises my own personal bar. Thank you to my very first client, Jeanne Omelia, for trusting me to support you to rock out your art career!

Thank you to Ocean Robbins, your family, and your father, John Robbins, for believing in me. Ocean, you are a gift in my life and a brother on the path. Thank you for committing to showing up for me and my business as if it were your own. I wouldn't be where I am without you.

Thank you, Ocean, Ryan Eliason, and Susan Peirce Thompson, for being on my board of directors . . . thank you, Susan, for showing me what big commitment means as a client and now dear friend. Thank you, Ryan, for being my first coach.

Thank you, Patty Gift, for the beautiful, feminine midwifing of the book that you provided; and deep gratitude to Wendy Sherman, my incredible and insightful literary agent, and to Melanie Votaw for writing this book with me. Melanie, you are a magical wordsmith of magnitude, and this book would not have happened without you.

Thank you, Vrinda Normand, for being a sister on the path. Women living at a different time in a different space with businesses like ours would be competitors . . . but we are collaborators, and I'm so proud to walk this path alongside you.

Deep appreciation to Maggie Ellis, Claire Stringer, and Nicole Young. Women Rocking Business wouldn't be where it is without your compassionate and wise contributions over the years. Thank you for being with us in the early days.

Thank you to my mom and dad, Linda and Jim Rice. Mom: You never cease to amaze me with your unstoppable ability to be proud of your daughter. You have been by my side every step of the way. I wouldn't be who I am without your love. Dad: Thank you for your unique ability to listen and support me when things get hard. Thank you for always being there with unwavering strength and your deep, compassionate heart.

Thank you to my cousin Amy Stepec, with whom I've shared some of the greatest laughs of my life, and my nieces and nephews Jack, Henry, Evelyn, and Lucy, who have given me the gift of getting to be an auntie. Thank you to Nora and Kate, my stepsisters, and my stepdad, Gary, for being an amazing part of my family. Thank you to Uncle Steve and Julie for the north woods love, and to Nels, Steve Stepec, Josh, Aiden, and Jaden for always reminding me of the value of play time with family. I love you guys. Thank you, Eric Blanz, for being my was-band, my husband of 10 years but a member of my family for life.

Thank you to my incredible Santa Cruz family. Thank you, Heather Houston, for dragging my ass to my first Bali retreat after my divorce, for singing to me through the tears, and for putting me on a motorcycle and teaching me to live again.

Thank you to my women's group, with whom true wo-manifestation wouldn't be possible . . . Kerena Saltzman, Grace Gamboa, Debra Artura, Lisa Carlton, and of course Tery Elliot and her husband, Russ, for being my Santa Cruz auntie and uncle. Thank you to my circling group and to Ben Saltzman, Eric Schneider, Matt Chapman, and Steven Cervine for being incredible men in my life. Thank you, Mark Nicolson, for believing in me and loving me through all the chapters of our relationship.

Thank you to my mentors: Shanda Sumpter for being so dedicated to my success as a coach and a friend; Marci Shimoff for being beyond generous with your literary wisdom; to Justin Livingston for always having the answer; Jeff Walker for being the grandfather of Internet marketing; to Kendall SummerHawk for getting my business off the ground; to Jesse Koren and Sharla Jacobs for making a space for me at your table before I knew what the heck I was doing; to Claire Zammit for showing me what true, embodied Feminine Power looks like. Thank you, SARK, for bringing your creative, deeply aligned wisdom to me and to the world and for helping me straighten out chapter 1 . . . and boy, did it need straightening!

Thank you to Lynne Twist, Sara Vetter, John Perkins, and the founders of the Pachamama Alliance for helping me keep one foot in the natural world as my business has grown, for whisking me off to the Amazon rain forest, and for deepening my values to conservation and sustainability as we've worked together to support each other.

Thank you, Christina Morassi, for being by my side through the shadows and the light, and for taking this dynamic and bold photo of me that you'll see on the cover. I used to be afraid of photo shoots and will forevermore be more comfortable behind the camera thanks to you.

Thank you to my affiliate partners—you know who you are—for being behind my launches. Your support and belief in me is a limitless source of strength.

ABOUT THE AUTHOR

Sage Lavine, M.A., C.L.C., is a former schoolteacher from Iowa who moved to Santa Cruz, California, to start her life over as an entrepreneur. She now owns a home a couple of blocks from the Pacific Ocean, where she enjoys frolicking, beachcombing, surfing, and paddle-boarding with sea lions and dolphins as much as possible. Sage is the CEO of Women Rocking Business, a consulting and coaching organization that has touched and inspired more than 100,000 aspiring women entrepreneurs around the globe to build businesses that change the world.

Sage Lavine has seen firsthand through working with thousands of emerging female entrepreneurs that when women learn about marketing and entrepreneurship through the lens of women's values, they are better positioned to implement effective strategies and create success. Sage has taught tens of thousands of women entrepreneurs to scale up their careers, enroll clients and customers, create sustainable wealth, and step into the life they truly desire. She is a highly sought-after speaker, trainer, facilitator, and mentor and has shared the stage and worked closely with many of the top business and spiritual leaders of our time, including Neale Donald Walsch, Jack Canfield, Janet Attwood, Marci Shimoff, Claire Zammit, Jean Houston, Gregg Braden, Max Simon, Lisa Sasevich, Derek Rydall, John Robbins, Eben Pagan, and Marcia Wieder, to name a few.

Sage delivers keynote presentations and seminars on women's leadership, women and money, and women and entrepreneurship to groups and organizations around the globe and has been featured on Fox News, in the *San Francisco Chronicle*, in the *Huffington Post*, and at the Inspiring Women's Summit, the Shift Network, Big Vision Business, Liberia Educators Conference, Irresistible Marketing Academy, Woven Women's Conference, and the California Chamber of Commerce Women's Conference. She also holds a master's degree in education. Sage believes in purposeful entrepreneurship as a way to create a life of meaning and also as a way to contribute to social and ecological solutions for the planet. She and her clients have raised hundreds of thousands of dollars for the Amazon rain forest of Ecuador, the children of Liberia, and the women of Indonesia. Sage inspires her students to love themselves and one another so much that we can't help but all succeed . . . together.

To learn more about Sage's keynote presentations or training programs, please check out our website or contact our team at support@ sagelavine.com.

Website: www.womenrockingbusiness.com

HAY HOUSE TITLES OF RELATED INTEREST

YOU CAN HEAL YOUR LIFE, the movie,
starring Louise Hay & Friends
(available as a 1-DVD program, an expanded 2-DVD set,
and an online streaming video)
Learn more at www.hayhouse.com/louise-movie

THE SHIFT, the movie,
starring Dr. Wayne W. Dyer
(available as a 1-DVD program, an expanded 2-DVD set,
and an online streaming video)
Learn more at www.hayhouse.com/the-shift-movie

THE GAME OF LIFE AND HOW TO PLAY IT,
by Florence Scovel Shinn

*RISE SISTER RISE: A Guide to Unleashing the Wise,
Wild Woman Within*, by Rebecca Campbell

*SHE MEANS BUSINESS: Turn Your Ideas into Reality & Become
a Wildly Successful Entrepreneur*, by Carrie Green

*THANK & GROW RICH: A 30-Day Experiment in Shameless
Gratitude and Unabashed Joy*, by Pam Grout

WORTHY: Boost Your Self-Worth to Grow Your Net Worth,
by Nancy Levin

All of the above are available at your local bookstore,
or may be ordered by contacting Hay House (see next page).

We hope you enjoyed this Hay House book. If you'd like to receive our
online catalog featuring additional information on Hay House books
and products, or if you'd like to find out more about the
Hay Foundation, please contact:

Hay House, Inc., P.O. Box 5100, Carlsbad, CA 92018-5100
(760) 431-7695 or (800) 654-5126
(760) 431-6948 (fax) or (800) 650-5115 (fax)
www.hayhouse.com® • www.hayfoundation.org

Published and distributed in Australia by: Hay House Australia Pty. Ltd.,
18/36 Ralph St., Alexandria NSW 2015
Phone: 612-9669-4299 • *Fax:* 612-9669-4144 • www.hayhouse.com.au

Published and distributed in the United Kingdom by: Hay House UK, Ltd.,
Astley House, 33 Notting Hill Gate, London W11 3JQ
Phone: 44-20-3675-2450 • *Fax:* 44-20-3675-2451 • www.hayhouse.co.uk

Published and distributed in the Republic of South Africa by: Hay House SA (Pty),
Ltd., P.O. Box 990, Witkoppen 2068 • info@hayhouse.co.za • www.hayhouse.co.za

Published in India by: Hay House Publishers India,
Muskaan Complex, Plot No. 3, B-2, Vasant Kunj, New Delhi 110 070
Phone: 91-11-4176-1620 • *Fax:* 91-11-4176-1630 • www.hayhouse.co.in

Distributed in Canada by: Raincoast Books,
2440 Viking Way, Richmond, B.C. V6V 1N2
Phone: 1-800-663-5714 • *Fax:* 1-800-565-3770 • www.raincoast.com

Access New Knowledge.
Anytime. Anywhere.

Learn and evolve at your own pace
with the world's leading experts.

www.hayhouseU.com